NOT YET
"FREE
AT
LAST"

NOT YET "FREE AT LAST"

THE UNFINISHED BUSINESS OF THE CIVIL RIGHTS MOVEMENT

OUR BATTLE FOR SCHOOL CHOICE

ICS PRESS

INSTITUTE FOR CONTEMPORARY STUDIES
OAKLAND, CALIFORNIA

This book is a publication of the Institute for Contemporary Studies, a non-profit, nonpartisan public policy research organization. The analyses, conclusions, and opinions expressed in ICS Press publications are those of the authors and not necessarily those of the Institute or of its officers, its directors, or others associated with, or funding, its work.

Inquiries, book orders, and catalog requests should be addressed to ICS Press, Latham Square, 1611 Telegraph Avenue, Suite 902, Oakland, CA 94612. Tel. (510) 238-5010; Fax (510) 238-8440; Internet www.icspress.com. For book orders and catalog requests, call toll-free in the United States: (800) 326-0263.

Cover and interior design by Rohani Design, Edmonds, Washington. Book set in Goudy by Rohani Design. Printed and bound by Whitehall Publishers.

0 9 8 7 6 5 4 3 2 1

Library of Congress Cataloging-in-Publication Data

Holt, Mikel.
    Not yet "free at last" : the unfinished business of the civil rights movement : our battle for school choice / Mikel Holt.
        p. cm.
    Includes bibliographical references and index.
    ISBN 1-55815-510-4
    1. School choice—Wisconsin—Milwaukee. 2. Afro-Americans—Education—Wisconsin—Milwaukee. 3. Afro-Americans—Civil rights—Wisconsin—Milwaukee. I. Title.
    LB1027.9   IN PROCESS
    379.1'11'0977595—dc21
                                                    99-40712
                                                    CIP

CONTENTS

FOREWORD

In every age a book comes along that will shake readers to their senses. A hard-hitting, brutally honest book that "takes no prisoners." Mikel Holt has written such a book.

Not Yet "Free At Last" is an important work that walks readers through the *real* story of school choice in Milwaukee, a story that will shock, educate, and inspire anyone who cares about the education of our nation's children. This book goes beyond the rhetoric and rumors through which opponents and false prophets have attempted to politicize school choice. It provides a spirited intellectual ride on the new Freedom Train. The beauty of this book is that it is also a story about the folks: people who by most measures are ordinary but who accomplish monumental things.

While Holt's story comes from his personal experience and thorough research, it is also a practical manual that will shout out a critical message for today's and tomorrow's parents. What began many years ago as Holt's search for a better education for his own son became a journey that helped change the way that education is delivered across the United States for low-income people. Mikel Holt is a train conductor who isn't just *doing his job*; he loves and cares for his passengers as family.

As in any work that tells the truth, Holt's book will shame, anger, enrage, expose, and call people to accountability. This book shows the real fight, demonstrating what real freedom can be while beating back the myths and lies propagated shamelessly around the country by school choice opponents. Mikel Holt also helps readers understand how school choice benefits the low-income families who exercise this new option and why choice is the one thing that has caused urban public schools to change the way they view the education of the poor.

Not Yet "Free At Last" also highlights many of the people who have worked behind the scenes for many years to make school choice for low-income parents and guardians a reality. These silent heroes not only took on the education establishment but also faced enemies seen and unseen who were committed to stopping school choice at any cost.

Whether you are a teacher, politician, business leader, parent, or concerned citizen, this book will leave you asking for more. In addition to experiencing the pain and danger involved in the school choice struggle, you will feel the excitement and joy of people having the power to choose where their children will be educated— private or public, religious or nonsectarian. For Black people, this book will challenge their outlook on today and their dreams of tomorrow. Holt will give people—any people—a reason to rally and march toward educational freedom.

As you watch the wall of the status quo crumble from the pressure of reform, you will want to stand up and cheer as Holt tells the story of Milwaukee's school choice program and its effect on Milwaukee's future.

—Brother Bob Smith
President, Messmer High School

ACKNOWLEDGMENTS

T he African-American Freedom Train made an unscheduled stop in Milwaukee, Wisconsin, in 1989. Fortunately for Black America, while in Milwaukee the train changed conductors and engineers and, at the request of its educationally starved passengers, switched tracks as well.

This book chronicles the sojourn of those who commandeered the Freedom Train from conductors content with riding around in circles, and describes the seeds they planted along the new route. Their journey changed America, reshaped the cultural and political landscape, and turned the educational monopoly on its ear.

Analogies aside, the school choice movement is not just the result of years of frustration with a system that kept Milwaukee's African-American community in a state of perpetual socioeconomic and cultural stagnation. It is also the manifestation of a philosophy for self-empowerment and self-determination advocated by leaders on whose philosophical ground school choice supporters stood. I take this opportunity to pay tribute to Frederick, W. E. B., Martin, Malcolm, and Marcus. Likewise, respect and admiration go to their protégés and conduits: Louis, Conrad, Asa, and Robert.

My eternal gratitude to my local mentors: John "Grappa" Holt, James Baker, Brother Booker Ashe, Ruth Thomas, Walter Jones, Lincoln and Marie Gaines, and recently deceased protégés Joe Winston and J. W. "Baba" Walker. They collectively helped bridge the philosophy gap, linking the past to the present for me and other lieutenants in the school choice army. Our community's heartfelt thanks are, as a result, extended to our community leadership: Howard Fuller, Larry Harwell, Teju Ologboni, Oshiyemi Adelabu, Commander Mike McGee, Tyrone Dumas, Tony Courtney, Walter Sava, Brother Bob Smith, and Zakiya Courtney, the driving spirit force behind the movement. Likewise we recognize State Representatives Spencer Coggs, Antonio Riley, Scott Jensen, and Scott Walker, State Senators Gary George, Gwen Moore, and Alberta Darling, Congressman Tom Barrett, Mayor John Norquist, and Aldermen Fred Gordon and Marvin Pratt.

My lifelong admiration goes to two important women whose contributions to our movement were crucial: Polly Williams, a true African queen and the mother of school choice, and Patricia Pattillo, who held the faith and provided the mechanism through which we were able to "plead our own cause."

Much love also to the daily contributions of the *Milwaukee Community Journal's* immediate family: Harry Kemp, Bill Tennessen, Colleen Newsome, Carol McDuffy, Josephine Joki, and Cal Patterson. And most especially to Terry Mallard, my Girl (Sister) Friday, Monday, and Wednesday; Thomas E. Mitchell Jr., my other right hand; and Bob Thomas, whose triumph over medical adversity was inspirational— but expected, given his ability to convince a fly that it's really a dragon.

The seemingly endless hours put into this publication taught me the obvious: writing a book is a long way removed from conceptualizing it. Thankfully, there were always extended family close at hand who assisted with research and editing or who provided objective comments. That important resource included Greg Stanford, my forever militant "Uncle" Ronn Grace, and the researchers of the Black Research Organization (the catalyst and initial sponsor of this book): Kevin Walker, Larry Bandy, Virginia Stamper, Alicia Griffin, Warwees Holt, Taki Raton, and Muhammad Sabir.

And, of course, I'd like to extend my thanks to those of the Harambee Community School family who led the struggle over the decades—most recently, board members Tommie Alexander, Sister Callista, Rodessa Evans, Judge Russell Stamper, Leslie Johnson, Pam Bolden, Kathy Barnes, and Cleveland Lee. Special thanks also to Bob Hawkins, Governor Tommy Thompson, Bill Schambra, George and Susan Mitchell, Dan McKinley and the PAVE staff, Michael and Mary Jo Joyce, State Representative Scott Jensen, Charles Sykes, Dan Schmidt, Leah Vukmir, Jim Prather, Tim Sheehy, John Gardner, and Melissa Stein.

My gratitude also to the parents, activists, politicians, elected officials, and children involved in the school choice battle: we proved ten thousand ants can eat the mighty elephant. The aforementioned individuals represent a wide spectrum of ideologies—political, cultural, and religious. But they agree upon one thing: equality of opportunity is essential to our system of democracy and freedom. They understand the true meaning behind the African adage "I am because we are."

This book is dedicated to those who have defined and shaped my past, present, and future: to George and Sideena Holt, my parents, for providing me with an unshakable foundation, sense of purpose, and thirst for justice; my other mother, Eora Williams, for her faith and unconditional love; and my siblings Dwayne, Bernadine, Debbie, Johnny, and Clarence, for their support and encouragement over the years (and for watching my back).

To my wife, Warwees, for completing my circle, inspiring me, and sharing me with the movement. Of course, there's no *me* without *we*.

And, lastly, to my children: Gerald, Mia, Malik, Radiah, Mykel, and Adrian; and grandchildren: Ahmeer, Amari, and Vonn. You're my future, our future. Never forget that through your veins flows the blood of queens and kings, scientists and mathematicians, scholars and warriors.

May all of you stay in God's shadow.

Hotep.

Abbreviations and Acronyms

CORE	Congress of Racial Equality
DPI	Department of Public Instruction
MCJ	*Milwaukee Community Journal*
MMABSE	Metropolitan Milwaukee Alliance of Black School Educators
MPS	Milwaukee Public Schools
MSB	Milwaukee School Board
MTEA	Milwaukee Teachers Education Association
MUSIC	Milwaukeeans United for School Integration Committee
NAACP	National Association for the Advancement of Colored People
PAVE	Partners Advancing Values in Education
PFAW	People for the American Way
PFSC	Parents for School Choice
SDC	Social Development Commission
WEA	Wisconsin Education Association

A PERSONAL JOURNEY

I'm for truth, no matter who tells it. I'm for justice, no matter who is for or against it.

—MALCOLM X

"Say what I can't say," exclaimed Donna Rogers in an exasperated voice. "I gotta' speak the company line, but you're free to tell the truth."

We were standing offstage in an auditorium that held more than three hundred Milwaukee, Wisconsin, public school teachers. At the podium, a local television news anchor had just delivered his opening remarks, heaping endless praise upon the members of the Milwaukee Teachers Education Association for their "professional excellence" and the sense of commitment they exhibited in dealing with the "problems" that come with urban education.

I and my colleague Donna Rogers, a television reporter with one of the local network stations, could only look at each other in shock and confusion as we listened to this sycophantic diatribe. Our disbelief was rooted not only in the history of conflict between the union representing Milwaukee public school teachers and the Black community but also in the abysmal state of public education in general. The fact that the news anchor had been in Milwaukee for less than six months added to our consternation: by no stretch of anyone's imagination could he have acquired enough knowledge about the local education system, much less the history of Black protest, to have made such a statement.

But then again, the news anchor was White and obviously more interested in maintaining the status quo and appeasing the audience than in espousing truth.

As socially conscious African Americans who struggled through the civil rights wars that have forever scarred Milwaukee, both Donna and I understood that our roles transcended our jobs. We were not reporters who happened to be Black, but Black reporters with a vested interest and stake in the events we covered.

Among our joint ventures were many sojourns to the Milwaukee Public Schools administration building, where we gathered news of angry parents demanding better opportunities for their children. Or calling for an end to inequitable busing. Or protesting the closing of a Central City school. Or decrying the exclusion of African-American students from specialty and magnet schools. We had covered dozens of meetings on union and Milwaukee School Board (MSB) efforts to undermine school desegregation, derail educational reform efforts spearheaded by African Americans, and evade allegations of discrimination, conflicts, and confrontations between Black and White teachers.

Like most African-American journalists, we covered civil rights demonstrations for our respective media—and participated in them. We marched in protest demonstrations, then wrote about the events. We attended African-American organizational meetings and community forums both to participate and to collect data we would later use to educate our brethren and to advance the campaign for justice and equal opportunity.

Recently, we had found ourselves trapped inside a police-formed barricade at a Nazi rally held in Milwaukee's segregated Southside. I was able to dodge the dozen or so eggs thrown at the Nazis, which were also hitting the precariously close reporters inside the barrier. Donna, who had a noticeable limp as a result of a childhood bout with polio, was not so lucky. I helped to clean her off when she swatted away one egg-missile that she had intercepted.

So now, in this packed auditorium that the news anchor was trying to finesse, Donna said to me, "I'm not going to bring up that egg." As the stage lights fired up her Afro like a halo, she urged me on. "You know what you gotta' do, brother. Spread some truth."

I nodded in affirmation, took a deep breath, and turned my attention back to the podium, where the news anchor was concluding his presentation.

I had originally planned to discuss the reasons behind the growing African-American opposition to the school desegregation process. Many White civic leaders were taken aback by the disapproval expressed by the Black community since the inception of the desegregation process. Most of the community's complaints centered on the inequitable busing patterns, which placed the onus of the process on African-American children. They were also disgruntled about the closing of several Central City schools, which had fueled the busing plan.

Most recently, concern had been voiced about the high suspension rate of African-American students, the widening gap in achievement between Black and

White students, and the political posturing of the school superintendent and the MSB over demands to keep a new Central City high school—a neighborhood school—under community control.

As applause reverberated following the news anchor's closing remarks, I tried to prepare a new text in short order. Before I could formulate an opening, the emcee was announcing my turn to address the audience.

Wearing a half-smile as I peered out into the sea of predominantly White faces, I shook the emcee's hand and adjusted the microphone.

"Instead of my prepared statements, I thought I would like to take this opportunity to ask a few questions that are dear to my heart," I announced nervously. "Some of you obviously won't like the tone of my questions. And if I piss some of you off . . . well . . . take it with a grain of salt, 'cause this is serious business and I'm speaking from the heart."

After a long, pregnant pause, I continued: "I have a five-year-old son who's ready to take that educational journey, and I'm debating where to send him to school. And my decision is based on stories I've written or read, people I've talked to or about, and statistics that paint a picture that's not the most flattering in the world.

"So let me ask bluntly: why should I entrust my son, the love of my life and the future of my family, to your hands?"

I told the plain truth to the teachers in that auditorium: since the official start of the school desegregation process in Milwaukee, African Americans—with the blessing of the teachers union—had almost exclusively shouldered the burden for busing under the so-called voluntary integration program. Even so, criticism consistently came from teachers who used seniority systems to avoid schools where Black students remained in the majority. That obvious affront lingered in the minds of many Black people.

"Grade point averages of Black students did not climb, as we had assumed they would under 'integration,'" I said, giving the word a sarcastic tinge, "but instead took a nosedive."

Conversely, suspensions of Black students soared, many originating from what one sociologist called a cultural clash. Black students were suspended for carrying Afro picks, or for wearing what White teachers considered inappropriate clothing. Reportedly, two Black students had even been suspended for being too exuberant while giving each other dap, an intricate and often enthusiastic series of handshakes, body slaps, and hugs. A White teacher had thought that they were fighting, and an argument ensued when they tried to explain.

Allegations of racism or insensitive comments directed toward Black students at newly "integrated" schools were apparently filed in the same cabinets as actions taken against White hate groups that demonstrated outside schools where Black students were bused to meet desegregation quotas. To these civil rights affronts, there came nothing but silence from the teachers union—and from most teachers.

"Desegregation, which y'all keep erroneously calling integration, is by any name a farce," I told the startled crowd. "And I don't know who to really blame. I do know that very few White teachers have done what could and should have been done to make life more bearable for Black students or to use their positions to promote racial harmony. And that says something about the whole process and the mindsets of far too many teachers."

Pausing for a second to judge the audience's reaction, I quickly added that there are many excellent White teachers in the system. "In fact, the good educators greatly outnumber the bad. But there are also many incompetent teachers, many racist teachers, and many apathetic teachers whose presence is well known to Black children and their parents—and who are protected by the same union that keeps insisting that it cares.

"Of even greater concern," I continued, "is that union members have engineered a system that not only has been hostile to Black children and the Black community but also has undermined the core principles of public education."

The Milwaukee school desegregation process was sold to Black people as the cure-all for decades of fiscal inequities, inferior educational offerings, and other byproducts of sociopolitical apartheid. The process turned out to be an administrative boondoggle exacerbated by the resistance to change. Desegregation threatened teacher seniority, forcing some veterans to "ghetto schools" and "corrupting" their classrooms with undesirable ghetto children. A large number of teachers contributed to the desegregation placebo by resisting integration, or masking their attempts to under- or miseducate Black children. Their conspiratorial agenda again defined the failed education system and fixed the spotlight on the systemic racism inherent in Milwaukee Public Schools (MPS). By all determinations, MPS was indeed a microcosm of Milwaukee. And Milwaukee had a history of hostility toward African Americans.

"If nothing else, this has taught me and many other Black activists about the difference between desegregation and integration. It has taught us that the system doesn't care about us, that the two-tiered education system we fought so hard to change over so many decades remains as strong as ever.

"I know what I'm saying to you is shocking," I told the teachers, and from their stares and groans I could tell that my words had struck a chord, if not receptive ears. "But let's be honest—the history of this school district is not one that any of us can brag about, and the position of the teachers union has not always been what you can call pro-Black, or even pro-child. That's understandable. The teachers union agenda is the well-being of teachers, not parents, or children for that matter. If that were honestly told, it would erase a lot of confusion," I said. "My agenda has always been what's best for Black people—that's *my* union, the Black people's union, and I'm sure you can understand my agenda. We've lost a generation of Black children, and I don't recall the union stepping in to stop the bleeding.

"Now, on a more personal note: my prized possession is in need of an education. Who should I entrust him to? Can you guarantee me that you will treat him as if he were your own?"

I ended my speech by admitting that my assumption could be wrong; I knew there were many dedicated teachers in the system to whom I would eagerly entrust not only my son but also my life. But there were also people who simply wanted to pick up a check, there were racists who had no business being near our children, and there were incompetent people who should not be allowed in a school building. And the union protects them!

I closed by encouraging those who put children first to let their collective voices be heard, to lead by example, and to help weed out the bad apples.

There was an eerie silence as I ended my comments, followed by sporadic applause, primarily from small groups of Black teachers scattered throughout the auditorium, and a few Whites. Several feet away from the podium, Donna wore a broad smile as she looked down at her notes. The news anchor looked shocked and confused. If I had had the time, I could have briefed him on the long history of local educational politics, the reasons for Black disenchantment, and the ongoing struggle to secure the seemingly unattainable: a first-rate education for our children.

After the event, I left the convention facility and stepped into the warm fall air of Milwaukee's Southside, a community that I had marched to integrate a decade before, although few Black families had moved into the area since then. I crossed the hotel parking lot with a mixture of pride and apprehension. I was proud for having said my piece, echoing what I believe most Black folks would have said, given the opportunity. My apprehension came from the numerous generalizations I had made during my speech. Maybe the teachers were not at fault, I thought; maybe they, too, were victims of a callous school board and the vestiges of White supremacy. After all, Milwaukee's apartheid system had grown stronger through manipulation of the races, subsidizing a power base by creating and maintaining a caste system. Maybe the teachers, too, were victims of a self-serving political monster with its own agendas.

As I approached my car, my daydreaming was interrupted by a broken windshield and two slashed tires.

The following week I enrolled my youngest son, Malik, at Harambee Community School, a private, Black-owned academy in the heart of the Central City.

LOCAL BEGINNINGS

*When the missionaries came, they had the Bible and we had
the land. Now we have the Bible and they have the land.*
— WEST AFRICAN PROVERB

N othing is certain except death, taxes, and second-class citizenship
for Black people."

This culturally amended maxim has held true for African-
American Milwaukeeans for almost a century. On the brink of
Milwaukee's becoming a minority-majority city, various socioeconomic measurements suggest that it remains one of the least hospitable places for African
Americans to reside. Milwaukee's minority population is one of the country's poorest, and the city consistently ranks at or near the top in a dozen negative social
indicators, including teen pregnancy rate, mortgage loan rejection rate, male unem-
ployment rate, high school dropout rate, and the gap between Black and White
student academic achievement in the Milwaukee Public Schools. And despite composing nearly 48 percent of the city's population, Black men hold less than 4 percent
of private-sector middle-management jobs, according to the Urban League.

In fact, although it was once a stop along the Underground Railroad, today it
holds the distinction of being among the nation's most segregated cities. To understand the cause of this paradox, one needs only to look at the state of public
education and the antipathy of "educrats" to decades-long cries for quality education.

Many of the societal ills that plague Milwaukee can be traced to the apartheid
philosophy that underlies the education system. Nearly 60 percent of the city's
African-American population lives in poverty and an almost equal percentage,
according to the latest figures from the Literacy Services of Wisconsin, is functionally illiterate. Both the welfare rolls and prisons are filled with high school

dropouts. The U.S. Department of Justice reports that fewer than 25 percent of prison inmates hold high school diplomas,[1] and the Wisconsin Policy Research Institute declared in a 1998 report that the illegal drug enterprise has become the fastest-growing employment opportunity for young African-American males.[2] Although the vast majority are high school dropouts, they are evidently savvy enough to maintain complex inventory and accounting systems.

Some have tried to make a case that the crisis in Milwaukee's Black community is the result of our inability to take advantage of the educational opportunities before us, that Whites who attend the same public schools succeed, creating their own opportunities. This theory suggests that African Americans are genetically inferior and do not want the same things as White Americans. It suggests that Black parents do not treasure education and are apathetic about the futures of their children. Such assumptions are ludicrous for a variety of reasons. The most obvious is the four-decades-long struggle waged by Black parents and community activists to improve the inadequate and often hostile public school conditions that have confined and hindered Black children. A strong case can be made that the system of educational apartheid that defines Milwaukee is so debilitating, so obstructionist, and so intractable that most Black children do not stand a chance of success.

Someone once theorized there are no coincidences in the universe. Similarly, there are no aspects of the abysmal state of Black Milwaukee that can't be traced back to the education system. That many African Americans have escaped and have achieved in spite of debilitating conditions is a testament to Black survival skills and our ability to overcome the obstacles of apartheid. Unfortunately, most African Americans have not been so fortunate.

VENTURING NORTH: MILWAUKEE'S BLACK POPULATION

The battle for quality education for Black children in Milwaukee has been framed by institutional racism and financial inequities since the first African "American" established a home there in 1835. Jo Oliver was a cook for Solomon Juneau, who is considered Milwaukee's founder. Oliver reportedly was taken aback when he was denied access to what he assumed to be public documents at a trading post, and he was later ostracized from an organized mission bible study, despite the area's status as a free state. While "Mah nee-waa ka" was not a mecca for Black escaped slaves, it was considered a community where Americans took seriously their biblical mandate to treat all of God's children as brothers, regardless of race. But apparently that didn't mean that all were equal in White eyes, as Black people soon learned when they moved beyond simple courtesies to seeking equal access or treatment.

A trickle of Black migrants followed Oliver's residency, numbering somewhere around two hundred by 1840, according to state historical society records. Historians note that the "free Negroes" and some escaped slaves worked and lived among the White settlers, but were generally accepted more by Native Americans than by the German and English settlers who made Milwaukee their home. The Black migrants were restricted by artificial barriers rooted in slavery, even though that inhumane practice was outlawed in Wisconsin.

Some suggest that Milwaukee's abysmal record on race relations was cemented during this period, which coincided with passage of the Fugitive Slave Act of 1850. During this period, national attention focused on the circumstances of Joshua Glover, a runaway slave who had been given shelter in Racine, Wisconsin (a small community thirty miles south of Milwaukee), during his sojourn along the Underground Railroad, which ran through southeastern Wisconsin and continued up into Canada. Slave catchers learned that Glover was in Racine but were diverted by Racine citizens when they tried to capture him. Posse members, how-ever, bided their time and eventually were able to steal Glover away, transporting him to a jail in the original Milwaukee county courthouse until the slave catchers from Missouri could return him to the plantation from which he had escaped.

The residents of Waukesha, an area to the west of Milwaukee that was a hotbed of abolitionist fervor, heard about Glover's incarceration. Abolitionists marched the twenty-six miles from Waukesha to Milwaukee and broke him out. A member of their party was killed in the effort. Joshua Glover later returned to Wisconsin and, remembering his treatment in Milwaukee, settled in Racine. He was later involved in a court case to secure the right of African Americans to vote in Wisconsin.

A historical side note: at that time the Ripon Society, headquartered near Waukesha, formed a political party to carry out its antislavery, profarm politics. Thus the Republican Party was launched, and it quickly expanded into Illinois. An ambitious young Illinois legislator switched his allegiance from the noncommittal Whigs to the GOP. His name was Abraham Lincoln.

The Black population remained modest in Milwaukee until shortly after the turn of the century, when a steady, albeit modest, number of Black males migrated primarily from the southern states of Mississippi, Arkansas, and Georgia. In "Black Milwaukee: A Social History and Statistical Profile," historian and sociologist Ron Edari notes that the era of World War I saw a significant increase of Black migrants, including most noticeably an influx of professionals, a sizable percentage of whom were "mulattos":

A good many of these mulattos, as they were referred to then, represented the skilled and better-educated blacks who had left the South after the installation of the Jim Crow system and the institutionalization of white terrorism following Reconstruction. They came to Wisconsin in spurts, establishing communities in the northern areas of the state where they farmed and established trades. Many settled in Milwaukee, establishing small businesses or working as paraprofessionals and educators.[3]

Racism, a cornerstone of the Milwaukee culture that continues to this day, was a staunch reality that curbed Black opportunities. Blacks were limited primarily to menial occupations, and even though mulattos were afforded more opportunities than their darker-skinned brothers, statistical data shows that in 1910 only a handful lived in Milwaukee. In 1910, fewer than thirty Black professionals were listed in city statistics, fifteen of whom were educators restricted to teaching almost exclusively in segregated public institutions or in church-run private schools. These circumstances existed although just fifteen years earlier these same professionals had worked with progressive Whites to see the passage of the Wisconsin Civil Rights Act of 1895—a measure that, at least on paper, banned the segregation of public facilities.

Milwaukee's African-American population grew significantly just prior to World War II, aided by two major migrations. The draw was Milwaukee's thriving industrial base, which included such factory giants as International Harvesters, American Can, and A. O. Smith. Milwaukee was also considered the brewery capital of the world, with abundant employment opportunities at Pabst, Schlitz, and Miller brewing companies. While the city itself was segregated, the wages and benefit packages offered by employers were among the best in the country and thus a powerful incentive for Black southerners, no matter how illiterate.

In Alabama, Georgia, and Tennessee, editorials and advertisements in Black newspapers promised higher pay and a more humane lifestyle up north. In some communities southern politicians banned those newspapers, not because of their love for the potential emigrants, but because of the demand for sharecroppers and the cheap labor that supported the southern economy. However, banning Black newspapers, particularly the *Chicago Daily Defender*, which called on Black southerners to flee from Jim Crowism, did not slow the migration. From 1948 to 1953, industry giants recruited Black workers from Georgia, the Carolinas, Kentucky, and Virginia. A second major migration of African Americans from Tennessee, Mississippi, Arkansas, and Louisiana followed in the mid-1950s, swelling the minority populations of not only Milwaukee but also Chicago, Detroit, and Gary. Edari notes that "between 1950 and 1960 . . . the Black population increased from 21,772 to 62,458, a percentage change of 186 percent."[4]

For those who ventured north with families in tow, the job opportunities provided the foundation for a social and cultural lifestyle far superior to what could be obtained in the Deep South. There, the whip had been replaced by cattle prods, slavery had given way to Jim Crowism, and plantation servitude had led straight into institutional racism and sharecropping. But in Milwaukee, a large percentage of the Black community owned homes, and they left their new cars unlocked near their well-manicured yards.

SEGREGATION—AND A CLOSE-KNIT COMMUNITY

Wisconsin Historical Society collections suggest that in the late 1940s, racial coexistence—if not integration—was the norm. Black Milwaukeeans lived in a small area north of the downtown business district, which was jointly occupied by low-to-moderate-income German, Polish, and Jewish Americans. Sixty years ago, what is now considered Milwaukee's ghetto was a bustling middle-class neighborhood with thriving business strips that not only anchored the city's property base but also defined its ethnicity and culture.

However, as German, Polish, and Jewish people moved to the northwest and Southside, African Americans were pushed further north of downtown, creating a Black community—known to Black residents as Bronzeville—which also served as a system of containment. The city openly maintained ordinances that perpetuated segregated housing and denied Black Milwaukeeans access to many government jobs.

The city's hypocrisy is illustrated alarmingly well by the Milwaukee Braves' baseball team: although Whites were proud of Black stars such as Hank Aaron who made the team what it was, Black players were not allowed to dine at most downtown establishments. It was not unusual to find Aaron or visiting Hall of Famers like Willie Mays listening to Dizzy Gillespie at a jazz spot in the Walnut Street business district—not only because they enjoyed the be-bop but also because they were restricted to that area by societal rules.

Black elders still tell an apocryphal story about a scuffle at a prissy hotel that illuminates the dichotomy of Black life in Milwaukee. Although baseball great Willie Mays left White Milwaukee in reverence when he hit four home runs in a single game at Milwaukee County Stadium, he was denied a table at a prestigious Milwaukee hotel later that evening because of his color. However, this didn't stop the management from begging him for autographs. And upon hearing that Mays was in the lobby area, many patrons left the hotel's show, which featured a nationally renowned Black performer—reportedly Sammy Davis Jr.—to greet him. But not one of them was bold enough to offer him a seat at his or her table.

Black Milwaukee was a community of interest in the 1950s. In terms of economics and education, the Black community operated somewhat like an African village. Ironically, segregation solidified the Black city-within-a-city, which was run by a hierarchy of Black professionals, tradesmen, and clergy. Networking was the key—neighbors were considered an extension of family and organizations such as the YMCA provided strong community support.

Black churches provided tutorial programs, summer programs, and even recreational programs. Local chapters of the National Urban League and the National Association for the Advancement of Colored People (NAACP) as well as several business organizations, also played pivotal roles in the upbringing of Black children, contributing books, staff, and other resources where needed. Black children like me grew up in Milwaukee knowing our schoolteachers also as Sunday School teachers, neighbors, and community leaders. Held in high esteem, teachers were frequently called upon to represent Black interests in city hall, to function as consultants for businesses, and to serve on the boards of civic and community organizations. Some of Milwaukee's most prominent elder citizens today were educators and pioneers during this period and in most cases set themselves up as mentors and tutors for those who followed. They did so not only in the public schools but also in community and Freedom Schools, the YMCA, and the churches.

Black parents, many of whom were first-generation escapees from the South, knew a deep-seated hunger for a better overall quality of life devoid of the fear and trepidation that was commonplace in the South. They longed to establish better circumstances for their children.

The vehicle for that dream was education.

A MILWAUKEE EDUCATION

There is little recorded history of educational opportunities available to the first Blacks to arrive in Milwaukee, but it is a certainty that they were not allowed full access to the limited public education system of that era. The Catholic Church reportedly set up a quasi-public education system that was considered adequate for the times, if not equal to the offerings of White residents. Black "public" schools were reportedly subsidized by Black churches and civic organizations, which received modest funds from tax appropriations.

Segregation and inequitable financing apparently sparked a debate four decades before *Brown* v. *The Board of Education,* and sixty-five years before the school desegregation settlement. Because there was no mechanism through which Black Milwaukeeans could seek redress and because to protest was to invite mob violence, the debate was limited to occasional appeals for additional financing. For the most part, Black Milwaukeeans knew their place. If they forgot, the local branch of the Ku Klux Klan—although mostly inactive—was always there to remind them.

The migration period of the '40s and '50s presented new challenges in the educational arena. There were few places north of the Mason-Dixon line in which segregation was indeed equal, and fewer still, outside of private schools, in which integrated classrooms were the norm. In Milwaukee, the setting was particularly disturbing: not only were resources unequal but the school board was blatant in its disregard of the Black community—Black students in particular—prompting a growing militancy that would erupt in the next decade.

As Whites fled the Central City in droves, abandoning their housing to the Black migrants, local government, including the school board, put into place covenants and policies that contained and restricted Black movement and educational and professional opportunities. In many respects, the system that was put in place was similar to South Africa's infamous apartheid system, providing fodder for lawsuits two decades later. Those lawsuits clearly showed conspiratorial policies that locked Black adults out of public-sector jobs, restricted available housing to the six-square-mile Central City area, blocked Black children out of specialty education, and provided far less funding for educational programs. The least-tenured teachers were assigned to the oldest and most poorly equipped Central City schools. It was common for Black children to share classrooms with rats and mice.

To some emerging Black leaders, the solution to this crisis was integration through litigation: Black children would be better off if allowed to attend so-called White schools with those schools' superior teachers, facilities, and equipment. Others felt that the solution was to equalize resources and to build the best educational opportunities available within the confines of the covenants. Many thought it wasted energy and effort to mingle with people who hated you because of the color of your skin. Subjecting your child to hostility from fellow students and to the low expectations of prejudiced teachers made little sense. Proponents of this separate but equal philosophy noted that even within segregation's circumscribed environment, Black children were excelling because Black teachers cared and Black administrators made the most of the dollars. Community and school spirit were remarkably high. "Give us equal resources and we'll achieve in unprecedented numbers," said proponents.

A clear distinction was made between desegregation—equalization of resources that would set the stage for voluntary multicultural integration—and integration/ assimilation, which was being advocated by the NAACP as a moral mandate. For the next two decades, these distinctly different philosophies would continuously go head-to-head. For some time, advocates of integration emerged at the vanguard, although those with more pragmatic, nationalistic views waited in the shadows, their beliefs firmly entrenched. Thus in the 1950s, while the nonviolent movement later to be headed by Dr. Martin Luther King Jr. was a strong force in the African-American community, an undercurrent of militant, nationalistic thought was building. Desegregation was appropriate as a vehicle for equal access and resources, said the nationalists, but integration was both unrealistic and unwelcome.

For the moment, however, the masses responded to a King-inspired vision—one grounded in the belief that integration/assimilation was a cure-all. The issue of educational equality was but the tip of the iceberg: this battle was intertwined with the open housing movement as well as with the quest for economic empowerment and access to public-sector jobs. It was becoming clearer that the Black Freedom Train's track ran right through the Milwaukee School Board, which meant constant danger of bureaucratic and political derailment.

Essentially led by Black professionals like Vel Phillips, the first Black councilperson, Isaac Coggs, the first Black state representative, and Lloyd Barbee, a talented attorney who eventually became a state representative, the campaign for educational equality challenged the status quo at every turn. The campaign first gained prominence in the mid-1950s, as the city's Black population reached what one Southside politician referred to as a point of "sizable nuisance." Milwaukee's Black population numbered thirty-five thousand, and nearly eighteen thousand Black students were confined to fewer than two dozen schools, such as Roosevelt Junior High School and Lincoln Junior and Senior high schools.[5] Leaders of the campaign looked at the educational deficits—overcrowded classrooms, outdated books, dilapidated facilities—and decided that Milwaukee's Black community would be best served by total integration.

Though underfunded and poorly staffed, the Black schools provided educational opportunities that exceeded those that had been available in the South. A strong case can be also made that the educational offerings of the '50s and '60s were superior to the offerings available since that time. Even though the resources available to the leading "Black" schools of the 1950s—including North Division and Lincoln High Schools—paled in comparison to all but a handful of White schools, the teachers assigned almost by default to those institutions were nonetheless dedicated and resourceful. Unencumbered by union obstructionism, most took the extra steps necessary to provide in substance what they lacked in material goods. Black teachers made the best of the situation—but that didn't mean that they were willing to *accept* the fact that Black schools received less than 70 percent of the funding allocated to White schools.

The growth of the Black population in the 1960s put MSB members and administrators in a quandary: how could they maintain the official city policy of segregated and separate institutions and still accommodate the steady influx of Black students? In the 1960s and 1970s, as Milwaukee resisted the national trend to desegregate, the education system was the battleground that defined the local culture.

One short-term, separate-but-equal solution to the overcrowding problem in the Central City schools was called intact busing: entire classrooms of Black students were bused to White schools, but Black and White students were never allowed to interact. The "Negro" students, who would arrive minutes after White students were tucked safely into their classrooms, were assigned separate bathrooms, and even had a separate recess period. Under intact busing, which took effect in 1958 and lasted until 1972, Black students ate bag lunches in the host cafeteria after the White students left or were transported back to their neighborhood school for a quick snack, then returned to the White school.[6] Three hours later, they would be ushered again into a chartered school bus for the trip home. They were also denied participation in extracurricular programs and activities.

Intact busing was an example of separate but equal at its best—or worst, depending on your point of view. The only certainty was that it did separate the races while solving the overcrowding problem, just as school board members had planned. To ease overcrowding, the board also resorted to leasing space in nonschool facilities and contracting with social service agencies and even some private schools. Rumors circulated that administrators were even encouraging Black students to drop out and were assisting them in getting jobs.

The contrasts between Black and White educational opportunities were so sharp they prompted protest upon protest and eventually civil disobedience.

THE PROTEST YEARS

During the early 1960s, prayer vigils and community meetings gave way to demonstrations and protests as it became obvious that while the White Establishment may have offered sympathy for the blatant educational injustices, they offered little remedy. Even the mayors of that era (who included socialist Frank Ziedler and quasi-socialist-turned-Democrat liberal-turned-moderate-demigod Henry Maier) were silent on the obvious disparities in the education system, approving by city charter the school board budget. Ziedler, who lived in a Central City neighborhood, also voiced little opposition to the policy of segregation, while his successor, Maier, tried to brush it under the rug by saying he had no control over the education system.

In 1962, the antipathy of the White Establishment to the cries for equality prompted Black leaders of the day to set the stage for a decade of protest that forever changed Milwaukee. Black groups (including the NAACP) and a number of Black political leaders broached the question of inferior schools to every conceivable influential body: the MSB, the mayor, White businesses, civic communities, and the clergy. Their efforts were akin to spitting into the wind. Of the handful who responded with empathy, none were in positions to change the status quo.

In summer 1963 attorney Lloyd Barbee sought an audience with State Superintendent Angus Rothwell to discuss the segregated and inferior schools in Milwaukee. According to Michael Stolee's "The Milwaukee Desegregation Case," Superintendent Rothwell, in true political fashion, claimed that compulsory racial integration was contrary to state policy.[7] The following year, Barbee made an impassioned request to the MSB to end de facto segregation. As expected, his appeal went unanswered, sparking what was to become one of the most volatile periods in Milwaukee history.

In January 1964 the NAACP voted to boycott Milwaukee Public Schools beginning the following summer. In the interim Barbee offered his troops to the Congress of Racial Equality to start a series of demonstrations against segregation. The movement was kicked off with a march and demonstration at the MPS administration building: more than 350 parents and community activists braved the cold to demand equal opportunity for their children. MSB members ignored the group and left the building by the back door.

Exactly thirty days later, CORE and the NAACP paved the way for a splinter group that would coordinate a campaign against inequities. Lloyd Barbee was elected chair of the new organization, called the Milwaukeeans United for School Integration Committee (MUSIC). Barbee announced in spring 1964 that the organization would take to the streets, the legislative chambers, and the courtroom if necessary to end Milwaukee's system of educational apartheid. He declared that the only thing worse than the policies that denied equal opportunity to Black children was MSB members' blatant opposition to justice. The segregated schools were only part of a trend that permeated every aspect of local culture, he said, and MUSIC, along with the NAACP, CORE, and the Urban League would do all within their powers to dismantle brick by brick the foundations of institutional racism.[8] Two months later, MUSIC undertook a series of high-profile protests and demonstrations that dramatically illuminated the duel system of justice in Milwaukee.

Over the next few years, parents and social activists covered the gamut of protest methods, including writing letters, appealing to local government officials, and chaining themselves to school buses. By the end of summer 1964, more than seventy MUSIC members had been arrested for engaging in civil disturbances, and Barbee guaranteed local authorities that there was much more on the horizon.

The MUSIC protest coincided with a Black-student walkout that lasted for several weeks. MPS denied any sizable impact, but according to Michael Stolee, nearly fourteen thousand Black students were recorded absent during the period.[9] Most attended private schools or Freedom Schools set up for that purpose. The tactic did attract national attention, and although it wasn't enough to prod the MSB to accommodate even the most insignificant demand, it was recorded as a successful strategy that would be used again.

The battle continued, and on June 18, 1965, three weeks after learning that a letter he had written to the MSB asking for the discontinuation of intact busing had simply been filed away, Barbee filed a federal lawsuit against the MSB for maintaining segregated and inequitable public schools. The suit was filed on behalf of the parents of forty-one children, including nine Whites, charging the district with intentionally segregating the public schools in violation of Constitutional guarantees.

To punctuate that bold move, several hundred Black parents led by Barbee and Sister Marilyn Morehousen, a Catholic nun, took the unusual step of forming a human chain around school buses to demonstrate their refusal to accept the racist status quo. Eleven protesters were arrested, including Barbee. Stolee writes that after being arrested, Barbee said, "Let this MUSIC demonstration be a warning to the city that we will continue picketing, sit-ins, lay-ins, chains and any other kinds of '-ins' until the intransigent school board caves in." The human chain, which received national publicity but scant local coverage, simply met with the usual strategy of the powers-that-be and their propaganda machine: ignore the outcries when possible, infiltrate or disrupt when necessary.

Undaunted, a small contingency of CORE members showed up the next week at a board meeting and began to sing. Although they were arrested, a few days later they staged a sit-in outside the superintendent's office while Father James Groppi (the Catholic priest who helped lead the two-hundred-day-long open housing marches under the auspices of Black Alderwoman Vel Phillips) and a group of protesters chained themselves to buses in front of the 20th Street School.

Later, the Parental Educational Choice Plan and calls for African-centered schools and a Black school district in the heart of Milwaukee's quarter-million-strong African-American population would signal a turnaround in agenda and tactics, as the battles moved from the streets to the courts and legislative chambers of the state and nation's capitals. But for now, rare was a day that no protest or demonstration was staged. Some took place at schools; others were held at the MPS administration building and city hall. MUSIC under Barbee and Sister Marilyn was highly selective in choosing battlegrounds: unbeknownst to MSB members, they generally arranged to provide evidence of board policies that Barbee would use in his school desegregation lawsuit.

One of the most remarkable and eye-catching protests of the summer was the by-product of a joint strategy by members of MUSIC and a contingency of Black clerics. Before the national media and shocked and frustrated White civic and business leaders, *several hundred* Black and White protesters chained themselves to school buses. Some of the protesters chanted "integration by any means necessary," a play off a refrain issued two years earlier by Black nationalist Malcolm X. Malcolm's call was for justice and freedom under an umbrella of self-sufficiency. It is clear that he would have agreed with the demands for equal funding and accessibility, but would not have joined in the push for integration.

On December 5, 1965, the battle focused on an MSB plan to construct several segregated elementary and middle schools in the heart of the Central City. MUSIC targeted McDowell Elementary School for a major demonstration, which included dozens of activists chaining themselves to the construction equipment at the school site. While children chanted "no more segregation" and adults carried signs decrying the board's policies, police arrested twenty-one protesters after sawing them free from tractors and cranes.

The army Barbee and Sister Marilyn amassed consisted of a who's-who of Black political and civil rights leadership, including Reverend Leo Champion, Jeannetta Robinson, John Givens, Alderwoman Phillips, and Judge Clarence Parish, who in 1964 was elected mayor of Black Milwaukee—a ceremonial position created by Black community activists to protest city hall's antipathy to Black concerns. He relinquished this title only upon his death. Although their election was an outgrowth of Black frustration, Parish and the Black council never received the community support they could and should have had; key members and supporters of the concept found themselves splitting their time between marching and protesting for open housing and for school integration.

Occasionally a word of sympathy would emanate from the Catholic Archdiocese, a liberal politician, or a sympathetic civic leader. Whites, including students from Marquette and members of several socialist groups, joined the protesters on a number of occasions and attended some of the strategy sessions and prayer vigils. On one occasion, Sister Marilyn reportedly solicited the aid of a dozen White families, who publicly announced their desire to enroll their children in all-Black Central City schools. The White families were denied registration forms, adding further ammunition for Barbee's lawsuit.

But with only a handful of Black elected officials in Milwaukee County to raise the cry for justice on their respective legislative floors, there was little opportunity for a voice to be heard within the political status quo. The media, for the most part, was either apathetic or condescending in its reporting, despite the righteousness of the cause. Indeed, fighters for justice found themselves ostracized by the media, political leaders, and educrats. Even Barbee, considered conservative in Black circles, was labeled an anarchist by the media and White political leaders, who made it known through word and policy that Black Milwaukeeans were, and would continue to be, second-class citizens in Milwaukee.

Webster Harris, one of many soldiers in the education reform army, was to say years later after he joined the Republican Party, "Many of us were there for different reasons; not all of us were integrationists. But the issue was discrimination, which was pervasive throughout the city and in every vestige of life in Milwaukee. The schools were the most obvious, along with housing and trade jobs, which we were locked out of along with government jobs. We were second-class citizens, plain and simple, and the most obvious solution to that situation was to break down the barriers, brick by brick."

Debate raged at dozens of MUSIC and NAACP meetings as to how to accomplish those goals. Some soldiers pressed for continued demonstrations, mirroring nonviolent projects around the country, coupled with legal action, such as Barbee's suit. Others advocated more militant tactics. All were in agreement that direct appeals to the MSB fell on deaf ears. On a half-dozen occasions, members of the various groups joined neighborhood parents and Black politicians at school board meetings to espouse their disenchantment with and opposition to the board's plans, but to no avail. The Barbee lawsuit, which the NAACP joined but was unable to adequately pay for, was caught up in legal limbo, and prayer vigils and sit-ins were not moving the board much either.

Finally, more drastic tactics became the norm, with or without the endorsement or consensus of the coalition leadership. The first group to break away was the NAACP Youth Council Commandos. These young turks called for more direct action against the status quo impediments to a higher quality of life, and from their ranks sprang some of the astute and strident grassroots activists, politicians, and businesspersons who are still major players in the Milwaukee community today.

The Commandos' primary mission was to serve as police during the 200-day open housing marches. Many members grew angered and hardened by the rocks and bottles they intercepted daily from White racists, who carried signs encouraging the marchers to "Return to Africa" or to "Buy their nigger burgers" at a Southside restaurant. Getting beaten up on a daily basis while police ignored assaults or egged on the bigots didn't sit well with the council members, many of whom grew up in the shadow of Malcolm X and H. Rap Brown. A growing army of Black nationalists called for an end to the "begging and willingness to spit into the wind," as one leader described it.

Integrationists were ever hopeful that their protests and demonstrations would show concrete results, as they had in other major cities. Several meetings were convened to attempt to reach a consensus to put aside philosophical differences and to display a unified stance for the cameras and reporters. With the exception of a couple of militant groups—including the Republic of New Africa—that advocated a violent revolution, the consensus was to follow a time-tested path. As a result, nationalists stood beside integrationists for common demonstrations, including one in which a half-dozen organizations created another human chain, this time in front of school buses that carried White children to three new schools. That demonstration resulted in one of the largest mass arrests before or since the 1967–68 open housing marches. Nearly one hundred participants were jailed, and many were allegedly brutalized by the police.

Word of the incident fueled calls for a boycott of MPS, which occurred immediately thereafter. Once again, on October 18, 1965, more than fifteen thousand Black parents pulled their children from public schools. And again, the problem of school placement was resolved by the creation of a dozen Freedom Schools, supported by the Catholic Archdiocese and a group of White students from Marquette who called themselves Students United for Racial Equality. Indeed, an eye-opening letter from a contingency of Catholic priests stated that "when the needs of the children are not satisfied by the existing school system, it is within the rights of the parents to remove their children from the schools and place them in others."

While Black students were getting their first taste of freedom, MUSIC, CORE, and the NAACP were letting several school board members—including the board's president, John Foley—and the mayor know that it would no longer be business as usual. Each time they returned home from their hard day's work, they were met by protesters.

PULLING TOGETHER: BLACK INDEPENDENT SCHOOLS

The opening of the Freedom Schools had an unanticipated by-product: many Black leaders called for the abandonment of MPS and the creation of a Black school district. How it would be funded—or whether the state would even recognize the request—was unknown. What was agreed upon by Black activists in a fall meeting in 1965, however, was that the Milwaukee political structure was immovable in its desire to keep Milwaukee segregated.

Many of the militant Black activists declared that integration was a dream that would never fully materialize. Instead, the Black community should seek equality of resources, if not a Black-controlled district. The quest for integration was nonsensical not only because of the racial climate, but also because it would weaken Black institutions, undermine Black culture, and dilute the communal spirit. Focus instead on building a stronger community, they said; if integration materializes, let it be on equal terms. Black people should not seek to be assimilated into the White community. Let this be *true* multiculturalism.

Despite their compelling case, the militants were essentially drowned out by traditional leaders such as Barbee, Phillips, and Wesley Scott, executive director of the Milwaukee Urban League, who saw a greater value in knocking down the plantation walls and forcing accommodation.

Both sides did agree on the need to explore and create other opportunities for Black children. Nationalists pressed for the creation of independent Black and community schools; integrationists encouraged the enrollment of Black students in Catholic and Lutheran schools. The nationalists' cry for Black independence and control of institutions was soon answered.

Besides the filing of the school desegregation lawsuit and the subsequent passing of the Open Housing Ordinance in 1968, there were few headline-grabbing protests for a couple years, although less-publicized calls for the dismantling of the apartheid state in Milwaukee continued. That relative calm lasted but a short period as the movement's emphasis shifted from tearing down legal barriers to ensuring survival amid escalating police brutality and blatant acts of bigotry from Southsiders and representatives of hate groups, including the Nazi Party. It was inevitable that a spark would soon send Milwaukee into flames. And in summer 1968, riots not only changed the civil rights status quo but also further widened the racial divide. When the smoke finally cleared, a new wave of Black militancy stood tall, drawing the attention of a frustrated new generation of Black youth.

From that movement emerged an even stronger cry for Black power and a growing conviction that community control of institutions—or the creation of new Black ones—was the solution to social and political ills. In the early 1970s new leaders such as Michael McGee, Hubert Canfield, and Doris Green, who collectively started the United Black Community Council, found the community receptive to their calls for a more militant approach, which included a willingness to fight racism and police brutality with fists and fury instead of bibles and legal documents.

A half-dozen community institutes were established, including Harambee and Urban Day Community schools. Black leaders such as Reuben and Mildred Harpole—many of whom were at the forefront of the integrationist movement a few short years earlier—took advantage of the closing of several Central City Catholic schools in their quest to build a district within the public school district. Harambee, for example, was created when Black parents and activists assumed control of the former St. Elizabeth Catholic School after the Archdiocese withdrew its financial support.

Harambee's history of struggle during the 1970s and 1980s illustrates the depth of parents' and community activists' concern for and commitment to securing first-rate education for their children. At the first organizational meeting under the school's new administration, those in attendance battled for more than an hour over a name, offering such suggestions as "Malcolm X" and "Marcus Garvey." They wanted to identify with a Black nationalist and also make a political statement. Someone offered "Freedom Academy," and another suggested "African People's Institute."

Eventually, activist Ron Johnson introduced the term "Harambee," noting the importance of all Black people putting aside their differences and "pulling together," which is the translation of the Swahili word.

"They don't want us to educate our own," said Ron Johnson. "They don't want an educated Black community; we all know that. And if it's to happen, it's only going to happen because we commit here to ensure it happens. And that means we have to stop arguing and bickering and work together. We have to pull together to make this happen for our children. In the spirit of Malcolm, Martin and our forefathers who sacrificed for us, we have to pull together. Harambee."[10]

Smiles and nods of agreement filled the room, as did a commitment to educational excellence and a philosophy of Black children empowering themselves. That commitment was put to the test hundreds of times during the next decade as the school struggled to survive financially. Scarcely a week went by that administrators didn't have to hold off bill collectors ranging from the electric company to book suppliers. But the parents, joined by community activists and local politicians, did whatever was necessary to keep the school going. Often teachers went unpaid or collected percentages of their salaries. Parents were called to contribute dishes for school lunches.

Corn roasts, weekly neighborhood car washes, and Friday and Saturday fish fries were among the imaginative fund-raisers orchestrated by parents and supporters to offset costs, along with occasional door-to-door solicitations when necessary. No parents were turned away because they couldn't pay tuition, and the waiting list of prospective students attested to Harambee's excellence as an educational institution.

Instructors included retired MPS teachers, attorneys, an occasional college instructor, and a Pan-Africanist historian who taught the children about a homeland and an ancestry all but ignored by the public school system. Indeed, the hallmark of the Harambee Community School, like hundreds of Black independent schools around the country, was that it provided Black children with a strong foundation of self-esteem and Black pride. High expectations were the norm in this K–8 school, and, despite a scarcity of everything from books to desks, the students didn't just learn—they excelled.

Two students who attended Harambee in its early years were Joe Donald and Shawnee Sykes. Donald's and Sykes's parents saw something special offered at Harambee, an intangible quality that only private schools, particularly those founded by parents with a shared vision, provide. The children were viewed not just as recipients of education, but as vessels for a new tomorrow. They were treated as future community and world leaders who, much in the vision of W. E. B. DuBois, were the Talented Tenth, the 10 percent earmarked for leadership and greatness by circumstance and opportunity.

Both Donald and Sykes met those expectations and today are role models and leaders for another generation. Joe Donald went on to attend St. Lawrence Seminary, excelling both academically and athletically. After graduation he pursued first a bachelor's and later a law degree from Marquette University. After a decade of service as an assistant city attorney for Milwaukee, in 1997 he accepted a gubernatorial appointment as a Milwaukee County circuit judge. He currently serves in juvenile court, where he witnesses society's failures daily and administers justice to those who didn't have access to the education and support mechanisms he was fortunate enough to enjoy.

At a retreat for Harambee Community School board members in April 1999, Donald recalled how he emerged from Harambee with a "can-do" attitude and a sense of individuality and purpose that many juveniles who appear before him in court don't have.

"They taught us to be proud of who we are and that we had a purpose and responsibility to our community. There are so many children who come before me who lack self-esteem, something we had in abundance," he said to fellow board members during a meeting to explore options to expand the school. "I'm for expansion to enable us to embrace more of these kids; to give them the foundation I received."

Shawnee Sykes took to heart the teaching of the Sisters of Notre Dame who had stayed on when St. Elizabeth became Harambee Community School and decided that she would enter the convent. She attended Divine Savior Holy Angels Catholic High School after graduating from Harambee, then accepted a scholarship to Spellman College in Atlanta, where she earned a bachelor's degree in nursing. Sykes then earned a master's degree in Pastoral Studies. In 1997 she resigned from her post as the director of African Ministries for the Catholic Archdiocese of Milwaukee and she is currently on sabbatical as she completes doctoral work at St. Louis University.

Both Sister Shawnee Sykes and Judge Joe Donald are assisting current Harambee students to follow their examples: Judge Donald serves on the school's development board and Sister Shawnee is a mentor and lecturer. Sister Shawnee also serves on the Messmer High School board.

There are dozens of equally impressive success stories. As school board President Tommie Alexander explained to Dr. Alexander Lockwood Smith, New Zealand's minister of education, during Smith's visit to the school several years ago, "Harambee's graduates are changing the world, making an impact wherever they are. They are politicians and engineers and teachers and police officers. Most importantly, they are parents who are impacting the next generation, doing positive things and fulfilling the dreams we had for them."

Harambee and its sister school, Urban Day, proved to be beacons in an otherwise dreary educational environment. Indeed, it has long been said that public school educrats and teachers unions have fought Black independent and parochial schools because they feared that the community would make comparisons that would illuminate the public schools' deficits. The public school teachers and educrats did not want to be put in a position of explaining why children from similar "dysfunctional families" and socioeconomic backgrounds failed under their charge yet excelled in Black independent schools.

Why have the Black independent schools had such success? It surely has not been the result of technology; there are no state-of-the-art classroom environments. It can't be because of avant-garde teaching techniques. No, the answer is much simpler.

At the private institutions, more is expected of students, and the teachers teach because they love children more than paychecks. Equally important, they are given a sense of self-actualization—Black pride if you will—and are told they are keepers of the flame. They are told that their ancestors didn't mysteriously appear on Earth as slaves, but were creators of science and math and the arts.

Parents are involved in the process at Black independent schools because they feel they have a voice and a role in the process, that their input carries weight. They participate in classroom instruction, call teachers with questions and concerns, and serve on the school boards. Thus, the schools bring forth future Black leaders with a sense of self, purpose, and commitment to community.

While independent schools were attempting to fill the educational void, the protests of the 1960s defined Milwaukee and its resistance to change, but achieved little more. The MSB never moved, the civic community simply hid its head in the sand, and the body politic just turned its back. In subsequent years, Black Milwaukeeans worked both within and outside the school system to overcome the obstacle of entrenched institutional racism. Freedom Schools flourished, as did enrollment in parochial schools, most notably Catholic schools. In fact, it was because of the unavailability of seats in the Catholic school system that several Black parents explored the possibility of state-sponsored vouchers as a means to an end.

The year was 1970, and while the voucher effort succumbed to a quiet death, it planted a seed that would bear fruit two decades later.

THE FIGHT FOR VOUCHERS

Wisconsin's first campaign to enact a school choice program began when a group of Black parents met to discuss the ramifications of proposed closings or mergers of several Central City Catholic schools. The schools were operating at a deficit, in part because few of the thousand or so Black families with children in Catholic schools could afford to pay full tuition—and most were not Catholics. Because scholarships were rare in Catholic schools, the Archdiocese absorbed the costs as part of its mission of outreach. But as Whites left the city in droves, the economic base was proportionately undermined and the burden on the Milwaukee Catholic Archdiocese grew. Declining attendance at Central City Catholic churches and efforts to consolidate resources prompted the Archdiocese to begin a politically scarring process of cutting financial support for its Central City schools.

Hundreds of Black students reportedly ended up leaving the Catholic school system as a result. Several hundred others were absorbed when Black parents elected to assume control over two Catholic schools and convert them into Black independent schools. How many fell by the wayside, however, is anyone's guess.

The solution to the quandary was found when a Black parent read about a federal program to fund a voucher program and introduced the idea of a coordinated campaign to lobby either for a grant through that program or for state or local funding through MPS. The premise of the latter idea was that the district could save money by paying for the tuition of Black students attending Catholic or independent schools.

The Black parents' group was led by Jesse Wary, a well-known community activist and coordinator of the Federation of Independent Community Schools. Wary and his group of parents, joined by several community activists including renowned activist Donald Sykes, executive director of the Social Development Commission (SDC), the state's largest antipoverty agency, put into motion a year-long campaign to introduce a voucher program in Milwaukee—a campaign that energized the Black community and some White MSB members and ultimately earned the endorsement of the *Milwaukee Journal*, Wisconsin's largest daily newspaper. The campaign came within a hairbreadth of success.

In an August 20, 1970, *Milwaukee Sentinel* article Wary revealed that the group had been studying the idea of vouchers "for months as a pilot within MPS." Seven private Central City schools—Bruce Guadalupe, Martin Luther King Jr., St. Boniface, St. Francis, St. Leo, Michael Community School, and Harambee Community School—had agreed to be part of the pilot, said Wary, in order to "give parents a choice. If MPS does not participate, we would go ahead on our own and try for the funds" through the federal grant. Harambee and Bruce Guadalupe would eventually become participants in the country's first voucher program, although it would not be initiated for another two decades.

The parents' group, which received seed money from the SDC, focused its campaign around securing a $5 to $8 million Office of Economic Opportunity (OEO) grant. The grant was part of a federal pilot project that sought to study the impact of vouchers on poor communities over a period of five to eight years. It was to be awarded to only one city. During the pilot, the number and types of participating schools were to be determined by local authorities but could include religious schools. And herein lay the catch: the pilot would have to be coordinated through a local government authority—in this case, the MSB.

The easiest part of the campaign was securing public support. Wary's group found a responsive audience wherever they traveled in the African-American community and even found some support among the Establishment, including parents and the civil rights community, particularly the Urban League and the Social Development Commission. They also found receptive ears in two school board members, John Stocking and Donald O'Connell, who helped organize the Committee for Educational Vouchers.

An informational hearing about the OEO grant in early October 1970 revealed broad-based support for vouchers, which would have included both parochial schools and specialties run by the board or by third parties.

Robert Bothwell of the Center for the Study of Public Policy in Cambridge, Massachusetts, was brought in to advance the possibilities. During an October 18 appearance on *Public Conference*, a television show produced by the Milwaukee Public Library, Bothwell announced that the possibilities for vouchers were endless: "You might have schools concentrating on art and music or new Montessori schools springing up. The more diverse and attractive these schools are to parents, the more pressure there will be on the system to make changes."[11] Bothwell noted during several speaking engagements that the vouchers would allow up to twelve thousand students to attend any participating school that the parents so designated and thus would provide for healthy competition between private entities and the public schools.

Vouchers would force the educational monopoly to reassess itself, Bothwell theorized, and would compel public schools to improve in order to attract or retain students: "Good schools might have money to expand and bad schools might be forced to close. There hasn't been any urgency to change before unless parents became incensed. This would provide an alternative [to demonstrations]."[12]

In an interview published in the *Milwaukee Journal*, MSB Director John Stocking stated that competition would be good for Milwaukee Public Schools. "This system would reward those schools that would produce for the children," he said, "and would discourage and cut off those schools that did not."[13]

Wary and Bothwell stressed that the voucher program would provide parents with true power by permitting them to send their children to schools they felt met their educational needs rather than relying on bureaucrats to make decisions based on ambiguous or racial guidelines.

Moreover, the voucher program would be a much-needed source of funding for community schools engaged in a desperate struggle for survival. Wary noted that "the program would give us a source of funding to put into practice some things we've been talking about. It would give the community a chance to educate its children in the way we think is actually relevant in today's world."[14]

Despite growing public support, pressure from the local and national teachers union and other special interests ultimately swayed a majority of MSB members to derail the proposal. Thus, after a lively two-hour hearing before a packed house, the MSB's Appointment and Instruction Committee voted to reject a proposal to seek the grant. However, the 3 to 2 vote did not deter proponents. After the meeting, the board's two "yeas" vowed to press on for a feasibility study that they hoped would sway their colleagues.

Armed with a broader base of support secured in the course of a month of informational meetings, the two board members introduced a compromise plan. Ironically, a key component of the proposal was the elimination of parochial schools from participation, a decision that appeased some skeptics but eroded some Black support, particularly from Wary's group. To offset that loss, Stocking and O'Connell invoked the aid of the Milwaukee Urban League and several noted academics from the University of Wisconsin. An effort to pull the NAACP into the organizational structure fell flat. The SDC eagerly joined the fight—a coup of sorts, since at the time it was the premier antipoverty/Black empowerment agency in the state. The SDC was created by the city of Milwaukee and Milwaukee County as a quasi-public venture with the express purpose of tackling poverty and building the Black community through self-sufficiency programs. SDC head Donald Sykes argued for the voucher during the school board hearing, noting "This is not a reflection on the superintendent or the board; but the state of urban education in America is in trouble. This is an opportunity for Milwaukee to become a leader in terms of education. This is one of the few federal programs where you would be free to design a program not fettered by federal guidelines. We are asking for the opportunity to sit down and explore the opportunities a voucher system would provide here."[15]

As the debate over vouchers was reaching a head, Harold Jackson, the lone Black MSB member who had been appointed several months earlier, issued an eye-opening assessment of internal politics that had the Black community in an uproar. Announcing that he did not know how long he would be able to serve on the board given its politics, Jackson charged that MPS "instills negativism, despair, and a feeling of inferiority in its Black children."

The noted attorney, who would a few years later be named a circuit court judge in Milwaukee, went on to charge that Black children were being "canceled out" at some point in the educational process, so that when they reached adulthood many of them "believed they were genetically inferior to Whites." He called this scenario "absolutely lethal."[16]

A week before an MSB meeting to reconsider the grant application, the Committee for Education Vouchers released a report that made a strong case for the program, with input and endorsements from a cross section of the city. "The essence of a voucher program is to develop alternative school curricula and to help parents choose which ones their youngsters attend," declared the report. "The Milwaukee Voucher Program will not endorse the notion that merely giving out money can, by itself, improve the quality of school programs."[17]

The report recommended limiting the vouchers to low-income students and creating a lottery to ensure fairness in selection of the applicants. It also called for the creation of an agency to oversee the implementation of the program as well as to "develop common goals for all schools, develop specialized schools, provide public information about the schools, and supervise, evaluate, and regularly accredit programs, including private schools."[18]

The report was well received throughout the city, so much so that it drew an unlikely endorsement from the subjectively liberal *Milwaukee Journal*, which noted in a front-page editorial that discontent with America's public schools is "deep, widespread, and probably growing. It is essentially acute in big cities where some of the nation's best schools have in recent years become among its worst. Surely, it is no time for school officials to plug their ears and close their minds [to reforms and innovative ideas]."[19] Yet that was exactly what was happening in Milwaukee, where the board had declined the opportunity to look at vouchers as a viable stimulus and reform: "Allowing parents to select their children's schools (public or private) by giving them vouchers in the amount of their community's per-pupil school expenditure, in theory, would increase parental options while stimulating healthy competition between public and nonpublic schools."[20]

But on November 10, 1970, the hopes of Black and low-income parents, educational reformers, and a growing number of politicians were dashed against the bureaucratic wall when for the second time in two months, the MSB's Appointment and Instruction Committee voted against further study of the voucher proposal.

The derailment of the school voucher campaign again shifted the movement's direction to a variety of other fronts, including a campaign to elect Black Milwaukeeans to the school board. Some activists were also calling for a separate Black school district or appealed to the governor for a state commission to run the public schools. Seeing the writing on the wall and urged by corporate heads and city hall, the school board voted on August 3, 1971, to end intact busing—a major victory for MUSIC. The MSB hoped the policy change would stymie growing unrest and a parade of protests, which brought to the city negative public relations, threats of a second riot, and the prospect of funding losses from the federal government.

The decade-long protest to destroy the apartheid education policies in Milwaukee had sparked one of the largest protest campaigns in state history, complementing the campaign to end legalized segregated housing. Maybe because many of the same leaders were involved in both campaigns, these protests emphasized integration over desegregation. Many Black leaders erroneously believed they could somehow legislate morality and were willing to go that route even if it meant destroying Black institutions in the process.

A splinter group of Black nationalists disagreed with the assimilationists and fought to end segregation with the express purpose of erasing barriers to equality. They sought to knock down the barriers while building a stronger Black community upon elements of African culture, creating mechanisms to empower the Black masses. If integration were then to occur, it would occur among equals based upon mutual respect. However, the nationalistic movement would have to wait its turn, as the 1970s witnessed the inevitable culmination of the civil rights litigation of that era: the Milwaukee school desegregation lawsuit.

CHAPTER
3

WHAT WENT WRONG
WITH THE SYSTEM

The most potent weapon in the hands of the oppressor is the mind of the oppressed.

—STEVE BIKO

In the early 1970s, Black children found themselves at the short end of a dual public school system that was governed by tactics precariously close to apartheid. How to change that reality, however, was subject of much debate. Grassroots organizers and more militant naysayers fought to secure resources denied their children, not to integrate or to achieve admission to predominantly White schools. Some within that group advocated for fiscal parity, site-based management, and control over the neighborhood school system. For them, separate—if truly equal—would suffice.

As Organization of Organizations head Larry Harwell would recall in a 1997 interview with a *Milwaukee Community Journal* reporter,

The desegregation battle is nothing more than a farce. Too many of us have been duped into believing that if our children are bused across town and allowed to sit next to a white kid, something magical is going to happen; the white air will swell the black brain. That's not only ridiculous, it's racist. The only thing our black child will learn is that he is being taught to believe he is inferior, must go outside his community to learn, and that black teachers can't teach him, or that he can't be taught in a Central City school.

The reality is we did okay while segregated and given less of everything. What we want now is the opportunity to excel; we want equal resources to raise our plateau to that of white kids. Imagine where we would be [if we had the same resources as the white kids]. [Politicians] also keep selling us the lie

that this [process] is integration, when it's really desegregation. They say it's
voluntary, when it's not voluntary, at least for black children. Why don't they
equalize the resources and make the busing equal, if it's voluntary?[1]

While many in the Black community agreed with Harwell, their voices were
generally drowned out by the chorus of integration supporters, whose numbers
included the city's most prominent Black leaders. Fronted by the NAACP, CORE,
and MUSIC, they advocated integration of the schools as a major step toward
knocking down the various barriers that locked Black people out of Milwaukee
society. School board policies were consistent with other infamous city covenants
that included segregated housing, insurance and home mortgage redlining, and a
criminal justice system that led Black citizens to utter sarcastically that "there are
two systems in Milwaukee: there's justice and JUST US." Breaking down one barrier, the integrationists said, would cause a domino effect that would bring the
entire edifice of enforced second-class citizenship crashing down. NAACP leadership felt that the best way to change the status quo was to destroy the problem at
its core and thus pressed a class-action school desegregation lawsuit. Lloyd Barbee
served as lead counsel for the lawsuit, which lasted for over a decade.

The desegregation lawsuit provided the opportunity for Black leaders to push
forward the assimilationist agenda: if you lived, worked, or studied next to Whites
long enough, they would recognize both your uniqueness and your commonalities,
and friendships would emerge. This was the only way to make America truly a
color-blind nation. Whether or not it was possible to legislate people to like you
apparently received little discussion.

MSB MAKES ITS MOVE

In mid-1973, after a decade of political posturing, the MPS desegregation case
picked up steam with the replacement of Robert E. Tehan by Judge John Reynolds.
A well-known liberal and supporter of civil rights causes, Judge Reynolds sent out
word of his frustration with the school board's posturing and let all parties know he
wanted to bring the lengthy case to a conclusion—in favor of the plaintiffs. That
fact was not ignored by the MSB, three members of which were Black. The racist
views of the MSB were summed up by Director Lorraine Radtke, who said desegregation would introduce chaos because Black children "can't understand our
plumbing. [You'll] have urination in water bubblers."[2]

While the majority of MSB members were opposed to integration in any form,
given the piles of evidence against them they were pragmatic enough to know that

a ruling for the plaintiffs was a certainty. The prevailing assumption was that White Milwaukeeans did not want to integrate with Black people and were adamantly opposed to any program that would erode their comfort level and cultural stability. The task before the MSB was to craft a desegregation program that would appease both White Milwaukee and the courts—one that would maintain the White power base and avoid the violence that had followed desegregation orders in other cities. Forced busing, for example, could spark violence or White flight, both of which would be detrimental to the city. And time was of the essence: either the courts or Madison lawmakers could intercede with plans of their own.

One of the most promising—albeit controversial—proposals that emerged was crafted by future mayoral candidate Dennis Conta. State Senator Conta's plan called for the creation of cluster districts that joined parts of Milwaukee's school district with two suburban districts, Shorewood and Whitefish Bay.

The Conta Cluster Plan drew significant support from pockets of the African-American community, which was desperate for quality education at any cost and envious of the resources enjoyed by White suburbanites. MSB members, however, were quick to lambaste the proposal, expressing fears that the Milwaukee district would be absorbed in the process. Suburban lawmakers were also skeptical, though their opposition was mostly fiscal and territorial: merging districts not only would strip autonomy and fiscal stability from the suburban districts but also would eventually open the door for a metropolitan school district. If such a plan were implemented, would it not mean that eventually there would be no suburbs, no middle- and upper-class haven, no separation from the horrors of urban life? The Conta Cluster Plan had to be defeated at any cost—on this point Republicans and Democrats agreed.

The Conta Cluster Plan was doomed from the start. However, it did serve to frame the debate as well as pave the way for an eventual compromise on intradistrict desegregation transportation. It also let Black people know in no uncertain terms how so-called liberal suburbanites really felt about them.

LIBERAL HYPOCRISY

I was made brutally aware of liberal hypocrisy while covering one of my first assignments in 1975 for the Milwaukee Star Times, a Black-owned weekly newspaper. I was an idealistic Black reporter who bought into the rhetoric of liberal-leaning suburbanites. Surely my liberal suburban friends—those who begged for an end to Vietnam during my tour there, criticized Milwaukee Mayor Henry Maier for his apathy toward Black inequality, voted for the Democratic Party

1975
Eastside
meetn

in large numbers, and spoke out boldly against segregation—would jump at the chance to put their money where their mouths were. I was certainly naïve—and about to receive my first lesson in the varying shades of gray when it comes to Whites' views of Black people.

The hearing on the Conta plan drew hundreds of liberal Eastsiders who filled to capacity the large meeting room on the University of Wisconsin campus. When I arrived there was not a seat to be found and I was forced to stand against the wall near the entrance with a dozen other participants. Only a handful of the two hundred or so people in attendance were of color.

Having flirted with socialism and attended numerous meetings where liberal White Eastside suburbanites championed the causes of equal opportunity, I felt totally at ease in the room and was scanning through my notebook when I heard a White man telling the panel, which included Lloyd Barbee and Dennis Conta, that Black children were "deviously inclined." I looked up and to my amazement, witnessed a casually dressed White man spewing a hate-filled diatribe about how "savage" Black children were and how they would bring their "barbaric culture" to the suburbs.

I was shocked, not just by his racist comments but also by the nods and acknowledgments they drew from the audience. And that turned out to be one of the less vivid commentaries of the hearing!

For nearly thirty minutes I listened not only in shock but also with a bit of fear as these so-called liberal Democrats mixed a strong brew of racist epithets. In their twisted, hate-filled minds, Black people would rape their daughters and spread cultural disease, illegitimacy, and immorality in their virgin environment. Several suburbanites did stand up to the diatribes—one man almost ended up in a fistfight with a neighbor over a prejudicial statement. One stately gentleman who reminded me of Ward Cleaver from Leave It to Beaver chastised the racists in the audience for their "un-Christian and un-American comments." He received modest applause. But most in attendance remained silent and through word or gesture seemed more supportive of the opposition, leaving little doubt that the same bigotry that has stereotyped the Deep South was also alive and well in Milwaukee's supposedly liberal suburbs.

I don't know how the hearing ended. After another five minutes I eased out of the room to keep from exploding in rage. There was no doubt that I would be "lynched" by these Eastside liberals if I protested too loudly. So I left, shuddering in anger and brought to tears by the realization that my so-called friends were in truth no different than the KKK and the Nazis who frequently held rallies in Milwaukee. As a resident of Milwaukee, I was accustomed to racism, but this revelation was particularly disturbing. It meant that Black Milwaukee was all but friendless. Sure, there were still the Ward Cleavers of suburbia, and chances are a large percentage of those who remained silent in the audience were not racists. But if they were afraid to rock the boat, they hindered our cause as much as the hate-spewing bigots did.

For reasons I can't fully understand, I found myself trying to justify the crowd's behavior while driving the four miles west to my Central City home. Maybe these people were victims of the White media propaganda. Maybe only the racists showed up for the hearing. Or maybe I had left too early. Surely others would stand up and support integration. After all, these were liberal Whites, not the Southside bigots who threw bricks at my parents and siblings during the open housing marches of the mid-1960s, and whose children carried signs telling us to "go back to Africa."

But it didn't take long for the truth to overwhelm me: many, if not most, liberal suburbanites were hypocrites at best, covert racists at worst. They liked to project an image of open-mindedness and self-righteousness, but when push came to shove, their true colors came to the surface. They loved our music, quoted Dr. Martin Luther King Jr., and could sing every word of "We Shall Overcome." But when it was possible that my Black child would sit next to their White child, all bets were off. The suburbs were not just a haven for middle- and upper-class Whites, not just a sanctuary from poverty: they were an escape from Black America.

Strange that I did not see it before. Most of the Whites with whom I associated were truly liberal college students, Central City residents "Blackanized" by association, or members of socialist groups, including the Worker's World Party, the Socialist World Party, and the Communist Party. The true allies of Black people were actively involved in civil rights; they often stood with us at protest marches and even took the lead in fighting police brutality. But few, if any, were suburbanites. I couldn't envision any of them fighting the Conta Cluster Plan, school desegregation, interracial marriage, or Black control of community institutions, but I was to learn in the coming years how wrong I was.

DESEGREGATION BY ANY OTHER NAME

Even as the Conta plan diverted public attention, the MSB was secretly crafting what members felt was a desegregation plan that would both appease frightened Whites and placate teachers fearful of losing their seniority and privileged assignments. Continuing a costly court battle and inviting the possibility of a federal takeover and court-structured desegregation plan simply did not make sense.

To ensure that the desegregation process would be effective—which meant not putting any undue burden on Whites—the board closed several predominantly

Black schools, converted several others into citywide specialties, worked out secret deals with teachers union representatives over seniority, and gutted the neighborhood cluster pupil assignment programs.

Two decades later, the U.S. Commission on Civil Rights noted that what was unveiled as the cure-all desegregation settlement in 1976 was only a placebo. Not only did the plan fail to deliver on the promises of quality education for Black students but it resulted in another two-tier school system that gave White students access to the best schools—and forced most Black students on long bus rides to nowhere.[3]

Under this plan, an overwhelming majority of the students involuntarily bused for desegregation purposes were African American. The majority of the Whites who did board buses were assigned to specialty schools. More than 70 percent of Black children were bused out of their neighborhoods while fewer than 5 percent of White students were bused to Black neighborhoods. Milwaukee Public Schools was reimbursed for busing and also received a bonus of up to $4 million when it exceeded a certain quota. MPS had created a busing monster that was fed by state dollars and was increasing its appetite by millions each year.[4]

Under the guise of voluntary integration, the school desegregation program forced many concerned parents to send their children to schools dozens of miles from their homes. Simply getting to those institutions was often a herculean task: fewer than 40 percent of Milwaukee's low-income families owned cars, and often bus service left them miles away from the school in a neighborhood where people of color were justifiably afraid to travel.

School inaccessibility—not apathy—limited parent participation in parent-teacher conferences and other school activities. That point was illustrated several years ago when MPS educator Muhammad Sabir, assigned to an elementary school deep in the all-White Southside, suggested that the school's parent-teacher conference be shifted to a Northside location in the heart of the Central City. Although participation by Black parents had averaged less than 30 percent, when the next conference was held at a church in the heart of the Central City, attendance nearly tripled.

Logic would dictate that administrators would respond to that impressive attendance by shifting conference locations on a permanent basis. Of course, the opposite occurred. Teachers complained about having to travel to the Central City area, and administrators thought that the change could set a precedent that wasn't cost-effective. So in grand bureaucratic fashion, the proposal was dropped and business as usual prevailed. The next parent-teacher conference drew attendance of about 32 percent.

Not coincidentally, MSB members and the NAACP never responded to letters detailing the parent-teacher conference experiment, which in the eyes of many parents and educational activists was proof positive that the public school system was unwilling to prioritize the needs of parents and students over those of educrats and teachers. Some suggested that the system was set up to put as many impediments as possible in front of Black and poor parents, thus ensuring a permanent underclass to supply the service industry.

In a December 8, 1976, document entitled "Comprehensive Plan for Increasing Educational Opportunities and Improving Racial Balance in the Milwaukee Public Schools," School Superintendent Lee McMurrin stated that the program would include both voluntary (for White students) and mandatory (for Black students) busing, and the intent was not even to meet the court-ordered goals, but merely to balance schools up to a 50 percent minority standard and then to exercise a variety of alternatives beyond that point. These included "transferring minority students out and majority students in under the suburban exchange program" and establishing a "similar kind of relationship with private schools in the city." Not only was the program not voluntary but its methodology was rooted in appeasing White families, not forcing their children to attend schools where Black students were in the majority.[5]

Hypocritically, McMurrin stated: "We believe that through the exercise of these alternatives the system need not balance minority/majority beyond the 50 percent standard. Moreover, the psychological guarantee of not having to attend a school that is predominantly minority will tend to stabilize the population of the city."[6]

McMurrin and the board's sole challenge was to withstand criticism as their plan was being implemented. And since the White media was in their pocket and the only protests came from disgruntled parents, that goal was not difficult to accomplish.

The desegregation settlement finalized in 1979 by Judge Reynolds called for 75 percent of the system's students to be assigned to "racially balanced" schools that could be no more than 60 percent Black. According to the U.S. Commission on Civil Rights, prior to 1976 only 14 percent of schools met the court-ordered definition. By 1979, through allowed quotas for Whites at specialty schools and forced busing of Black children, 79 percent met the definition.[7] But from that point, an unexpected White exodus reduced the number of White students in the program, forcing more Black students to assume the busing burden.

One study of the plan, conducted by the National Institute of Education and released three years into the desegregation process, created a stir when it revealed that Black students were bused in a bizarre, inexcusably complex system.[8] For example, in one elementary school attendance cluster, Black students were bused to twenty-six different schools in White areas, even though there were available seats at their neighborhood schools. The study showed an astronomical 3,100 exchanges of students between elementary schools, confirming what many had already assumed: the busing plan not only was excessive and contrived to benefit White Milwaukee but also wreaked social havoc on Black families, in some of whose households four children were each bused to a different school.

A foundation-shaking *Milwaukee Magazine* exposé written in 1986 by reporter Bruce Murphy and freelance writer John Pawasarat announced that

> On paper, in the desegregation literature, the Milwaukee plan became known as a national model; in reality it was a bureaucratic nightmare—one of the most inefficient and inequitable plans ever devised.
>
> In theory, desegregation was seen as a way of stabilizing the school system and preventing white flight; in fact, about one-third of elementary school-age whites left the city [following the settlement], and of those who remained, fully one-half attended private schools. . . . [A]s a result of demographic changes that were compounded by the Milwaukee desegregation plan, a system that was once majority white and middle class is now just the opposite: The majority of Milwaukee Public School students are from low-income, minority and single-parent families. Together, these students make up a vast underclass of children whose level of achievement is well below that of other students and who may never receive a proper education unless the school system is fundamentally changed.[9]

In their prophetic assessment, Murphy and Pawasarat went on to say:

> Small wonder that education has become perhaps the number-one issue in Milwaukee today, even as it remains the most misunderstood. For the fact is, Milwaukee has a completely different school system than it had 10 years ago. Still, [School Superintendent Lee] McMurrin and the school administration remain locked in the policies of the past, policies that can be traced back to the widespread local fear of what happened in Boston. In 1976, when the state's Democratic politicians set out to integrate the city's schools, the last thing they wanted was a "Boston situation" in Milwaukee. The result was a very different kind of failure.[10]

DESEGREGATION AND THE WHITE COMMUNITY

Advocates of integration such as the NAACP and some Black politicians hailed the settlement. The NAACP, with a vested interest in the desegregation process and a blind eye toward the inequities, embraced the process wholeheartedly, as did

groups like the Coalition for Peaceful Schools, an integrated group whose sole purpose was to ensure that Milwaukee did not follow Boston's racial explosion, and the
Committee of 100, which was created by the school board and fell under the thumb
of Superintendent Lee McMurrin. The Committee consisted of one hundred Black
and White parents and handpicked citizens and was supposed to be an advisory
group for MPS and the desegregation process, but it was just a placebo. Its recommendations went nowhere.

Once school desegregation was introduced, the MSB's top priority was to
appease disgruntled and obviously scared White Milwaukeeans. At stake was not
only the comfort zone and prejudices of White Milwaukee but also the future of the
city. It was often said behind closed doors that desegregation—the threat of Black
children sitting next to White children or eventually living next to them—would
chase White middle-class families and their taxes from the city.

The White press put the best face on school desegregation. The Milwaukee
Journal and Milwaukee Sentinel, the city's two dailies, downplayed the busing
inequities. Even though the methodology and results suggested otherwise, the press
referred to the program as one of integration, not desegregation. It seemed to make
no difference that the legal remedy for segregation is desegregation, not integration. Courts can only order the movement of bodies and an end to fiscal inequities.
They cannot order integration, which is a natural, voluntary process that generally
evolves over time.

Superintendent Lee McMurrin, the chief public relations instrument for the
district, constantly confused the issue, provided erroneous and misleading statistics,
and even managed to downplay a racial confrontation involving Nazis at a desegregated school. McMurrin's strategy was to deflect attention away from the board
and the desegregation process by challenging groups like the NAACP to toe the
line. He used his Committee of 100 as a sounding board and rubber stamp for his
plans. Few complaints from the Committee of 100 or other reform groups ever
found their way into the pages of the White media—another obvious example of
the "Black-out" of opposition to desegregation. Eventually, the Committee of 100
imploded out of frustration.

Yet the White media apparently loved McMurrin, lies and all, rarely looking
behind the statistics and the Black success stories he offered as examples. In fact,
at various points the White media was accused of being a propaganda arm of MPS
and the superintendent.

In fall 1978, I confronted McMurrin during his annual State of the Schools
press conference, noting the inconsistencies in his busing statistics, and challenged
him on his use of the term "voluntary integration." I pointed out that fewer than 8

percent of the children bused for desegregation were White and that most of them were assigned to specialty schools, which was in itself a strong example of the bias that tainted the program. I also asserted that since Black schools were closed, the process was not voluntary for Black children, who never received their first or second choices, and that the courts had repeatedly stated that the process was one of desegregation, not integration.

A red-faced McMurrin responded that I was confused and apparently out of touch with reality. In fact, anyone who questioned the process was a usurper who wanted to undermine a sincere effort to bring about peace and harmony in Milwaukee. As for the inequities in busing . . . well . . . "You people asked for it!"

But if the media, White politicians, school administrators, and McMurrin thought that the Black community would remain silent, they were mistaken.

DESEGREGATION AND THE BLACK COMMUNITY

One might ask whether Black leadership had any inkling of what was in store: the inequities of the system they approved and the burden that would be shouldered by Black students. Milwaukee historian and philosopher James Pugh believes that they did, and lectures to this day that "Black leaders of that era compromised even before they negotiated. They couldn't see the forest for the trees. I don't fully blame them, because it was obvious there were many factors at work. The courts brought in a White attorney, Irv Chaney, and mandated he assist Barbee. Pressure was on everyone to get this done peacefully, and with as little interruption to White citizens as possible." However, once the smoke cleared the Black press and a majority of Black politicians positioned themselves against the plan or let it be known that they were skeptical of it.

Black politicians such as State Senator Monroe Swan, who authored a state bill to reorganize MSB to provide greater Black representation (the bill backfired, and the number of Black board members was actually *reduced*), attacked the system for discriminatory policies that undermined efforts to secure quality education. Further fueling opposition were several reports from State Senator Swan and other cynics that pointed out the inequities in busing.

Even MSB members acknowledged as much. One board member admitted, "State money, in the form of consensus, was the driving force behind the desegregation process." Joyce Mallory, another Black board member, called the program "unnecessarily massive and discriminatory."

Groups such as the Organization of Organizations and Blacks for Two-Way Busing grew out of the disenchantment, pushing not only for equalization of busing but also for a curtailment of double standards for Black students, who were disproportionately disciplined and earmarked for "exceptional" educational programs.

It was no coincidence that attendance at parent-teacher conferences took a nosedive following desegregation, nor was it happenstance that minority suspension rates soared while self-esteem and academic achievement plummeted. Black parents found themselves dozens of miles away from their children's schools, which were often in hostile environments where they encountered angry—sometimes violent—Whites. Their children were suspended for carrying Afro-picks (which teachers thought were weapons) or were disciplined because their vocabularies and cultural mannerisms were perceived as hostile or threatening to White teachers, some of whom had never before come into contact with a Black person. Many teachers, naïve and prejudiced by a media intent on painting a picture of Black people as illiterate and morally bankrupt, had low expectations for their charges. Who could learn in these conditions, let alone reach his or her full potential?

School desegregation accentuated this travesty by destroying neighborhood schools, the cornerstone of the Black community. Opponents saw the inequitable burden on Black students, the closing of the neighborhood schools, and the refusal of the Establishment to address the ever-present problem of White hostility, and cried foul.

Community forums, news articles, and investigative reports in the Black press supplied a steady flow of information that MPS could not contain.

The Black press, particularly the *Milwaukee Community Journal* (MCJ), which was founded in 1976—ironically the same year as Judge Reynolds's ruling in the school desegregation case—waged an ongoing battle with MPS and its steady parade of superintendents over the so-called integration process.

From the onset the MCJ attacked the program's inequities. We at the newspaper also openly questioned whether the program was achieving its numerical goals, citing local and national studies such as the National School Board Desegregation Research Project, which described Wisconsin as one of the country's most segregated states. A decade after the desegregation settlement, only 70 percent of Black students attended desegregated schools, and that number was dropping as White children continued to leave the system for private and suburban schools. Repeatedly we editorialized against school closings in the Central City, the prejudiced conduct of teachers, and efforts to move more and more Black students into remedial programs.

By 1980 it was becoming increasingly obvious that a majority of Black parents disapproved of the desegregation program, and even the most optimistic Black leader was no longer calling it a voluntary process for Black children. Black board

members were openly challenging the status quo, militant Black leaders were calling for an overthrow of the district and a transfer of Black students to Freedom
Schools, and Black teachers were decrying racist policies of their own union, which
they said condoned incompetent teachers.

The pendulum of grassroots support in the African-American community had
begun to swing in a new direction.

THE SAVE NORTH DIVISION CAMPAIGN

From that chorus of protest emerged State Representative Annette "Polly" Williams,
a fiery social activist who had cut her teeth fighting for predominantly Black electoral districts under reapportionment.

Williams, a former welfare mother and Urban Day parent, wanted for Black
Milwaukee what she had had: options and opportunity. Williams believed that education provided the seeds for empowerment, the central ingredient of Black
independence. Community control of institutions was the path to self-determination and self-actualization. Like State Senator Monroe Swan, Williams was a
strong critic of desegregation, not only because it placed the burden of busing on
Black children but also because at the end of a two-hour bus ride in predawn hours
in subfreezing temperatures, Black children received an inferior education—even
when compared to the system under segregation. Among the more startling statistics that fueled Williams's anger was that one decade after court-ordered school
desegregation, the high school dropout rate for Black nonspecialty school students
had increased by 40 percent, an all-time high.

Williams also revealed that during the first eight years of desegregation, the percentage of Black students who were demoted at the middle and high school levels
had increased by 300 percent, a change she attributed to racism. White teachers,
she noted in reports she published monthly, were often afraid of Black children or
had low expectations that doomed them. There was also growing concern over the
irreparable psychological harm to Black students who were told they must be in the
proximity of Whites in order to achieve. In addition, the desegregation order dispersed Black teachers throughout the system. Whereas Black teachers were once
concentrated in schools where their commitment to Black children could be max-
imized, under desegregation they were rationed throughout the district, and a quota
cap was placed on assignments to any one school.

Williams was certain that the MSB would have little, if any, sympathy for the
plight of the Black community's children. Historically, the MSB had turned a deaf
ear to the cries from the Black community and advanced legislation that benefited

the White community almost exclusively. It was with those factors in mind that Williams joined community activist Howard Fuller in fighting the MSB about converting a neighborhood/attendance-area school to a specialty school and later in advancing a call for a Black school district.

Not only was North Division High School one of the oldest schools in the city, it was a historical marker for Black Milwaukeeans. Parents and community leaders petitioned the MSB for nearly a decade to construct a new facility on the site of the deteriorating school. Yet despite their promise to maintain North Division's status as an attendance-area facility after its reconstruction, the MSB—after considering recommendations to relocate the school from its site at 12th and Center streets to 7th and Center streets (this idea was premised on a concern that White students would not travel too deeply into the Central City, and 7th and Center was adjacent to the expressway)—decided to convert North Division into a citywide medical/dental specialty. Under the MSB plan, North Division would be closed as an attendance-area school at the end of the 1979–80 school year, and the health specialty would be implemented in 1980–81 for grades 9 and 10, adding grade 11 in 1981–82 and grade 12 in 1982–83.

So, three years later to the day after Judge Reynolds issued his final decree on Milwaukee's school desegregation, Fuller led a group of more than five hundred students and activists in a protest march to the MPS administration building.

Fuller's first speech in the Save North Division campaign shook the status quo and set the terms for the future debate on desegregation: "We thought that all a Black student had to do was sit next to a White student and he would get an equal education. But we found that there were all kinds of ways to belittle Blacks. We have gone from discriminating against Black kids by containment to discrimination by scattering them all over. In Milwaukee, we turned the *Brown* [v. *Board of Education*] decision on its head."[11]

To understand Fuller and his community's affection for North Division, one has to understand not only the importance Black Milwaukeeans put on education but also the role Black schools had in providing stability to Black neighborhoods. North Division High School and Lincoln High School (the latter of which the MSB closed as part of its desegregation scheme) were the cornerstones of the Black educational experience in Milwaukee during the '50s, '60s, and '70s. Many of today's Black elder statesmen, including several of the Black political figures and the most prominent and successful business leaders, were products of Lincoln and North Division, which often won the state basketball championships and were the sites of community forums, social gatherings, and political meetings. To this day the schools' rivalry is played out in an annual alumni basketball game, which is a major scholarship fund-raiser for the Black community and which, in many respects, is one of the city's most notable "family reunions."

Fuller was one of a dozen city notables who had attended North Division High School, although for him the battle to keep the school a neighborhood institution involved more than just keeping history alive. An early advocate of site-based management and Black empowerment, he understood the importance of a strong community support mechanism to enhance educational opportunity. The MSB's disregard for Black demands to make the school an area-attendance school was a personal and community insult that irked him all the more because a Black man, Leon Todd, served as the MSB's point man on the issue. This frustrating and often confusing scenario appeased the White media, but left a sour taste in the mouth of the Black community.

Fuller and Williams, however, refused to give way and used their organizing skills to build a broad-based community network to fight the board's plans. Dozens of community meetings that were advertised in the Black newspapers, in church bulletins, at community sessions, and on Black radio soon drew hundreds of supporters whose frustration over years of board apathy fueled their desire to stop what they considered yet another insult to a community on the brink of explosion.

Todd's position against keeping North Division a neighborhood school and his personal attacks against Fuller and Black parents who opposed his views made him a focal point of the campaign and earned him the title of "Uncle Todd." Todd symbolized everything that was wrong with the system, including the complicity of African Americans within the educracy who were willing to sell out their communities for money or accolades from Whites. The fact that Todd's primary support base was the White community told a story of its own, as did his inflammatory comments about Black single parents.

Fuller, the proclaimed-revolutionary-turned-intellect, had grown up in Milwaukee, but upon leaving the city after attending college on a basketball scholarship he headed a social/political organization in Durham, North Carolina, and founded Malcolm X University in the same state. Upon his return to Milwaukee, he worked as an insurance salesman before entering the political arena as a spokesperson and Black leader.

Apparently content to live outside the public eye after hanging up his revolutionary cloth, he found himself drawn back into the fire not only by the North Division battle but also by a campaign to end police brutality.

An unprecedented string of police murders of Black citizens (each under controversial, if not openly suggestive, circumstances) and the chief of police's racist stance led Fuller to join Michael McGee, grassroots organizer and former Black

Panther, in forming one of the most successful and powerful movements in Milwaukee—the Committee for Justice for Ernie Lacy.

Lacy, a twenty-year-old Black man, was arrested for a crime it was later learned he did not commit. During a struggle with police, officers pinned the unarmed man to the ground with their knees on his neck, killing him. Although the death was underplayed by Milwaukee's White media, the Committee for Justice for Ernie Lacy drew thousands to rallies and pulled together one of the most unique coalitions in Civil Rights movement history: motorcycle gang members, Hispanics, and socialists joined Black clergy, nationalists, Pan-Africanists, and integrationists in a common cause.

Eventually, the Committee emerged victorious, having won a slew of important civil and political battles, including a settlement to the Lacy family and a change in state law to restrict the tenure of the chief of police. Fuller went on to tackle educational issues, and McGee successfully served two terms as a city alderman until he threatened to undertake a campaign of civil disobedience if the city didn't move to tackle the myriad problems facing the black community, particularly joblessness and inequitable educational opportunities. White Milwaukeeans interpreted "civil disobedience" to mean a violent outbreak, prompting city official and business leaders to oust McGee from political office by gerrymandering his district.

In the Save North Division campaign, the strong community support mechanism put in place by Fuller and Williams emerged victorious, and the MSB relented—at least on paper. For a period it appeared as if the community had won a major victory, which was epitomized both by the decision to keep North Division a neighborhood school and by the rejection of LeonTodd at the polls shortly thereafter. But the victory was short-lived; the MSB put in huddle after huddle to ensure that the school would not be successful. The board refused to follow through on its commitment to make the school a true site-based-managed institution, one in which parents and community leaders would have a say in the curriculum, staff, and administration of the school, and instead made the school a virtual dumping ground for disruptive and problem children. To top things off, the board fired two consecutive principals who were making headway in improving the quality of education.

Black board member Joyce Mallory challenged the policy of dumping disruptive students on the school, and Texas Bufkin, one of the fired school principals, later sued the MSB and won a settlement estimated at $1 million. Eighteen years later, Bufkin used part of her settlement money to start a private school that is a participant in the Milwaukee School Choice Program.

HOW DESEGREGATION FAILED OUR CHILDREN

Soon after the North Division battle, Fuller turned his attention to a new, albeit almost identical, crusade, this time to keep Roosevelt Middle School a neighborhood-attendance facility. He took his case to the court, but was shot down when U.S. Magistrate Aaron Goodstein ruled against parents, saying that while the desegregation process was unfair to African Americans and in fact created a new form of discrimination, it was legal and previously agreed upon by plaintiffs and defendants. The defeat further soured relations with the school board and sparked a renewed call for alternatives to MPS.

Fuller vowed to strip from MPS the veneer of unbiased, quality education. Two years after the crusade to save Roosevelt Middle School as a neighborhood school, the fiery activist was named Secretary of Employment Relations, a gubernatorial cabinet position. However, it wasn't state relations Fuller was interested in. Seeking a platform from which to alter the educational status quo in Milwaukee, he pressured then–Governor Tony Earl into empowering a commission on education and pacified the business and civic communities in Milwaukee by putting at the head of the body two prominent business leaders, George Mitchell and William Randall.

Sixteen months later, in early October 1985, their research was presented to the governor, the state superintendent, and other key state officials under the title "Study Commission on the Quality of Education in the Metropolitan Milwaukee Public Schools: Better Public Schools." They had about a week to brace for the uproar that was to ensue when the report was published in the press, which set off a chain of events that altered the course of educational history in Milwaukee.

The report pulled no punches. It provided indisputable facts showing that contrary to the rosy picture painted by McMurrin and the educational Establishment, school desegregation was no cure-all. In fact, Black children were probably worse off than at any time in local history. The report noted:

> There is an unacceptable disparity in educational opportunity and achievement between poor and minority children on the one hand and nonpoor and white children on the other.
>
> Although commendable examples of effective programs and high scholastic achievement are found in public schools throughout the metropolitan Milwaukee area, thousands of young people are leaving these education systems limited in their capacity to participate—either as effective citizens or productive workers—in contemporary society.[12]

The report went on to reveal that "poorly prepared youth in the metropolitan area comprise a significant segment of the population, enlarging the burden of our local economic and political systems to support those incapable of supporting themselves."[13] Under school board policies including desegregation, Black children were lagging seriously behind their White counterparts and were dropping out of school in record numbers.

Among the abysmal facts noted by the commission:

- By the fifth grade, a significant majority of poor and/or minority children were performing below the national average on achievement tests.
- There was a significant gap in math scores between boys and girls. MPS longitudinal data showed large drops in math scores from grade 7 to grade 10 for girls of all races, and particularly for Hispanic and black girls.
- Black achievement in the ten high schools meeting the desegregation criteria was abysmally low. Black students received Fs in 26 to 43 percent of their courses and only eight of twenty-one black students exceeded national test average.
- The average grade point average in thirteen out of Milwaukee's fifteen public high schools was less than a 2.0, or a C average.
- More than one-quarter of the courses taken in MPS high schools ended in a recorded grade of F or U for unsatisfactory. In seven of the MPS high schools, the percentage of Fs was above 30 percent.
- MPS had a dropout rate more than double the state average and higher than any suburban school, with most dropping out before the eleventh grade.
- The suspension rate rose in six schools with large black populations; the percentage of black students suspended was twice that of white students.
- Attendance fell in half of the desegregated high schools.
- For the grades tested—second, fifth, seventh, and tenth—the percentages of students in MPS below the national median ranged from 45 percent in second grade to 58 percent in tenth grade. Of all suburban students tested, the percentage below the national median ranged from 17 percent in second grade to 29 percent in tenth grade.
- While one-half of the suburban district enrolled between 5 and 17 percent minority students, minority teachers in the suburbs represented only .5 percent of the total teaching staff. In 1983–84, 18.5 percent of the MPS teaching staff were minorities as compared to a 59 percent minority student enrollment.[14]

There was little school officials could do to dispute the findings, especially since the data, collected on more than sixty thousand students in fifteen districts, was analyzed and broken down by race, gender, and family income. The research provided this startling highlight:

> The commission's research demonstrated clear differences in school performance between racial and income groups in both the city and suburbs. Differences existed on a number of performance indicators, including test results, dropout rates, and grades. The differences all were in the same direction: low-income students did less well than non-low-income students, and white students did better than minority students.[15]

While Black children were excelling in private and parochial schools, the research showed that in the public schools' second grade "70 percent of white children were at or above the national median achievement level, while only 43 percent of black students were. In the fifth grade those figures were 62 percent for whites, and 29.9 percent for African Americans. In the seventh grade, the numbers were 64 percent and 30.9 percent and in the tenth grade, they closed slightly from 62.2 percent for whites and 22.3 percent for black students."[16] The report caused such a stir that Black leaders from both sides of the political and civic aisle began a chorus for reform that shook the very foundations of the school administration building.

To frustrated Black parents, MPS's response was as predictable as it was disappointing: the MSB and Superintendent McMurrin questioned the validity of the data and criticized the agenda of the Democrat-appointed task force members. As expected, McMurrin challenged the value of any research that put a bad face on Milwaukee.

Even supporters of MPS were shocked by the response from the educrats, which had an air of denial and antagonism. The attack on commission members also created a stir—after all, they included not only influential businesspeople but also prominent Black and White civil rights leaders. But more was to come. Provoking sensationalistic headlines in the local media, McMurrin engaged in a month-long verbal battle with commission cochair George Mitchell. Eventually, Mitchell emerged unscathed, but the superintendent had driven another nail into his own career coffin: McMurrin's posturing was drowned out by Mitchell's eloquent denunciations of the status quo and the lie that had been perpetrated against the Black community.

With the commission study as more fuel to the fire, MPS was desperate for an avenue to divert growing public sentiment and "solve the Negro problem," as one board member put it. The solution came in the form of Chapter 220, an intradistrict public school choice transfer program that was literally thrown in

MPS's lap by then-former State Senator Dennis Conta through a group he formed called the Metropolitan Integration Research Center (MIRC).

The MIRC threatened the MSB with a new desegregation suit and later encouraged the members to initiate their own lawsuit against two dozen suburban school districts over their segregation policies. Unlike the Milwaukee desegregation suit, the suburban district suit quickly reached a compromise that was beneficial to MPS and proved to be lucrative to the suburbs as well. MPS would be able to divert thousands of Black children to the suburbs, thus avoiding a new desegregation lawsuit that would force greater involvement by White children. As Whites left the Milwaukee public schools, MPS was increasingly faced with the prospect of equalizing the busing formula to meet court-ordered desegregation goals. The new suburban transfer program settlement provided a way around that problem.

The suburban areas, although callous in their opposition to a Black "invasion," faced a fiscal crisis because of declining student enrollment. Since they were essentially stuck with a fixed tax base, it was possible that the districts would receive less state aid—and could eventually go bankrupt. Chapter 220 solved that problem by providing districts with matching state aid for every Black student accepted. Moreover, the districts could essentially cream off the best Black students—both academically and athletically. (This stipulation prompted State Senator Monroe Swan to call Chapter 220 a bounty program.) Also as part of the settlement, districts that exceeded modest enrollment quotas would receive bonuses far exceeding the cost of education, and a provision set aside seats for suburban White children in Milwaukee's best specialty schools. The fact that the quota took away even more seats from Black students at magnet and specialty schools wasn't broached.

Everyone seemed happy with the deal: the suburbs, MPS, Black civil rights groups like the NAACP (which received a sizable grant as part of the desegregation process)—and even Black parents. Middle-class Black parents, eager to escape MPS and the cost of private schools, signed up their children in large numbers, despite the fact that a former MPS board member, now a board member in a suburban community, had readily admitted to the press that if it weren't for the money, the suburbs wouldn't have had anything to do with these Black kids. But any problems with Chapter 220 were superficial compared to what board members were soon to discover was their latest challenge: the effort to create a Black school district.

A BLACK SCHOOL DISTRICT?

In spring 1987, a campaign to carve out a separate Black school district rode the coattails of the Save North Division campaign. Some of those involved in the new campaign were converts from the desegregation battle who had learned the hard way that sitting next to a White child does not ensure that a Black student will receive a first-rate education. What they shared with their more militant brothers and sisters was a desire for Black achievement by any means necessary and frustration over the Milwaukee School Board's obvious resolve to ignore a problem that, like a cancer, was eating away at the foundation of public education in Milwaukee. So activists and parents who just a decade before ignorantly assumed nationalists to be "separatists and radicals" now joined them in pressing for an annexation to the system they previously sought to integrate.

State Representative Polly Williams came into her own while campaigning for the Black district. The proposal was to enact legislation that would establish a separate school district in Milwaukee consisting of two high schools and a dozen elementary and middle schools. The district would have its own board and state funding based upon existing funding allocations.

The North Division School District Plan had its detractors—particularly the NAACP and older, more traditional civil rights leaders—but the majority of African Americans seemingly felt that the plan had merit, if for no other reason than its ability to give Black people control over the institutions that affected their lives. Fresh in their minds were the Commission report findings, coupled with a slew of more abysmal statistics supplied by Polly Williams and carried in the Black press.

Interestingly, Governor Tommy Thompson let it be known that he, too, supported the North Division School District Plan. In fact, during the *Milwaukee Community Journal's* first interview with the gubernatorial candidate, Thompson acknowledged his support, albeit with the condition that such a plan would have to come from the Black community—not from Republican leadership.[17] His rationale was simple: the North Division Plan would be construed by some liberals as an effort to resegregate Milwaukee public schools. Thus to publicly endorse it would be political poison for Republicans—or even progressives, for that matter.

Ironically, Thompson's sentiment framed the position on school choice for many Republicans. It's an age-old controversy that has plagued and undermined efforts to build bridges between the Black nationalist and conservative communities. Black nationalists also fear the connection, feeling that support for issues identified with conservatives—from abortion to school choice—will taint their effectiveness.

Working with Larry Harwell, formerly the head of the Organization of Organizations (which was dissolved in the early 1980s), Polly Williams put together a communitywide parent organization that lobbied for the North Division Plan. Their strategy, which they would duplicate a decade later in the school choice campaign, included letter-writing campaigns to White state lawmakers, presentations at public hearings, weekly press conferences, and petition drives. Strategy and organizing meetings were held weekly at area churches, and other Black leaders and politicians were solicited to add strength to the demand for an autonomous district.

Again, Mitchell added a positive voice from the sympathetic White community with a *Wall Street Journal* article that was circulated throughout Wisconsin.[18]

Mitchell called the North Division School District Plan an effort that challenged "the way urban schools are governed and would mean a transfer of power from bureaucrats and union leaders to parents, principals, and classroom teachers. If successful it could cause a reappraisal of how American cities address the minority education crisis."[19] MPS had reacted to the plan as any monopoly would, Mitchell said:

[MPS] has tried to crush any discussion that might legitimize the proposals, which include either a new, independent school district or more autonomy within the current system. These reactions highlight the dual crisis in American public education—the failure of most poor minority children to learn and the stubborn refusal of urban school leaders to discuss reforms that research shows could make a difference.

The North Division School District is centered on a goal of increased academic achievement, resulting from more parental involvement, more accountability to parents, and greater autonomy for educators at the school level. . . . Research shows these factors are conducive to learning and usually exist in small systems not dominated by authority-conscious central bureaucracy.

Another essential ingredient for learning is high expectations. Inner-city parents deserve educational leaders with confidence in the ability of their children to learn, yet many of those running the Milwaukee public schools lack optimism. The district's last official plan projects that blacks won't score as well as whites on achievement tests for ten years.[20]

Joyce Mallory, former president of the MSB, scoffed at the suggestion that Black students could not do as well as Whites from the suburbs, wrote Mitchell.

These educators explain their low expectations by focusing on problems beyond their control—broken homes, teenage pregnancy—thus attempting to insulate themselves from blame, Mallory contends.

One impetus for the proposed district is research by a blue ribbon state commission I chaired that studied public schools in Milwaukee and its suburbs. The commission's report identified which schools were working, which were not, and why.

The study disclosed a dramatic disparity in learning between minority children from poor families and white students from middle- and upper-income homes. The gap is widest in the high schools, most of which are integrated. In Milwaukee, the odds are that black or Hispanic children will drop out of school or be graduated with a D average.

More significant was the finding that educational failure among poor minority children is not universal in the Milwaukee area. The Milwaukee research mirrors studies elsewhere, summarized by U.S. Education Secretary William Bennett in publications called "What Works" and "Schools That Work." The evidence is that learning occurs across the economic and racial spectrum when certain conditions are present. Among those conditions are parental involvement and teacher perceptions of parental involvement, high expectations, and strong school leadership.[21]

The North Division district could bring those components to the fore. Supporters of the North Division School District Plan didn't believe decentralization was a cure-all; they felt that "the key is a true transfer of authority and responsibility." This was demonstrated by four nonsectarian Milwaukee private schools with an 80 percent minority enrollment that achieved better results with low-income minority students than did the public schools—at a fraction of the public school budget. Parochial schools in Milwaukee, with a 25 percent minority enrollment, also consistently reported better achievement for minority students:

> The Milwaukee proposal also emphasizes giving poor parents more choice in school selection, the kind already held by many middle- and upper-income parents. Parents in the new district could enroll their children outside it if they felt a better education would result. Proponents state in their literature that no child would attend a school in this district if his or her parents did not make that choice.[22]

Mitchell went on to acknowledge that race has been the source of controversy in discussions of the new district:

> For years, school officials quietly condoned the segregated status of the schools in question. The same officials now shout "racism!" at the blacks who propose the separate district and accuse them of wanting to undo civil

rights progress. The school board's attorneys have labeled the plan uncon-stitutional, although it has not even been drafted in bill form yet. And after Republican Governor Tommy Thompson expressed interest in the pro-posal, city school officials threatened to sue the state. Proponents of the new district say it will encourage and enable white parents outside the dis-trict to transfer students to the schools. The proponents believe this will happen when the schools become effective.[23]

As expected, the school board fought the proposal tooth and nail, as did the teachers union. They were joined by the NAACP, which saw the plan as a road-block to integration, even though the schools considered for the plan were segregated anyway, in obvious violation of the school desegregation order. The floor debate for the North Division School District Plan took place in August 1987, about the same time a settlement was reached between twenty-four suburban dis-tricts and MPS over an intradistrict school desegregation program. The North Division School District proposal debate showed Polly Williams at her best, impli-cating the teachers union as an impediment to quality education for Black children and imploring Democrats and Republicans alike to "give us a chance to educate our own." Let the North Division School District be a pilot—if it fails, no one is worse off than they are now, she said. But if it succeeds, use it as an example of what can be done, a challenge for MPS. Unless they believed that Black children are intel-lectually inferior, it was the system—teachers and the administrators—who are responsible for the failure of Black children. Let Black parents control the system and they will weed out incompetent teachers and administrators, replacing them with caring educators. Then we can eliminate the excuses, argued Williams.

Much to Willams's—and her opponents'—surprise, the assembly approved the North Division School District Plan, setting off a firestorm of disgruntlement. That concern intensified as word circulated that if the senate approved the measure, Thompson was to fulfill a campaign promise and sign it into law.

During the next few weeks the Milwaukee Teachers Education Association (MTEA) and MPS pulled out all the stops to undermine the legislation in the senate. When the smoke cleared, the measure had been killed. But they couldn't kill the vision nor unearth the seed that had been planted.

The campaign for a separate Black school district should have been a wake-up call for the school board, but as in most cases before and since, the Black commu-nity's cries fell on deaf ears. Board members came and went, along with two new superintendents who tried in vain to effect change, but to no avail. Following the reign of apologist and spin-master Superintendent McMurrin, the MSB retained its first African-American superintendent, Hawthorn Faison. Faison, however, killed any hope of permanency when he committed the cardinal sin of engaging in a series of meetings with parents and community activists in the hopes of developing a consensus on school reform. Independent thought has never been a commodity of praise for superintendents, and soon Faison was looking for work.

The MSB then turned to the East Coast and Robert Peterkin, an African-American reformist with big ideas but little knowledge of Milwaukee-style politics and culture. Peterkin was receptive to ideas of decentralization, community partnership, and parental involvement in education, which probably put him at odds with some board members even before he penned his first proposal to reform the splintered, decaying district. Like his predecessors, however, MPS Superintendent Peterkin faced a board without a consensus or a true vision, a teachers union that all but controlled board policy, a frustrated business community that in far too many cases found itself forced to accept an undereducated and functionally illiterate "product," and an angry citizenry—particularly Black and poor parents whose cries for quality went unanswered.

The failure of the North Division School District Plan did not discourage parents or Black leadership. In many respects the defeat invigorated and inspired them in the drawn-out war to secure quality education for their children. Black parents and educational leaders had secured an unprecedented victory with the assembly approval of the self-governing measure: no bill of such magnitude had ever made it that far in the political process, providing proponents with the belief that they were one step removed from a major victory. That thought was even more comforting given the fact that the North Division Plan had received support from both sides of the political aisle, including the governor.

Education, Malcolm X once said, is the passport. The partial victory in the North Division School District fight implied that White legislators did not reject the idea of vesting Black people with the power to control the processes that determined their children's future. They had listened as Williams issued the challenge to allow Black parents to do what every other ethnic group had done: educate their own. They nodded in agreement when Williams explained that no one has ever done—or would ever do—for us what we would and could do for ourselves. And finally, beholding a sea of Black families who had missed a day of work to take a stand against failure and mediocre education, they pushed the "yea" button.

CHAPTER

4

SOUNDING THE TRUMPET

These are the best children we've got; their parents aren't send-
ing us any more and they can't be traded in for better models,
and we have to educate them as they are. The Parental School
Choice movement takes that as a given and doesn't shrink from
the task or use conditions they have no control over as an
excuse for why kids can't learn.

—HOWARD FULLER

From the doorway, Polly Williams quickly surveyed the room, then made her way to the head of the conference table. A few feet behind her, loaded down with papers, followed longtime community activist-turned-legislative aide and confidante Larry Harwell. There were seven of us at Urban Day School that first Saturday of August 1989, including representatives of Harambee and Bruce Guadalupe Community schools (Bruce Guadalupe is the city's leading Hispanic private school). All eyes focused on the neatly dressed middle-aged Black woman whose fiery expression of her nationalistic philosophy had often put her at odds with her Democratic Party colleagues.

Williams didn't waste any time. After positioning herself behind a chair at the head of the conference table and quickly acknowledging and greeting each of us by name, she got right to the matter at hand.

"I guess you all know why we're here. I've talked to most of you individually, so you know where I stand. Now it's just a matter of what *you* want to do." She explained that many parents had contacted her since the defeat of her Parental School Choice bill several weeks earlier, suggesting that she reintroduce the meas-ure. "I'm not opposed to that, but just being right ain't enough. I can't do this alone—*if* we decide to do it. In fact, *we* can't do it alone. We're going to have to find support on the other side of the aisle, and even then, there're no guarantees. It's an uphill fight at best and to be honest with you, those people who say they're your friends be plotting and stymieing behind the scenes to keep us down just like the other folks.

"Sometimes I don't think we have any friends up there [in Madison]. White folks got their agenda, and some of us get a few crumbs every now and then, but for the most part, we're by ourselves. But don't let me get started on that," she added, catching herself. "Y'all know what's what. The question is, do you want to do what's necessary to give us a chance to get this?"

Williams put down the pen she had been using like a conductor's wand to emphasize her points. She scanned the room, awaiting a response.

Eventually Zakiya Courtney, Urban Day school parent liaison and parental involvement coordinator, broke the silence.

"Well, I guess I can speak for everybody here when I say we're a thousand percent behind you," Courtney said. "Some of us ain't got the bitter taste outta' our mouths from the defeat of the last bill, but we're ready to go to war to get this through. We'll do whatever's necessary. Not just us in here, but our parents here and at Harambee and Bruce Guadalupe. And I assume thousands of parents throughout our community. We're ready."

Williams took in the nods and acknowledgments. She smiled and turned to Larry, who opened a folder containing a draft of the recently defeated Parental School Choice bill, along with various legislative maps, MPS statistics, and several pages of talking points and legislative summaries of related public education proposals, including the Chapter 220 suburban desegregation program.

"This is where we start," he said, as Williams stepped away to take off her jacket and roll up her shirtsleeves. "I think we can get some support from the Republicans that supported us before, and a handful of Democrats. The governor supported us before, and I'm sure I can get him to support a new measure, which would mean a lot, particularly if we can get him to lobby his folks. But this has got to be our bill, our campaign if it's gonna' work, which means the governor won't have ownership. I don't know if he'll let Black folks steal his thunder, but we'll see.

"But from there it's going to be an uphill climb," he said, handing out the documents. "There's going to be a lot of work. We got to rally our people, and then get them to make this an issue. And once we start, there's no turning back. This has got to be a massive people's movement if we're gonna' be successful. We gotta' use this to break the chains once and for all."

The meeting lasted for more than two hours. Each participant offered suggestions on the new proposal: recommendations ranged from a full voucher program to a version of the original bill limited to only a handful of students to "get our foot in the door." The scaled-down version of the School Choice bill was soundly rejected, as was a call for a program that would include religious schools and eliminate income restrictions. Enthusiasm grew as the meeting progressed and soon we were speaking in terms of when, not if. We finally settled for a program of one thousand students with family incomes below 150 percent of the federal poverty level.

"We can do this," school board President Tommie Alexander whispered to me as Harwell explained financing options to the educators and activists who made up the new steering committee. "We can get Harambee parents and Urban Day and Bruce Guadalupe parents and the hundreds who are waiting on lists and all those who are waiting on scholarships and get them all involved, and we have a movement," he said, his words fueled by the enthusiasm of his vision. "These are our children, and they deserve the right to go to school where they can get a real education. That's what we'll tell those fools up in Madison. What's good for the goose is good for the gander. We want the same for our children that they want for theirs. Money and color shouldn't determine whether you get a good education."

GOVERNOR THOMPSON'S SCHOOL CHOICE PLAN

Two decades after a small group of Black parents broached the subject of school vouchers as a mechanism to provide private school tuition to poor Central City residents (see "Vouchers," chapter 2), Governor Tommy Thompson included a full voucher program in his state budget proposal in January 1988. Following in the footsteps of an effort to carve out a separate Black school district, Thompson's proposal essentially targeted the same children, but would have armed them with a state grant of $1,000 to attend any private school in the Milwaukee area.

His legislation generated moderate interest in the African-American community after the *Milwaukee Community Journal* editorialized in support of it, following up with several stories examining vouchers as an alternative to school board apathy and the failing school system. A small group of Black parents suggested the bill could force Milwaukee Public Schools to address the problems plaguing the district: if enough parents opted out of MPS, the system would be forced to change itself. Vouchers could also fund an alternative school district; if the state wouldn't provide the community with the authority to control the public schools our children attended, perhaps we could create our own district from private schools and accomplish the same goal.

As it happened, the problem with the bill rested not in its goals or provisions, but in Thompson's lukewarm reception among African-American leadership, the major media, and opposing organizations, who accused the bill and its author of attempting to undermine the school desegregation effort and usurp the state constitution.

 The governor had made a tactical error by neglecting to solicit support from the targeted community. As a result, the bill was perceived as a partisan endeavor from an individual whose political stripes overshadowed his intent. After all, the governor was a Republican, a member of the party that not only had engineered repeated attacks against the civil rights community under the leadership of Ronald Reagan but had all but turned its back on the poor. In fact, it was pointed out repeatedly that the voucher program was originally introduced by Reagan, whose policies were considered anti-Black and antipoor. Democrats made use of that strategy, denouncing the bill despite its benefits to the poor. And given the Democratic control of the assembly and senate, it was not surprising that the governor's choice bill died a quiet death when it was brought before the Joint Finance Committee.

Despite this defeat, Thompson vowed to reintroduce the proposal after the fall 1988 elections, hopeful that Republican victories in the assembly would be sufficient to sway the vote or at least give more life to the bill. Thompson assigned his top aide to rewrite the legislation, this time with input from key African Americans, and gave the go-ahead to start floating the draft long before its projected introduction in the spring. His new legislation specifically targeted low-income Milwaukeeans and excluded parochial schools. The proposal also included a public school choice provision that allowed limited intradistrict transfers. By excluding religious schools from the private school voucher program and limiting it to low-income students, Thompson hoped to circumvent opposition that focused on the constitutionality of his previous bill as well as charges that he was providing an educational tax credit to the middle class.[1] After scrutinizing a draft, the MCJ boldly endorsed the new choice plan in a January 1989 editorial.

Thompson also planned to solicit Democratic cosponsors for the measure—details of which he leaked during a January 1989 speech in Washington, D.C.—and to entice MPS Superintendent Robert Peterkin to support the measure. This time around, Thompson made the strategic decision to enlarge his base of support. The best way to do that was to market choice in Milwaukee. Toward that end, the governor put together a conference on educational reform.

The conference, held on the downtown campus of the Milwaukee Area Technical College in March 1989, drew more than four hundred citizens of all economic, political, and ethnic backgrounds. The highlight of the conference, attended by several hundred Black parents, was a debate over school choice. The panel consisted of national school choice proponents John Chubb, senior fellow at the Brooking Institute, and Terry Moe, senior fellow at the Hoover Institute and associate professor of political science at Stanford University, as well as local educators Walter Farrell, a professor in the School of Education's Community Education Department at the University of Wisconsin–Milwaukee, and Howard Fuller, then Dean of General Education at Milwaukee Area Technical College.

Many believe it was this forum that served to establish school choice in the minds of Black activists as a major educational reform strategy.

Proponents clearly made the stronger case, offering an alternative to parents dissatisfied with the offerings of MPS. Chubb pricked up the ears of many Black parents when he asserted that current efforts to reform public education would leave most Americans terribly disappointed. Public schools, he said, are products of their environments, and as such, are controlled by outside forces that are slow to change, or are unwilling to grant the necessary power to reform public education. The better schools have more academic programs of instruction, clearer goals, and higher expectations. They usually also have strong, supportive teaching staffs and principals who are more oriented toward education than administration.

Private institutions, Chubb explained, feature similar systems that are more effective because principals and administrators "have to please parents or lose the students." Autonomy, he said, is the key, because public school bureaucracies and teachers unions make it all but impossible to achieve that end.

Terry Moe said he believes strongly in the voucher system, adding that most efforts to reform public educational arenas will not work because they are not based on a coherent sense of the causes of problems. "In the long run, they make matters worse, because reform often brings more rules and stricter constraints, which means you're relying on the fundamental problem to resolve the problem."

Clearly, a defining feature of the debate was an exchange between Fuller and Farrell, the only two Black men on the panel and well known as philosophical and personal adversaries. They took opposing positions on vouchers: Fuller asserted that school choice would empower Black parents and provide unique options to poor families, and Farrell claimed that choice didn't address the larger problem of inadequate education for MPS's ninety thousand students.

Farrell then gave another reason for his opposition: poor parents' inability to shift through the various educational brochures in order to make informed decisions about their children. In a nutshell, Farrell suggested that poor Black parents were too illiterate to make intelligent choices. Farrell's prejudicial comments—and the murmurs and hissing that following them—may have done more to push skeptics over the edge than anything else said during the morning-long session: a survey taken by coordinators and the MPS following the debate showed overwhelming support for vouchers.

Among those expressing support for Farrell's comments was a small group of NAACP representatives who had clustered near the stage. After the debate, one member of that group, Milwaukee Branch NAACP President Felmers Chaney, said, "if they're talking about anything to resegregate the public schools, we're against it. This whole idea smacks of racism to me. And if the Republicans are for it, that's what it is."[2]

Although the school choice initiative began to gain a foothold in the African-American community, Governor Thompson never had an opportunity to allow a wider audience to debate the merits of his bill. Shortly after its introduction in February 1989, the measure was removed from the budget bill by State Representative Walter Kunicki and State Senator Gary George when it came up for review in the Joint Finance Committee. Before Thompson could initiate a counteroffensive, however, two other choice bills were grabbing the lawmaker's attention.

Within months of Thompson's failed legislation, MPS Superintendent Robert Peterkin and his deputy superintendent Deborah McGriff initiated a series of meetings with representatives of several community schools, including Urban Day, Bruce Guadalupe, Highland, and Harambee, to introduce an MPS school choice proposal. The proposal, he told the community school representatives, would entail a scaled-down version of the Thompson bill under the direct auspices of MPS. State financial aid would continue to be routed through the public school system, but would then be redirected to the private schools, which would accept select students from MPS.

Peterkin, whose modest reform efforts had met resistance from the still-conservative MSB, was a strong believer in forging community partnerships with private schools and saw this proposal as an opportunity not only to bring successful private schools under the MPS umbrella but also to slice many at-risk students from the MPS apple pie. Initially, independent school officials were receptive to the proposal and, as Zakiya Courtney noted in a letter to fellow independent school administrators, were impressed by Peterkin's sincerity: "He comes from a background where alternative education means building contractual scenarios with community groups, and that's appealing to us, for a variety of reasons."

Urban Day's reasons for support were different from those of Bruce Guadalupe and Highland, both of which were strapped for financial resources. In fact Bruce Guadalupe, near bankruptcy, sought an influx of money to prevent it from having to close its doors. Urban Day, on the other hand, was merely carrying out its mission and approached the proposal as an opportunity to expand. Urban Day officials were in discussions with the Catholic Archdiocese to purchase a Central City Catholic school as part of its expansion plans, and the Peterkin proposal not only served that end by providing financial resources but also would enable Urban Day to tap into the long waiting list of poor parents without the financial wherewithal to pay even its comparatively low tuition.

The MPS plan was to be advanced through legislation drafted by State Representative Tom Seery, and all seemed well until the teachers union reportedly got involved and began to add troubling provisions to the legislation. The new Seery bill circulated for cosponsors was much more restrictive than Thompson's plan, placing income ceilings for participation and limiting schools to nonreligious institutions. Of particular concern were provisions that called for 80 percent of the children to be categorized under one of seven "at-risk" criteria, such as learning disabled, or to exhibit a variety of social stigmas, such as being born out of wedlock. The legislation also included provisions that placed private school teachers under the thumb of the teachers union and gave MPS power to oversee the schools' curriculum. And to remove any doubt as to how else this bounty program would benefit MPS, Seery added provisions that would allow MPS to take a 10 percent administrative fee out of state aid redirected for the program and to incorporate participants' grades in their attendance-area school's cumulative grades.

Such provisions prompted Harambee and Urban Day to withdraw their public support. As Zakiya Courtney noted in an interview during the negotiation period, the Urban Day board began to view the legislation as "a process through which the public schools could dump all of their problem children on us. They just wanted to use us. Not so much Peterkin, but the board, union or both. And then to top it off, they wanted to control who would teach and what we would teach. What they put on paper was far removed from what Peterkin had initially approached us with. This new measure would also take away our autonomy, making us nothing more than MPS satellites."[3]

But even without Harambee's and Urban Day's public support, the Seery bill continued to find receptive ears among several private schools, and that was enough for MPS to justify advancing it. After being notified of the strange provisions of the bill and its rejection by Black independent schools, the MCJ editorialized against it, not only because it stigmatized participants but also because it sought to undermine private schools in the process. The MCJ also noted how ironic it was that MPS sought a provision through which it could use the grades of choice students to enhance its own failing statistics.

Not surprisingly, Polly Williams soon joined in the criticism and after unsuccessful attempts to persuade Seery to amend his proposal, she took the bold step of drafting a very similar bill that eliminated the controversial provisions.

POLLY WILLIAMS'S BILL

To Polly Williams, school choice was to education what Kwanzaa is to Christmas. It was not a replacement for public education but a supplement adding cultural flavor, empowering Black America with an African-centered view. School choice served the duel purpose of providing an option and forcing accountability by the monopoly. Black parents would be educated in the process, and those who remained in the public-school setting would be strengthened and invigorated by our successes.

So Williams, a longtime advocate for school reform and critic of the Milwaukee Public Schools desegregation fiasco, took her own bill to the people. Surprisingly, the measure received overwhelming support wherever it was introduced, as the frustration over the quality of education available to Black children became increasingly antagonistic.

For example, one meeting held at Ebenezer Church of God in Christ drew more than three hundred Black people, most of them parents of school-aged children who almost unanimously endorsed the measure. Many of the speakers at the meeting called for more drastic measures to turn the tide of educational inequity. One speaker called on Williams to reintroduce a proposal to carve out a separate Black-controlled school district. Several talked about recall elections of school board members and the school superintendent, who just happened to be a Black man. One elderly gentleman received a standing ovation after chastising all of those in attendance who "believe White people will ever educate y'all kids. They want you and y'all kids stupid, and you should be 'shamed of yo'selves for thinkin' the same people who forged the chains want to teach you how to pick the lock." Leaning on a cane, speaking in a manner that belied his second-hand, tattered clothing, the elderly man who for an hour had been seated quietly in the back of the meeting hall went on to say, "Where I grew up we weren't allowed to go to school with White folks, so we created our own, and what the government didn't pay for, the churches and better-off people in our community did. We were taught the regular teachings, but we were also taught to fear God, respect our elders, and be proud of who we are. These White folks ain't going to teach that. We got to teach our own.

"We got to support our Black schools and create more of them. Every church should have a school, and they should have Black people who love our children, teaching them the three Rs and the other three Rs: responsibility, respect, and reparations. Yeah, I support Polly, but it's just part of the solution. And ain't nothing ever going to free us until we control everything."

Williams ended each of her meetings with a prayer and pledge to take the school choice army's concerns to Madison, although generally most of those in attendance carried with them only the faintest hope that Williams's political colleagues shared her vision or concern. As a rule of thumb, very few measures of any great significance introduced by Black Milwaukee legislators ever saw the light of day, not only because of institutional racism—which reared its head frequently in

Madison—but also because out-state legislators tended to have a bias against Milwaukee, which is the state's only first-class city and thus receives a disproportionate amount of resources. Despite control of the assembly and senate by Democrats, Black concerns have never been high on the priority list.

That point was illuminated annually as legislators routinely rejected State Representative Marcia Coggs's efforts to make state investment and pension boards divest of stocks that directly benefit South Africa; the lone African-American state senator's attempts to fortify an affirmative-action program and minority business development set-aside program for state contracts and services; and Williams's struggles to reform the public school system, including a measure to make the school desegregation "voluntary" busing program truly voluntary by requiring the district to solicit parents' permission to bus their children. Williams challenged her Democratic colleagues to show their sincerity about Black concerns by supporting this busing measure, which they—of course—did not. The bill died in the assembly despite significant Republican votes, prompting Williams to issue the first of many heated diatribes offering an assortment of new adjectives to describe her so-called liberal colleagues, including "missionary" and "plantation overseer."

Clearly, Black Milwaukee could justify with voting records the assumption that their concerns would not find receptive ears in Madison, which said as much about the level of institutional racism in Wisconsin as it did about the political realities of composing less than 6 percent of the state's population. Democrats could routinely vote against Black bills secure in the knowledge that they didn't have to entertain any "Blacklash": the Black population was clustered in one small area of Milwaukee represented by four Black assemblymen and one Black senator. There were only four Black votes to contend with, and, regardless of the significance of the legislation or the Black sponsors' oratory skills, those votes were effectively drowned out by snores and bad jokes. Republicans, on the other hand, could continue their policy of benign neglect and apathy for essentially the same reason.

Both parties, however, would occasionally use a piece of legislation to showboat or nudge the other party's level of sensitivity toward the downtrodden and the poor. Nothing was different on July 5, 1989, when Williams and Seery found themselves at center stage on the assembly floor arguing for their respective school choice bills.

Both lawmakers made compelling arguments. Williams had the advantage of speaking on behalf of future prospective participants, and Seery was armed with the blessings of the MPS administration and, apparently, the Milwaukee Teachers Education Association. Lobbyists had made their rounds through the legislature, planting seeds and fertilizing past relationships as they went. MPS under Peterkin,

Magnet Schools *fee*
also *Fuller*

a former East Coast administrator with hopes of easing reform past a myopic board, viewed the choice initiative as serving the dual purpose of lowering class size and appeasing those who demanded education options. The best schools in the system fell under the category of magnets, which ranged from elementary language immersions and creative arts to college preparatory schools. The problem was one of space. The schools' long waiting lists most adversely affected Black students—under an agreement reached over the suburban school transfer program, a percentage of all seats in Milwaukee public schools were set aside for suburban White children. And, of course, they usually enrolled in the best magnet schools, leaving Black students on the outside looking in.

Peterkin viewed community-based schools, with their emphasis on Black studies and the basics, as specialties of a sort. He also praised the Black independents—out of earshot of his bosses on the school board—for their dedicated teachers, strong disciplinary guidelines, and community support. Not coincidentally, he was never at the vanguard of the debate over the MPS legislation, even though it was assumed that he was its catalyst. The teachers union's support, although never publicly admitted, was no doubt rooted in a view that the MPS bill was the lesser of two evils. While school vouchers were a serious threat to the union's stranglehold over Black children, the MPS choice program could actually undermine private schools by making them satellites of MPS.

State Rep. Seery's case was strong and apparently appealed to many of the Democratic legislators whose endorsement and financing from the teachers union was common knowledge. Williams, however, ripped his bill to shreds, noting the hypocrisy of MPS's provisions and focusing on the stigma of the seven at-risk criteria. School choice should be offered based on income, not social demagoguery, she said. Finally, she appealed to her colleagues' sense of justice, noting that MPS had failed an entire generation of Black students who lacked the financial resources to seek a private school education. Williams stated that her choice bill could also be a wake-up call for MPS, forcing its board to address the concerns of Black parents and compelling its teachers—80 percent of whom were White—to take seriously their duty to provide a quality education to every single student, regardless of race, color, or creed.

Both bills were eventually shot down, although Williams could take pride in noting she received more votes, 54-44 to Seery's 58-41. More important, though, Williams's bill was the beginning of a movement that would eventually shake the nation.

A week after the defeat of her school choice legislation, Williams called me to express her gratitude for my support and to note that she had been bombarded with calls from parents, ministers, and community activists about her bill. Most encouraged her to reintroduce the measure, this time providing an opportunity for a community-based movement to support her along the way. Williams said she was giving thought to that request, but was taken aback by criticism she had received from several Black supporters of the Seery bill.

"One of them said I killed choice by splitting the vote," she said, frustration and hurt in her voice. "Me! I killed choice. That's ridiculous. Even you said Harambee and other schools wouldn't participate under the MPS bill because it would kill your schools. That was the point, I was pushing choice."

I tried to envision Polly Williams, that bundle of energy and determination, sobbing on the other end of the telephone line. In the years I'd known her I had witnessed her explode on a number of occasions, particularly in legislative sessions where her fiery expression of Black nationalistic philosophy often put her at odds with Republicans and Democrats alike. It was hard to imagine that some of the political drama might get to her.

"You know, Polly, I agree with those folks who say you should do it again," I told her. "Your bill gave me hope, and I saw enthusiasm I hadn't seen for a long time. It's something we can focus on, something all of us can identify with. And it's just so cut-and-dried. How can anybody who talks about equality and justice justify stopping poor kids from getting quality educations, particularly with so many failing in MPS? If nothing else, we can show them for what they are if they vote against it. We can put them and MPS before the public."

Before I could finish my sentence, Williams interjected that she wasn't interested in going through the long legislative process just to make a point. "Every year Marcia [Coggs] introduces her apartheid sanctions bill, and every year they shoot it down. She does it to make a point. I don't want to go through that. I don't want to mislead people. If we do this, I want to win." She continued, more deliberately, "You know, maybe we can win this. Maybe I can forge an alliance with some Republicans and a few out-state Democrats. It could be a dangerous process and they could really get me then for breaking party tradition, but I've never put them before what's right for us anyway."

She took a deep breath and paused for a minute before saying, "I don't know . . . I'm tired of this. I'm getting too old for this stuff. I have to think about it."

"Well, I'll tell you what," I responded. "I'm behind you, and our paper's behind you, and I can get Harambee and other schools behind you. You know I don't get caught up in that partisan politics stuff, they're all the same to me, but you have to weigh your future. If push comes to shove, I think you can win as an independent, and I'll knock on doors if necessary to make sure you don't have to worry about that end. I hope you go for it, and if you want, I'll help bring some folks together. You know how I feel about Black independent schools, and if there's a way we can bring more families into the fold, I'm all for it. Anything we got to do to stop the hemorrhaging, I'm for."

RALLYING THE TROOPS

Assembly Bill 601, called the Milwaukee Parental Choice Program, was cosponsored by thirty-six Republicans and eleven Democrats, including State Representatives G. Spencer Coggs and Gwen Moore, two African-American lawmakers. Polly Williams and Larry Harwell set into motion an organizational structure that would provide the troops for the school choice army and play a vital role in seeing the legislation to fruition.

The new army underwent weekly training sessions, generally held at Urban Day, which involved briefings, strategy meetings, and work assignments. Indeed, the group took on all the trappings of an army, with a chain of command and battle plan. Zakiya Courtney was named logistics officer, Harwell became operations officer, and I was appointed propaganda/information officer. Williams was the general, and when not barking out assignments—which could range from operating an information bank to carrying a picket sign—the impassioned lawmaker was hitting the political trail, drumming up support, or neutralizing opposition.

The key to the stratagem was communication. We were in constant communication with each other, and through our network, tentacles touched every corner of the African American community. From barber shops to beauty salons, Sunday services to cultural festivals, we enlisted people everywhere. Once involved, our soldiers quickly moved to enlist other soldiers.

The central nervous system of the process involved our newspaper, and an intricate telephone system reminiscent of the tribal African drumming system. As complicated as it was effective, Williams's telephone network involved a core group of a dozen parents and activists who were each assigned to phone two or three individuals, who in turn would call an equal number to rally the troops. Officers or subchiefs would be assigned to call peers or subordinates. Calls were made on a regular basis whether or not there were new developments, and information was related as simply as possible to prevent misinterpretation. Most importantly, the system enabled leaders to rally a large number of people on short notice.

While we worked hard at the grassroots level, Williams lobbied from her office to include school choice as a subject of discussion at forums and conferences. She also invited guests, including parents and educational experts like Howard Fuller, to speak about the benefits of school choice and the ongoing battle for quality education in the public school arena. Not a week went by without a voice proclaiming support for school choice.

One of the most significant and far-reaching examples of that strategy took place on February 7, 1990, at the tenth annual Black Women's Network Conference. The Network, considered one of Milwaukee's most influential African-American organizations, consisted of a who's who of local Black women—membership included most Black female elected officials as well as some of the most prominent Black business and civic leaders in the city. The Network took leadership positions on a variety of civil rights and women's issues, earning the attention of the media and Establishment powers.

Williams was among the founding members of the Black Women's Network, and it was no coincidence that this year's conference, "Parental Choice: Making Choices in the 1990s," featured a series of workshops and forums on school choice. The conference, held at the Pfister Hotel in Milwaukee, drew hundreds of participants, including such national figures as Robert Woodson, executive director of the National Center for Neighborhood Enterprise, and Dave Richardson, president of the National Black Caucus of State Legislators. State Senator Gary George and Thompson were among the speakers at the conference, which drew national press.

Thompson's appearance at the first workshop guaranteed that the session would be well attended by the Network's movers and shakers as well as by the White media. The governor wasted no time in getting to the heart of the matter during a not-so-impromptu speech before the audience of three hundred. He questioned whether those who describe themselves as friends of the Black community were really sincere or instead were selfishly blocking the doors of educational opportunity for poor Black children. In an uncharacteristically strident tone, he declared that African-American families should have the same educational options as White middle-class suburban families. To a chorus of amens and applause, the governor went on to say that Representative Williams's bill would provide low-income families with that option. School choice was a civil rights imperative that offered opportunities for African Americans to break the cycle of poverty and join the mainstream.[4]

Not only did Thompson's address set the stage and tone for the two-day conference, but it probably did more to endear him to Black gatekeepers than any prior event. Many of those who approached Thompson after his presentation did so with a totally different perception of the Republican and how his agenda could complement that of those who sought to empower the Black community. One audience member's question framed the moment: "Choice won't be enough . . . it's an important step, but there are not enough private schools. What about the majority of

Rest of Kids?

Black children left in the public schools, in places where the teachers don't care and where administrators look at them as numbers?"

Without ducking or dodging, Thompson responded, "That depends on you. I'm for many of the initiatives I hear coming from the Black press and some Black leadership. There's no doubt the system is failing you, but I can't come in here and dictate unless I have you in my corner. You tell me what [to do] and let's move for consensus. But don't let me or my party be the focus. Let education be the focus. I'll stand on principles and support you if you support [my efforts on your behalf]."

For the next two days, a steady parade of national and local educators and politicians expressed support for parental school choice. Several local activists and political figures also took advantage of the opportunity to decry state lawmakers' unwillingness to advance Williams's bill from an assembly committee where it was being held hostage.

The Network conference was a turning point both because it focused media attention on the issue of school choice from a Black perspective and because it showcased political and community-based support for the movement. Neither the White media nor the organized opposition—the teachers union and status quo Democratic Party machine—could continue to lie that the choice movement did not have Black support or that it was orchestrated by the GOP or Conservative Right. It was *our* movement, and the convention showed that we had local support from a cross section of Black Milwaukee as well as favorable national attention. We had momentum, focus, and political savvy. We were on our way.

MARSHALING SUPPORT

Two weeks after the Black Women's Network Conference, State Senator Gary George and School Board Director Jared Johnson added their names to a growing list of political leaders endorsing the Parental Choice bill. The involvement of George, the state's only Black senator, was a key coup not only because his name added further credibility to the campaign but also because he was a powerful and crafty political veteran—some went so far as to call him the smartest and most-feared politician in Madison. With a brilliant mind and a unique ability to orchestrate political agendas, George had climbed in one term to cochair of the most powerful legislative committee, Joint Finance. From his seat of power, he could advance or kill legislation. Only half-joking, a White politician once referred to him as King George.

At one point George had been groomed to make an eventual bid for national office, but he fell out of favor with Democrats for making pragmatic remarks about working with Republicans. Nevertheless, as he began lobbying both Democrats and Republicans on behalf of the initiative, which he intended to sponsor on the senate side, it soon became obvious that George was an invaluable resource for the choice movement. He seduced, induced, and threatened to get his agenda across, and although he rarely went on the public stomp to advance the choice agenda, his work behind the scenes took on monumental import as the campaign heated up.

As George, Williams, and State Rep. Spencer Coggs—one of the first politicians to publicly state his support for school choice—worked the legislative halls, the foot soldiers stepped up efforts to get Williams's bill out of State Representative Barbara Notestein's Urban Education Committee for a public hearing. The opposition's plan was obvious and insidious: refusing to hold a public hearing on the bill would effectively cause it to die a slow death in committee. The urgency of undermining that strategy was not lost on us. While some soldiers were assigned the task of rallying dozens of supporters to call Notestein, others lobbied members of her committee to raise the issue of a public hearing. All attempts seemed to fall on deaf ears.

Notestein was a classic missionary liberal who had worked as the coordinator of a poverty agency prior to entering elective office. One who touted herself as knowing what was best for Black people, her patronizing attitude could be offensive. I did my part, both through public presentations (including a rally held at a Northside church during which I referred to Notestein as the Bull Connors of the 1990s for what I considered her racially motivated, missionary attempts to block the doors of educational opportunity for Black children) and through an editorial in which I queried whether "so-called liberal politicians want to empower African Americans or in any way allow them an avenue out of the enslavement we find ourselves in."[5] The editorial was published following an interview with Notestein during which I told her that she might find herself subject to a demonstration outside her home, complete with signs suggesting that she was a racist. She expressed both shock and disbelief that she could be portrayed in such a way, given her "long history of work in the Black community."

Williams copied each article I wrote and circulated it through the assembly. Harwell posted the articles throughout the capital to make sure they were read, underlining in red the most incendiary points. The constant bombardment must have gotten to Notestein—or at least drowned out the support she received from choice opponents—because within days of a scheduled demonstration outside her home, the White liberal who had once called herself a supporter of Black interests announced that she would schedule a public hearing on AB-601, the Milwaukee Parental School Choice bill.

2/18/90

Notestein scheduled the Urban Education Committee hearing on February 18—a weekday morning—at the MPS administration building. In the next issue of the *MCJ*, I called this scheduling an obvious attempt to undermine the process by holding the hearing in the lion's den at a time when most Black parents would be at work. But Williams advised me to focus my efforts elsewhere, saying, "Trust me, she could schedule the hearing for four in the morning at the KKK headquarters, and I wouldn't care. This is our time, and we're not going to let them stop us now."

Within hours of the announcement of the hearing, word was circulating throughout the African-American community via Williams's telephone network. Soon there were few within the school choice army who were not privy to the new development. All that was left was to provide transportation for those who needed it and prioritize the order of speakers, keeping in mind that it was a well-known tactic of legislators to cut hearings short. Notestein and the teachers union would seek to stack the hearing with opponents of choice, so it was important that we intermingle our "experts" with parents, ensuring that their testimony would fill all loopholes and answer all conceivable questions.

Not one seat in the auditorium was empty—a rarity for a school board meeting. In attendance were children and adults, young and old, middle-class and dirt poor: a sea of Black faces. Some held up handwritten signs calling for school choice. I couldn't help but beam with pride upon seeing so many parents, activists, and children making a collective statement to which I could only hope the entire would nation pay heed.

The committee members were clearly surprised by the turnout. Even before the hearing was officially called to order, it was clear that this was not going to be business as usual. Indeed, the atmosphere was closer to a Baptist church service than a political hearing. The auditorium was filled with people rubbing elbows and making happy small talk, and off in one corner, one of several ministers in attendance led a small group in an impromptu prayer. Several children huddled together reciting a poem I could only assume they had prepared for presentation.

Of the members of the panel, only State Rep. Spencer Coggs looked comfortable in his position on stage. While he engaged in casual conversation with several of the Black parents, the other legislators fiddled with papers or surveyed the crowd. Of the legislators, only State Representative Kim Plache of Racine (a small city south of Milwaukee) had an ongoing relationship with African Americans, and none had ever participated in a hearing with so many Black folks—much less Black folks showing this crowd's enthusiasm on a cold winter morning.

I couldn't help but wonder how much prejudice these panelists brought to the hearing. Did they believe, as many Whites do, that Black parents don't care about their children? Did they have the same low expectations for our children as most public school teachers? How many of the panelists would seek to derail choice simply because it empowered Black families? Did they fear giving up control over even a few thousand of our children? If this grand experiment worked, and we were able to provide for our children what the public schools refused them, what would that say about MPS?

Of the fifty or so people who provided testimony during the three-hour hearing, only a few expressed opposition to school choice—and they represented the teachers union and MPS.

One after another, parents strode to the podium and called for options for their children. One mother of three said she would use school choice to send her youngest child to a private school because he could receive the type of education there that he was denied at the public schools, where he was considered slow.

"I know ain't nothing wrong with him 'cept that he don't get the kind of attention he needs. I can't afford to send him to private school now, but with choice I could." When asked if she felt choice would hurt public schools, this parent mused for a moment before answering that "it works for some of my kids, but not the youngest, and I'm not gonna' throw him away or let him become a statistic."

A mother of a sixth-grader announced that her son had been earmarked for special education. She was told by school administrators that he was learning disabled and emotionally dysfunctional. "But I put him in Urban Day, and he's doing wonderfully. His grades are up, and the teachers say he's a joy to work with; no problems and ain't never been suspended. If you people pass this bill, I can keep him in there. Lord knows what will happen to him if he has to go back to public school."

Still another parent nervously challenged the panel to "allow our own, those who know and care, who love our children like their own, teach them. [Our children] deserve the chance to be taught in nurturing places, where folks ain't scared of them, or feel they can't learn. If they can't or won't, let us take ours to where they can and will."

Notestein interrupted the testimony on several occasions to order the crowd to withhold their cries of "amen" and "right on," and "you tell 'em, sister." But when Polly Williams approached the podium, Notestein's voice was drowned out by resounding applause. Williams took center stage in what must have been a defining point in her political career. Propelled by the energy of dozens of parents and their children, she rose to the occasion in a grand, articulate display of sincerity that could have moved even the staunchest critic.

"This is a step in the right direction toward dealing with the problem of education in our city." she told the committee. "[The bill] empowers parents to make the ultimate decision for their children. None of the other things [legislators can do] will make a difference unless they empower parents."

Williams angrily rejected a committee member's contention that "low-income parents don't have the aptitude to choose alternatives to the public school system," decrying its racist implications. "I've heard the excuse: if you poor, you're stupid. Until you have parents as part of everything, until you incorporate them, nothing will change. We must reorganize our priorities [to incorporate parental involvement]."

Responding to another committee member's fear that the proposal would pull the most concerned parents and top students from MPS, Williams responded, "Are you concerned about the 70 percent White flight from MPS or Black students who leave MPS for the suburban schools [through the Chapter 220 transfer program]? It's ironic that the only time concern is raised is when poor people talk about educational alternatives."

Williams waited for the roar of applause to die down before continuing. "Why penalize poor parents, saying you have to stay and keep the system alive. The state is spending a lot of money to help middle-class families make more choices, but when it comes to poor people, it's a different standard."

Larry Harwell spoke after Williams, explaining that the program would be funded by a state grant of $600 per student, supplementing the general state aid of $2,400 already allocated for Milwaukee students. There would be no additional costs to local property taxpayers and no fiscal burden on MPS. In reference to a concern raised by the local teachers union that the private schools would not be required to meet state educational requirements, Harwell challenged the state superintendent to compare after one year the academic achievements of the participating students with their counterparts in MPS.

When one assemblyman questioned the logic behind the random student selection process that participating schools would use under the program, Harwell drew laughter from the crowd by stating that the provision in question was taken directly from current wording of the Chapter 220 suburban transfer program—a program, Harwell noted, that the assemblyman had not only embraced but also praised.

"Don't force stronger polices than 220 on us," Harwell cautioned. "Issues like the selection process, aid formulas, and other provisions of the bill are open to debate," he said. "The only issue we won't compromise on is MPS choosing the schools."

Doug Haselow, governmental relations coordinator for MPS and the only board representative to express opposition to the bill, often found himself on the hot seat. After Haselow asserted that the bill would take valuable monies from MPS, committee member State Rep. Spencer Coggs questioned how that could be true if the money followed the student: "The state's formula is based on the number of children in MPS. If a thousand students [leave, drop out, or] die the money would not go to MPS. The same holds true for this bill, so how can you assert MPS is losing money?" Haselow didn't respond, prompting a question as to whether Haselow was misleading the committee when he claimed MPS would be required to supplement the aid package.

Surprisingly, Haselow stated that MPS supported choice as long as the program was under the control of public school administrators and MPS could collect a percentage of the state funds. He reminded the committee that the year before, MPS had spearheaded the Seery choice bill, which allowed for direct contracts between the public school administration and a select number of private schools: MPS would pay the schools 80 percent of the state aid package, keeping 20 percent for administrative costs. The assembly rejected this proposal during the budget debates, but in the past several months, MPS reportedly sought a sponsor for a new parental choice initiative that was patterned after Williams's bill, except for strict criteria imposed on participating private schools.

Howard Fuller, director of the County Department of Health and Human Services and a longtime community activist and civil rights leader, surprised many with his attendance at the hearing. Fuller asserted that policy makers must begin to redefine public education to include all educational institutions that receive public funds. At one point, he said, he felt that choice would be the "death knell for public education," but he now believed "choice can be the savior of public education. The key to reforming the bureaucracy is progressive leadership at the top and empowering parents at the bottom. Williams's bill would empower parents to make one of the most important decisions they can make for their children."

Fuller rejected Haselow's assertion that the proposal would hurt MPS's desegregation efforts, stating, "It's sorry and sad that every time Black people come up with something [to improve the quality of education], MPS comes up with the boogeyman of segregation. The question we must ask is, are the institutions most important or the people they are supposed to serve? I want to see parents make the choices for change and not the bureaucracy," he said to shattering applause. Noting that from his past experience as a state official, he knows that lawmakers can either come up with a "thousand excuses not to endorse a plan," or an equal number to support one, Fuller encouraged the committee to "do the right thing and judge the proposal on it merits. It may be just a small step in changing a system that is currently in need of major overhaul, but we need a pilot like this to show what can be done."

VICTORY!

Two weeks later, on March 8, 1990, the Urban Education Committee met to discuss the school choice legislation. It seemed as if all of Black Milwaukee held its breath awaiting a call from Williams on the outcome of the committee vote.

"They passed it!" Williams yelled into the telephone. "My God, they passed it!"

I could practically hear Williams jump out of her seat, pounding her small fist against the table, unable to contain herself. I don't know if I was the first or the fiftieth person she called, but I'm sure each was treated to a similar burst of excitement.

"It's going to the full assembly. God bless 'em, we're going to get our day. They put some other stuff in there," she said hurriedly, "a sunset provision and a cap on the number of students who can participate, but we can deal with that later. The important thing is they passed it. The teachers union was there, MPS had people there, and a couple of top Democrats were there. They left the committee meeting mad. Larry and I left jumping down the hallway. I know White people were thinking we were crazy. Who cares?"

SIGNING IN

While Black citizens were holding their collective breath following the committee hearing, Williams and Coggs had undertaken an extensive lobbying campaign to sway committee members into supporting the measure. They felt that they had the support of Peter Barca, which guaranteed six votes—one short of the majority needed—and two other members leaned toward approval. But nothing was certain, particularly given Notestein's vehement opposition to the initiative and reported animosity toward Williams, whom she linked to her recent travails with the Black community. Moreover, with the exception of Notestein and Coggs, none of the committee members had any ties to the Milwaukee area, thus a negative vote would not adversely affect them come election time.

Given this state of things, everyone—including Williams—was caught by surprise when the key vote in favor of the bill came from State Rep. Kim Plache of Racine. Some theorized Plache was taken aback by the sea of Black faces that filled the MPS administration building to express their support for school choice. Certainly Plache was moved by the outpouring of support. It doubtless impressed her that Milwaukee parents' sentiments mirrored those of African-American residents of Racine, who, although small in number, were growing increasingly vocal about the failures of public education.

In the end, we chalked up Plache's support to one word: conscience. The Racine Democrat bucked the party line and jeopardized her friendship with Notestein because her conscience told her that providing poor parents with another educational option was the right thing to do. She was keenly aware of the abysmal state of public education in Milwaukee and the plight of poor Black children. Democrats had long called themselves the champions of the poor and disadvantaged, but generally their response had been to enamor us with programs that ease the pain but rarely cure the disease. Often the remedy was as bad as the problem. But this time Plache could vote to empower: instead of giving poor Black families a fish, her vote provided them with a pole, bait, and a fishing lesson.

During one of the weekly rallies, Polly Williams and Zakiya Courtney had spoken of the importance of a strong show of support by Black parents and community leadership.

"They really don't think you care," she said. "They don't think you care about your children, and they don't think you understand the political process. But this is our day—God is on our side—and we have to let them know it. Let them look at your beautiful Black faces and say you don't have a right to control where your children go to school. Let them stare you right in the eye and say 'we know what's best for you, and what's best for you is to send your children to failing public schools while we send ours to private schools.'"

And so several weeks later approximately two hundred Black parents, children, and community activists boarded chartered buses to travel the eighty miles from the heart of the Central City to the state capitol for the assembly session which would determine the fate of school choice in Wisconsin. Several of the buses were subsidized by school choice supporters and Black bus company owners, and an impromptu fund-raiser made up for what supporters could not pay. Still, the sacrifices made by poor parents were enough to bring Courtney and others to tears as they watched Black citizens board the buses. Several welfare mothers spent food money on bus fare. Although they couldn't afford to, entire families took off from work. Children missed school to attend the session at a critical time in the semester, even under threat of suspension. One elderly woman who had to be assisted on the bus began humming "We Shall Overcome," and several others joined in. Children who didn't know the words faked it. It was a joyous moment as our community rallied to change public education as we had known it.

Williams was right: many out-state politicians didn't think Black people cared about their own children as White people did. They thought that we were uncultured, that being on welfare or food stamps meant we were morally bankrupt:

America's stratified education system was in place because there would always be three classes, and most Black people would always be on the bottom.

I only wished that those who believed in such prejudiced theories could see the parents aboard this bus. I wished they would travel with them to Madison, listen to their hopes and dreams for their children. Hear them talk about a future of opportunity.

This was many choice supporters' first time in the Capitol. The marble and granite building was indeed impressive. However, the goal was to add a meaningful chapter to the history book, not to provide a history lesson. Thus it was with stern and determined faces that some three hundred choice supporters—including dozens of community activists and other supporters who traveled to Madison by car and Greyhound bus—crowded into the assembly chambers or lined the corridors outside it.

Williams was to later say that impressive showing affected both Black and White lawmakers, particularly Marcia Coggs, the most senior Black state representative. Marcia Coggs, the widow of Ike Coggs, the state's first African-American legislator, was no less committed to equal opportunity and social justice. But Marcia Coggs, a diehard Democrat, rarely strayed from the party line, and reportedly had sullenly chastised Williams for forging an alliance with Republicans to push school choice forward. To Coggs, working with Republicans was akin to making deals with the devil; for the most part their agenda was seen as anti-Black and antipoor. The wall between the two parties had been put in place not by African Americans, but by Republicans who didn't want any part of Black America. It was a rich White man's club and they wanted to keep it that way. Although Coggs had refused to publicly denounce the school choice bill or censure Williams, many felt she would vote against the measure when it hit the floor. Her expression as she peered into the sea of Black faces on this early spring day, however, told a different story. Coggs was Black and no less a victim of societal ills and prejudices than those who stared at her on this day. Some say that the gaze of the Black children and their parents instantly swayed Coggs. Or perhaps she realized that the choice solution was long overdue in a school system that had alienated and then abandoned Black children. Either way, Marcia Coggs would not be a pawn of the Democratic Party, as some had feared.

The floor debate raged on and on. Williams appealed to the consciences of those who support justice and equal opportunity. As always, she was articulate, resourceful, compassionate, demanding, and forthright. She put her colleagues on trial, but allowed them to set their own sentence: permanent guilt if they voted against the measure.

Assembly
votes for
the bill

Finally, in a historic vote that changed the face of education in America, the assembly voted to support the Milwaukee Parental School Choice Program. The cheers and smiles of all the parents in attendance told a story all its own—a story about two decades of work to secure quality education and a long-overdue victory. A story about empowerment and justice and now opportunity.

For Black parents, this vote was just short of a second emancipation proclamation. It provided them with the freedom to avail themselves of educational opportunities that the assembly members could take for granted. But it was also a rare victory in the struggle for human rights—for rare indeed was it that Black legislation made it through the assembly.

"This is truly an historic occasion," said Polly Williams after the vote. "For the first time in history, African-American parents will have a true educational choice for their children.

"What makes this occasion even more significant is the fact that we had to go up against the labor union, MPS and even the Department of Public Instruction. But our parents fought all the way and now there is light at the end of the tunnel."

FURTHER STRUGGLES

When the jubilation simmered down, the process continued. Half a dozen amendments were offered with the sole intent of dousing—if not drowning—this new bill. The first challenge came from Assembly Speaker Tom Loftus, who in the following year challenged Governor Tommy Thompson as the Democratic candidate for governor (and lost dramatically, no doubt owing to his opposition to school choice). Loftus's amendments ran the gamut from sunset provisions to an attempt to remove funds from the provision. Only one Black lawmaker, Gwen Moore, voted with Loftus on that amendment.

However, despite these apparent setbacks, school choice moved to its day with destiny and into the hands of State Senator Gary George. George, cochair of the Assembly/Senate Joint Finance Committee had his hands full trying to get the choice measure through. Two problems confronted the rising star: he faced a possible filibuster if the measure came through as a regular piece of legislation, and the legislature was only in session for another couple of weeks, which limited his lobbying time. Having lost on the assembly side, opponents of school choice could use the filibuster to essentially tie up the entire legislative session for days. Even though it was assumed proponents had enough senate votes to pass the choice legislation, the filibuster could supplant that possibility by forcing the legislative body to table it to speed up the budget process. If that were to happen, there was a good possibility it would not reemerge from committee during the current session.

To head off that possibility, George reintroduced the MPSC measure as an amendment to the budget bill. Politically that removed it from the vulnerable position of being shot down as an individual bill and protected it in the larger budget bill, where it was all but immune to attack. At this stage of the legislative process, with only a few weeks left before the session drew to a close, lawmakers were limited in their ability to debate provisions of a larger bill, and as such, opponents would be forced to vote down the entire budget bill if they wanted to dislodge the choice provision.

Over the next week, George used his considerable political savvy to reject efforts to tie the bill up in committee. He did accept a costly amendment that reduced financing for the bill by $600 per student, but had an escalator clause that would ensure that financing would increase each year. More significant was the introduction of an amendment prohibiting low-income families with children currently attending private school from reenrolling under the choice program. That amendment was like a knife in the back of the parents who worked so hard to see choice through this far; it meant that few of them would be able to consume the fruits of their labor. Many parents sacrificed basic necessities to keep their children in private schools, and choice would have been a godsend. What made the matter worse is that no one, not even George, could explain how that amendment got in the bill.

George had not taken part in the negotiations with senate Democrats that had led to the amendment. Walter Farrell, who worked in a consultant capacity with George, later reported to Williams that this provision could force the measure to be tabled. Williams and Harwell were angry and suspicious: Farrell, who now publicly expressed support for choice, had previously decried it and had strong ties to the teachers union. In fact, word had it that Farrell, a professor at the University of Wisconsin–Milwaukee, was a paid consultant to the MTEA and was put in place to safeguard, as much as possible, the union's interests.

Wherever the measure came from, it certainly wasn't going to disappear, and eventually Williams relented. It was imperative that the bill be voted on the next day—March 22—or it would be sent back to the assembly, probably never to reemerge. "Go for it," said Williams.

On March 22, the budget was passed, including the school choice provision.

Despite the problematic amendment, Polly Williams assured upset parents that no one would be excluded. Within days a commitment from the Bradley Foundation and Michael Joyce to allocate $2 million to fund a major scholarship

Choice
Passes

program allowed her to keep her word. Business and civic groups later formed an organization called Partners Advancing Values in Education (PAVE) to serve as the funding mechanism for a private choice program to complement the nonsectarian program. Under the leadership of Dan McKinley, PAVE became the primary tool in providing scholarships for parents ineligible for choice or seeking parochial school education for their children. God does work in mysterious ways.

May 12, 1990, was set aside for the official signing of AB-601, the Milwaukee Parental School Choice legislation. Governor Tommy Thompson announced he would sign the measure into law during a ceremony to be held at Harambee Community School. Appropriately, the signing took place in Malcolm X Hall under a poster of the Harambee emblem, which represents the school motto: pulling together. The hundreds who filled the hall that day had pulled together to challenge the mighty teachers union, MPS, and the political status quo. It was a victory they would share with minorities and low-income people throughout the country.

AB-601 was not an experimental educational pilot but historic legislation that could set into motion similar efforts around the country, knocking down the educational plantation walls. The signing not only marked a major victory for parents but also signaled a new day for education reform in Wisconsin—and a jumpstart for a stagnated Civil Rights movement.

Chapter 5

IN OPPOSITION

As long as you keep a person down, some part of you has to
be down there to hold him down, so it means you cannot soar
as you otherwise might.

—MARIAN ANDERSON

P arental school choice was about empowering poor parents with the educational options to which most teachers have ready access, but it was
also a mechanism to dispel myths and racist stereotypes about why
Black children were not achieving. We in the African-American community knew that the underachievement was rooted in low expectations, sluggish
and disdainful bureaucratic procedures, an irrelevant and often racist curriculum,
and inept and prejudiced teachers. Our school choice victory, we felt, would finally
give us a chance to change the status quo.

Unfortunately, it didn't take long for the adversaries of educational reform and
Black empowerment to stick a pin in our balloon. Instead of resting after our battle,
we found ourselves forced to fight through propaganda and misinformation
advanced by our opponents. Among the lies we had to counter in the first year were
that choice participants were the "cream of the Milwaukee Public Schools crop,"
that their academic achievement wouldn't improve in a private school setting,
that choice hurt desegregation efforts, and that the new program stole money
from MPS. We quickly countered with facts. For example, University of
Wisconsin–Milwaukee and Wisconsin Department of Public Instruction research
showed that more than 65 percent of choice participants came from single-parent
households, a near-equal percentage were Aid for Family with Dependent Children
(AFDC) recipients, and most had actually been failing in the public school
system—so much for cream of the crop.[1] Several research projects showed that the

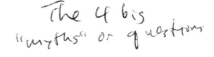

The 4 big
"myths" or questions

participants were, in fact, achieving in comparison to public school students—even given that most participants had been *behind* in their studies prior to registering for the private schools. Moreover, not only was MPS not losing money because of choice, it was actually gaining, both because the district raised taxes in anticipation of a loss that never happened and because MPS continued to receive property tax dollars for students who were no longer enrolled.

Despite these seemingly incontrovertible developments, staunch opposition continued from at least three directions: State Superintendent of Public Instruction Herbert Grover and his ally, the MTEA; Felmers Chaney, president of the NAACP; and Lauri Wynn, past president of the Wisconsin Education Association (WEA), the state teachers union.

HERBERT GROVER AND THE MTEA

As we soon learned, the teachers union and State Superintendent of Public Instruction Herbert Grover had worked out a contingency plan even as the choice legislation was weaving its way through the assembly. They apparently knew what we did not: that a majority of politicians on both sides of the aisle were solidly behind choice and were willing to buck the status quo to see the grand experiment to fruition. That certainty realized, union officials and Grover shrewdly shifted their focus from stopping the Freedom Train to derailing it as it left the station.

The first clue of this collusion came within days of the signing of the Parental School Choice legislation—in a May 2, 1990, speech, Grover suggested that the union and other opponents mount a legal challenge against the historic measure. The state superintendent said that the choice program "raises very difficult and disconcerting legal questions," adding, "right now, it's a legal holiday; this thing could be challenged so many ways."[2] A few days later Grover was quoted in the *Milwaukee Sentinel* as saying, "[School choice] is a disgrace. . . . Has the citizenry in Wisconsin lost its sense?"[3]

Grover went so far as to challenge opponents to file suit against him as the constitutional conduit mandated to implement the program, revealing that he would work aggressively to usurp and disrupt the program internally as they worked to challenge its legality. Grover's comments put a damper on an otherwise jubilant community celebration on May 12 in the Harambee Community School's Malcolm X Hall, organized by Polly Williams and a coalition of Central City private schools. The event drew hundreds of parents, community activists, and political supporters of school choice, who reveled in our accomplishments—which were made even more astounding by the political and financial power of the opposition. Tears flowed as Williams commended the parents for their hard work and perseverance against such formidable odds.

To rousing applause, Williams announced that what had been accomplished as a result of the community's unified efforts was truly momentous, not just because of its potential impact on education policy in Milwaukee, but because it would have a snowball effect that could change the face of education in the entire country.

"And we did it!" she shouted above the roar of applause from hundreds of parents and activists. "Poor people, community people, parents, and children. We sent a message that they couldn't ignore; a message that we care for our children, and we will do whatever is necessary to give them a chance to succeed—the same chance rich folks take for granted, the same choices teachers exercise but want to deny us."

But the fight isn't over, she said. "The forces of evil, those who oppose Black empowerment, will do whatever they have to do to stop us from making this a reality. We have to be ready for the next fight, and it will probably be in the courts."

In reference to Grover's comments of a few days earlier, she reiterated what she had told a *Milwaukee Journal* newspaper reporter: "The Department of Public Instruction has allowed the Milwaukee Public Schools to miseducate thousands of our children. *Our* children! This . . . freedom bill allows us to educate our own. [Grover and the unions] want to start a suit to cover up what they did to our children. They want to cover up their failure. But don't get down, we're prepared for this. God is on our side. Right is on our side. That's all we need," she said, smiling broadly. "We brought down the plantation wall, we ain't gonna' let them put shackles on us again."

Several other speakers echoed her message, including State Senator Gary George, who made a prediction based upon Grover's comments. "He's callously telling them what to do, which raises the question about his ethics and also his constitutional obligation to the people of the state of Wisconsin," George told the group. "The state has a constitutional obligation to educate all of the children of Wisconsin, and Grover is mandated to carry out that assignment. Whether he likes the law or not, his job is to follow the law, and for him to advocate for a lawsuit is tantamount to being a traitor," George said to thunderous applause.

Taking his cue from Williams's powerful oratory, George then declared it didn't matter who opponents allied with or how many lawsuits they filed—"They won't stop us!"

It would not be long before George's words would be put to the test.

FORMIDABLE OPPONENTS:
FELMERS CHANEY AND LAURI WYNN

There are essentially two reasons Black opposition to school choice continues and is almost exclusively middle-class: adherence to the philosophy of integration and classism as the cure-all and ties—financial or philosophical—to the status quo. To an extent, Milwaukee Chapter NAACP President Felmers Chaney and Wisconsin Education Association head Lauri Wynn's respective backgrounds provide particular insight into those reasons, and why the two emerged as the chief spokespersons for the opposition during the school choice debate.

Eighty-year-old Felmers Chaney's opposition to choice was rooted in an uncompromising adherence to the strategy of assimilation as the cure-all for American apartheid, ignorance of the cultural methodology and intrinsic worth of Black and community-based schools, and a misplaced aversion to the Black nationalist movement, which he referred to as misguided and separatist.

A retired Milwaukee police officer cited for bravery after a shootout left him with a bullet in his leg, Chaney had felt the slings and arrows of prejudice and bigotry throughout his life and had vowed at an early age to do all within his power to exorcise that cancer. His adamant hatred for institutional racism was equaled only by the hardship he and other Black police officers had to endure under the tyrannical reign of Chief Harold Breier during the '70s and '80s. It was often said that Breier's racist policies and disregard for the civil rights of Black Milwaukeeans were heaped upon the few Black officers on the force, many of whom stayed on the job only because they viewed themselves as their brethren's only buffer against police brutality. Promotions were rare (only one officer made it to the rank of lieutenant while Chaney was on the force), and choice assignments were out of the question. During Chaney's tenure the League of Martin, an organization of Black police officers, was formed to sue the department and city for decades of institutional racism. Although Chaney was not actively involved in the League of Martin lawsuit, he was testament to the tribulations Black officers endured during the Breier reign.

But it would be unfair to categorize Chaney as a conformist or one who silently accepted his fate under adverse conditions. As somewhat of an icon in Black circles, Chaney was actively involved in a plethora of social and economic ventures that helped to shape and strengthen the Black community. The police sergeant worked quietly behind the scenes in organizations like the NAACP and YMCA and held memberships in civic groups and neighborhood associations. He was a pioneer investor in Milwaukee's short-lived Black-owned brewery, People's Beer, became one of the founding board members of the city's Black bank, and was an early stakeholder in Halyard Park, a Black subdivision that became an enclave for Milwaukee's Black middle-class and a model of excellence for the entire city. In the era that spanned the turbulent 1960s and the transitional 1980s, Chaney's community efforts focused on what some would call nationalistic strategies that contradicted his adamant support for integration, but fit within the complicated and often paradoxical temperament of the Civil Rights movement in Milwaukee.

Growing up in one of the most segregated cities in the United States leaves one with the choice of either succumbing to second-class citizenship, praying for an encompassing moralistic change of heart on the part of the oppressors, or planting and nurturing seeds of self-determination. So while Chaney stood and shook his fist at the walls that segregationists erected to contain the Black community, he supported and advanced the Black institutions that prospered as a result. During Chaney's childhood of the '40s and '50s, the Black community was just that: a community. It offered not only a variety of Black service industries such as grocery stores and medical facilities but also entertainment establishments. Black movie theaters and nightclubs filled the Black community's Walnut Street business district, which was self-sufficient and prosperous despite surrounding racism. Black home ownership was common, Black churches provided outreach, and—even though schools were segregated—Black teachers were also students' neighbors and Sunday School teachers.

Outside of this concentrated Black community, life was hell for Black Milwaukeeans—only slightly better than conditions in the Deep South. Maybe a Black man wouldn't have been lynched for being on the wrong side of town, but surely he could have ended up assaulted first by racist White citizens and then by racist policemen. The unions blocked Black Milwaukeeans from membership, city jobs were few because of nepotism and institutional bias, and covenants prevented Black Milwaukeeans from securing housing or land outside the confines of the Black community.

Those realities shaped the mindset of Felmers Chaney and sparked within him a strong hatred of segregation and racial isolation. For Chaney, the opposite (that is, remedy and solution) of segregation, institutional bias and bigotry is *integration*, and in his mind's eye, anything all Black or Black-run was a manifestation of racism that must be destroyed in order to achieve the goal of inclusion. He took this philosophy with him as he assumed leadership of the Milwaukee branch of the NAACP in 1986 upon his retirement from the Milwaukee Police Department.

If Chaney had been considered unassuming during his years of departmental service, he atoned for it upon being elected to the NAACP presidency. Chaney was no longer bound by the mandate of silence that came with wearing a blue uniform, and he now spoke out comfortably against bias and institutional racism. During his reign, the NAACP waged successful campaigns to highlight racism within the U.S. Post Office, to compel area banks to honor Dr. Martin Luther King Jr. holiday (a campaign spearheaded by the MCJ), and to force the American Family Insurance Company to undertake a multimillion-dollar program in response to a redlining lawsuit. The local NAACP branch was also actively involved in the Milwaukee school desegregation process, which included operating a tutorial program funded with desegregation dollars.

Chaney's presidency was not without its critics, including board members and old vanguard life members who questioned office policy, the unavailability of staff to handle discrimination complaints, the heavy-handed administration, and Chaney's unwillingness to promote the type of programs that would attract new members—particularly young members. Some said the branch was stuck in the '60s and '70s and lacked the vision to adapt to the new millennium. The patriarch also incurred the wrath of female members when he announced after serving three terms that when he retired, he should be replaced by another "older man." Because of his sincerity, few ever challenged him on his opposition to school choice, although many officers of the NAACP—and obviously most of the organization's membership—voiced support for choice. At one point, Chaney stated that he opposed Black schools because they were segregated. When someone asked him if that meant the NAACP would take a position against the United Negro College Fund, he paused for several seconds in deep thought, then smiled, as if the dichotomy of the situation had finally dawned on him.

Lauri Wynn's opposition to school choice was partly a result of her unwavering support for the state and Milwaukee teachers unions and partly a manifestation of her fear that choice would undermine public education or lead to its destruction. School choice was a Republican Party conspiracy, she mistakenly believed, and all of the poor families who were not being served by the public school system were still better off than they would be if they had to navigate the oft-confusing array of private schools.

Like Chaney, Wynn was a product of the pre-desegregation era and a member of a network that followed the traditional civil rights path defined by Dr. Martin Luther King Jr., Ralph Abernathy, and (most recently) Rev. Jesse Jackson. This war was best fought in the courts and the union halls through vehicles such as school desegregation and affirmative action. Black nationalism—particularly Black control of institutions, buy-Black campaigns, and African-centered curricula—was a deviant aberration that weakened the movement by alienating White allies and other minorities. The Civil Rights movement was premised on a traditional strategy of assimilation—no matter how bumpy the road, how infrequent the tangible results for the masses. The best way to deal with poverty is not to be part of it, the old saying goes, and assimilationists believed that as the Black middle class grew, so would opportunities leading to a more just and equitable system.

In the eyes of those who followed this philosophy, Lauri Wynn proved that the strategy was plausible. Having worked up the union ladder as a teachers' representative, she was elected the first Black and female head of the WEA, which at the time represented a majority of the teachers in southeastern Wisconsin and thus was a major player in state politics. An articulate advocate for civil and women's rights, Wynn was soon offered a position as minority affairs advisor to Governor Tony Earl, a perch from which she was able to advance an agenda and philosophy that coincided with the NAACP's and made her among the most visible Black women in the state.

When a car accident left her one surgery away from losing a leg, Wynn refused to give into pessimistic physicians and instead fought to walk by undergoing a lengthy rehabilitation. Although she soon faded from the public eye, her courage and perseverance made her a role model for all citizens. Wynn was a fighter, whether for government policies that advanced the Civil Rights movement through Governor Earl or for more local endeavors such as fund-raising to ensure the continuation of a local program.

Wynn's reemergence as an ardent opponent of school choice was surprising but not out of character. Even though Wynn had sent her children to a private school—Urban Day—she was a traditionalist who could look past that contradiction. The issue, she said once, wasn't about the desperation of poor parents who wanted access to what she took for granted because of her economic status. No, the issue was the sanctity of the public school system, one of the few true remnants of democracy, which would be threatened if the poor abandoned it en masse. Despite its faults, the public school system provided Black children with an opportunity no other institution provided.

Wynn's views were cast in a status quo mold, and it became increasingly clear that her train was stuck at the union station.

ROADBLOCKS AND BULLDOZERS

While Chaney's and Wynn's views were understandable—albeit illogical from a Black nationalistic or civil rights perspective—at least they were motivated by honest beliefs, which is more than can be said of an effort by several city aldermen to put the Milwaukee Common Council on notice as opposing school choice. Yet this was the same council that had apparently taken a vow of silence during a decade of school desegregation, attempts by frustrated Black parents to carve out their own district, and even the early battle for school choice. The council members' action was obviously rooted in political rather than philosophical motives.

On March 28, Mayor John Norquist vetoed a Milwaukee Common Council resolution that denounced the school choice program. This new resolution had both public and private faces. On the public side, several aldermen claimed that they felt uncomfortable with this bold new plan to privatize public education, using the tired union line that choice would drain dollars from public education. Privately, the word was that these aldermen, who had been remarkably silent through the school choice debate, were being pressured by the MTEA to denounce the initiative. Apparently, the council was just one of several governmental bodies the union intimidated into opposing the school choice initiative. The school choice battle was waged even in political venues that seemingly had little control over legislation.

Norquist, however, was a maverick new Democrat who had bucked the union on a number of occasions and who announced that he would risk his political career over school choice. Although he recognized that the MTEA and the police union were the most powerful unions in the city, it was reported that during a staff meeting Norquist said he was willing to "write a check that the union could cash, but only at a risk of adding [his] name to the foes they were amassing en route to the bank."[4]

The mayor, who served several terms in the state senate before defeating former Governor Marty Schreiber in a hotly contested mayoral race in 1986, assumed a position at the vanguard of new Democrats who had not only expressed support for Milwaukee's choice initiative, but called for bolder programs to shake up the educational Establishment. In speeches and position papers issued throughout the campaign, the mayor had repeatedly asserted that Milwaukee government was politically impotent when it came to the city's single most important quality-of-life issue: public education. City lawmakers were legally empowered to approve or disapprove of the school board budget only in its entirety, and they had no input in policy or in the selection of a superintendent. Thus, both the mayor and the Common Council had to sit idly by as the system self-destructed, said Norquist.

Against this backdrop, Norquist advocated massive external reforms, including choice and school charters not only to provide options to parents but, more important, to "shake the political tree, to spark competition that will force the district to reform itself." Norquist hoped to work with several board members to press for

But do whites want it just to move $\star$ back in ^

reforms including decentralization and site-based management. A fiscal conservative, Norquist found himself at odds with the board over proposals to construct new schools, suggesting that a 1992 plan would bankrupt the city and do little to attract back to Milwaukee the middle-income families who had fled to the suburbs with the advent of school desegregation. Vouchers, however, were a step in the right direction, he felt, not only because they provided educational options but also because the initiative would change Milwaukee's image from a city with an educationally bankrupt public school system to the home of the country's boldest education initiative.

In fact, Norquist not only vetoed the Milwaukee Common Council antichoice resolution, but sent word to the council chambers that if aldermen were brave enough to override his veto he would put the union's threats on the table and take the fight to a public forum. A tenacious political fighter who was known to go for the throat when pressed, Norquist reportedly claimed that he would fight for choice on a racial platform: knowing that the upcoming census would prompt redistricting and expose the need for greater minority representation on the council, he would question the racial sensitivity of aldermen who voted for the antichoice resolution. He was prepared to put forth that over the past year none of these aldermen had sponsored any education legislation or otherwise involved themselves in the educational arena. Why try now to hinder school choice?

In a nutshell, Norquist, who had been backed by activist and former Black Panther Michael McGee in his bid for election, was willing to play racial hardball. Apparently, the mayor's threat struck a chord because aldermen didn't override Norquist's veto—in fact, they didn't even bring the matter up for discussion.

On May 30, state officials announced that only six private schools (Urban Day, Woodlands, Centro de la Communidad Unida, SER Jobs for Progress, Highland Community School, and Harambee Community School), approximately half of the expected number, expressed interest in participating in the program. The reason was clear: "The word is circulating that the teachers union is going to file a lawsuit to stop us before we get our paperwork through," Urban Day parent liaison Zakiya Courtney said during a teleconference from Urban Day. "Some of the other schools don't want to get caught up in a lawsuit or don't want to start getting students and then be forced to let them go in the middle of the school term. It's an awkward situation, and neither I nor Polly can tell them how to play this, aside from saying we predicted the lawsuit, and we're prepared."

Indeed, preparation wasn't the problem. The real challenge was to persuade school administrators to put aside their fears of legal entanglements. Choice supporters in urban communities around the country hoped that we would make a strong political and cultural statement by drawing at least a dozen schools, and hundreds of students, to the program.

As it happened, attracting students was not a concern. Based on calls to Williams's office and to the targeted schools, we estimated there were well over a thousand poor families ready to jump at the chance to send their children to a private school under choice—and that included only those who had kept abreast of the movement. Due to available space and participation restrictions imposed by the legislation, we calculated that we could accommodate a maximum of 850 students. However, the participation of only six schools would cut that figure by 50 to 60 percent.

Still, we were undaunted, and Williams kept everyone upbeat. She sent out word that not all of the Department of Public Instruction (DPI) bureaucrats were poised to block the schoolhouse door. In a *Milwaukee Journal* story, Steven Dold, assistant superintendent of public instruction under Grover, stated that he was "open-minded if not pragmatic about the program." He said that, based on DPI inquiries, as many as twenty-six private schools would eventually participate. Of course, his comments were made before rumors of a lawsuit, and flew in the face of Grover's open hostility to the program and his veiled attempts to usurp it. Indeed, Grover had all but ignored the legislative mandate to advertise the program—he had refused to send out a single press release—and had waited two weeks before the official sign-up period to notify the public.

Always a step ahead, Polly Williams told local forces to continue to carry out their plans while she worked at the state, local, and national level to draw attention to the school choice movement and the roadblocks it faced. "If they stop us, we'll let the world know how and why." she declared. "They won't shoot us from the weeds—it's going to have to be face to face."

She was confident that more schools would sign up for the program in its initial year if Grover's roadblocks could be legally or legislatively removed. Williams and Larry vowed that they would seek additional registration time through legislation or, if necessary, gubernatorial mandate. Thompson made it known in meetings and private discussions that he was willing to put on the gloves if necessary to see the initiative up and running by the fall.

A few weeks later, Williams drew international attention to the Milwaukee situation as European media publicized her participation as one of five panelists at a Brookings Institute Conference on Politics and Education held in Washington, D.C. Williams's remarks also caught the attention of the White House, which called school choice the next great educational battleground and Milwaukee the new Gettysburg. The centerpiece of the conference was the publication of *Politics,*

MJ
6/10/90
P 1

Markets, and America's Schools by John Chubb and Terry Moe, the same proponents who had participated in Thompson's workshop on school choice two years earlier. The book made a strong case for school choice and other reform programs that "made parents players in the education of their children."

The Conference on Politics and Education sparked a national debate played out in town hall meetings, political confrontations, and, of course, the media. News articles and editorials focused on the opinions of prominent Black and White leaders. These included Robert Woodson, executive director of the National Center for Neighborhood Enterprise, who, in a *New York Times* wire service article examining the school choice controversy in light of the conference, declared that, "my constituents are prepared to support Williams; to do whatever Williams needs us to do. She's speaking for thousands of low-income people all over the country. If necessary, we'll load up buses full of poor and disenfranchised people from around the country to travel to Wisconsin to show our support for this historic fight.[5]

Woodson, who had successfully maneuvered between political parties to push Black self-empowerment programs, applauded Williams's efforts to advance the fight for quality education to the Civil Rights platform and to raise questions about the motives of those who have traditionally led the movement: "[Williams's work] pulls the covers off this issue by recognizing that the people who are supposed to have been champions of the poor—the teachers unions, the NAACP—are really champions of their own special interests."

The *Wall Street Journal* added fuel to the fire by publishing a hard-hitting editorial that centered on Grover's efforts to derail choice—to "drive out Polly Williams's voucher plan with lawyers and strangling rules."[6] In a *Milwaukee Journal* response to the *Wall Street Journal* piece, William Bennett, former U.S. Secretary of Education and a proponent of school choice, called the initiative the "next great civil rights arena. It has to do with equality of education and opportunity. I think choice gives poor children the kind of opportunities that only middle-class and wealthy children have now." Although Wisconsin's school choice initiative was "restricted to too few students," it could serve as a catalyst for national educational reform and a public debate on education.[7]

"To engage the national conversation, you need a case, an issue. And this is it. Here you have this woman, whose politics as I understand it are quite liberal, aligning herself with the conservatives. The only plausible explanation is that she's trying to do the right thing to serve the well-being of children." But the fight would get harsher and more intense as the program moves forward, he predicted. "Monopolies never give up power willingly and the educational monopolists see Polly Williams and her small revolutionary band as a threat to bureaucratic control of [public] education that shifts power from the educrats to the parents. I think that we are now going into the second wave of educational reform and that we need nothing short of a revolution."[8] Milwaukee's School Choice Program could be the revolution's starting point.

President George Bush, visiting Wisconsin for a series of fund-raisers for Governor Thompson, echoed Bennett, calling school choice "one of the most interesting experiments in educational reform in the country. When schools compete to attract students, that can't help but to improve education."

LEGAL POWERHOUSE CLINT BOLICK

The Urban Day Community School cafeteria seats more than three hundred. On this Saturday morning in early 1990 not one place in the dozen rows of benches was unoccupied, and many people stood along the walls.

Anticipation and skepticism filled the air as all awaited the presentation of Clint Bolick, the lead attorney of the Landmark Legal Foundation for Civil Rights who had traveled from Washington, D.C., with an offer to represent parents in the lawsuits that would inevitably arise from the Parental School Choice legislation. Since his offer, two questions had been brewing: did he have sufficient expertise, and how was he to be paid? Some also thought it would be more appropriate to have a Black attorney.

No one could even estimate how much the legal fees would run, although it was calculated that more than $3 million had been shelled out for attorneys representing both sides in the decade-long Milwaukee school desegregation lawsuit. Just as in the desegregation suit, the defendants of the status quo—the MTEA, the NAACP, and MPS—would try to exhaust the resources of the pro-choice parents in a lengthy lawsuit, utilizing every legal maneuver possible to tie up the matter in the courts for years.

Had it not been for attorney Lloyd Barbee's perseverance and dedication in the Milwaukee school desegregation suit—which included investing his own resources in the case on behalf of parents—that legal struggle might still be pending. Barbee, who had served as a state representative for a dozen years, often found himself with a payment of "good will" when he approached the NAACP about money to file briefs or to bring in experts for depositions. On more than a few occasions he was forced to orchestrate fund-raisers to offset legal expenses, and he was a master at seeking out interns and law students to assist him in his work.

The MSB, on the other hand, could freely use the resources of the high-powered city attorney's office to defend itself even against the indefensible. The board brought in one of the most prestigious law firms in the Midwest to handle the case, and even after defeat was certain, it managed to buy time until it could prepare an acceptable settlement plan. Thus, a decade, $10 million (a good amount from taxes levied against the victims of the elected body's racist policies), and more than a mile of briefs, depositions, hearings, and consultations later, the desegregation suit was resolved (for good and bad).

Black parents certainly learned a lot from that struggle. If school choice miraculously passed, it was all but certain that *someone* would sue to kill the legislation and we would again face a long and costly battle. Just as in the desegregation lawsuit, the MTEA and MPS had the most to lose. Not only would school choice weaken their stranglehold on Black and poor children's aspirations but it could also illuminate publicly that Black and community schools were doing on a regular basis what MPS couldn't—educating Black children properly.

One of the few aces up the sleeves of Black parents that the board and teachers union didn't figure on was the large number of covert supporters inside the school administration and union. In fact, one of the greatest resources of the school choice army was the steady flow of information from Black people and progressive Whites who revealed board and union plans to undermine reform efforts.

Many Black teachers either voiced their support for choice or "at least didn't fight it," one of the teachers told us. "They know who it will benefit, but more importantly, they feel uncomfortable being pawns of the White-controlled union that has never worked in the interests of Black people anyway. That's why many of us crossed the picket line during the strike and fought plans to undermine desegregation. We're in the union, but not a part of it. What they come up with we're forced to accept, but there's always some grumbling." But if push came to shove, the union would unleash its resources to stop the educational choice movement in a legal forum, and, the teacher noted, the union's resources are immense. "They got half the legislature in their pocket, including Black representatives. They're like the Mafia, they have money, power, resources, and they can make offers you can't refuse. And they can afford the best attorneys in the state, and if that's not enough, they can go to the NEA [National Education Association] to get more of what they need."

Union informants revealed plans to discredit the school choice movement and its supporters, including Williams, Courtney, me, and others of influence; attempts to influence the media and Democratic Party state representatives, including threats to Black state lawmakers; and even boycott threats to MCJ advertisers.

Our sources told us that teachers were briefed on proper responses if they were approached about school choice. The statement was simple: it would harm public education, transferring money and resources to uncontrolled private academies. Parental school choice would take away money from poor minorities whose only hope was to remain under the scrutiny of those who cared and knew what was best for them—the public schools. We in the choice movement saw literature and memos before some of the intended recipients and were privy to meetings with lawyers, politicians, and State Superintendent of Public Instruction Herbert Grover, who was one of the union's major pawns and was the state's most outspoken and powerful opponent of school choice. The union controlled key Democratic Party legislators such as Notestein and Majority leader Tom Loftus, who were instructed to bury the legislation in committee or to kill it outright if it made it to the floor for consideration. As the legislation moved out of committee, the new tactic was to attack it at every turn. Herb Grover led the attack, a strategy that allowed the unions to distance themselves from the fight lest they ignite smoldering animosity in the Black community.

When we heard about the plans to initiate lawsuits when and if Parental School Choice became a reality in Milwaukee, we knew that we would need an expert defense. And so we found ourselves in the Urban Day cafeteria on this Saturday morning, face to face with Clint Bolick.

Bolick was conservatively dressed, well groomed, and very much Caucasian. Short, of medium build, and beginning to bald, he wore a gray three-button suit and an unimposing tie. He looked like a lawyer to me, although he didn't carry the aura of superiority and cockiness that has earmarked the profession. A small smile creased the corner of his mouth, offsetting the otherwise serious look on his face. His eyes darted around the room as if he were trying to establish a link with a skeptical jury.

Williams stood up from her bench. "Good morning," she said pleasantly. "I assume most of you know why we're here today. It's getting to that point in this struggle where we're going to need to fight as much in the courts as we have on the assembly floors. Today I want to introduce someone to you who I think can help us. Of course, it's up to you, but right now I honestly think we need somebody with the expertise and resources to represent us. And as I told y'all last week, we don't have the money it's going to take to defend what shouldn't even need defending. This gentleman is willing to take on the challenge, and it won't cost us anything but our hard work—if y'all give him the go-ahead."

Williams scanned the room looking for approval. She was honest in saying she would prefer a Black attorney, and had made efforts to secure one, but had fallen short—the attorneys she approached were too expensive, unfamiliar with constitutional law, or unwilling to go against the Establishment. One of Williams's friends,

Robert Woodson, had approached Williams about linking her with Bolick. Bolick came with many recommendations, and friends around the country had assured Williams that his firm, the Landmark Legal Foundation for Civil Rights, had a battery of sincere, honest, and committed lawyers. Parents and activists would have full authority to accept or reject strategies to be used in the case, said Williams, and she could require Bolick to hire a local Black attorney as an assistant.

Bolick talked about the suit in a calm, matter-of-fact manner, emphasizing that while "right is on your side," it did not mean that justice would be done. Opponents of school choice could be expected to pull out all of the stops and had the resources to take the case to the U.S. Supreme Court if necessary.

"This is a movement that has the potential to undermine the stranglehold of those who have your children trapped in a system that isn't working in their best interests. People profit from not educating your children and on the system works in their interests, not in yours," he explained.

Bolick said his strategy would focus on the Constitutional rights of parents to secure quality education for their children, and the discriminatory nature of public education. "If you have money, you have choices. If you don't, you're stuck with whatever they give you. And obviously, what they are giving you is inferior—otherwise they would have their children sitting side by side with your children."

Bolick suggested that his defense of school choice would lie within the same framework used for most civil rights cases: "It's about denial of fundamental civil liberties based upon income," he said "It's about discrimination."

For more than an hour the attorney explained his strategy in layman's terms. "[The case] will be won or lost with you," he said repeatedly, adding to the surprise of many that those who stood up for their children could expect to come under attack from those with a vested interest in maintaining the status quo. Opponents would attack the parents' credibility, their education, association with "militant groups"—even religious affiliations.

"If there are skeletons in your closet, they will find them," Bolick said. "That's their job. They will do anything and everything to discredit parents and particularly lead spokespersons. They will paint pictures of choice supporters as pawns of the right, of Republicans, of racists. They will use the NAACP to paint pictures of leaders of the school choice movement as radicals whose efforts would undermine decades of bridge building and legal challenges. School choice will harm integration, will cream the best students and thus further hurt MPS, and it will fuel segregation."

Bolick planned to counter every argument well in advance, choosing plaintiffs and witnesses who were above reproach, and propping up spokespersons who carried as much, if not more, credibility than the NAACP representatives. Bolick provided us with several legal precedents he would introduce, along with case studies. He was a legal scholar well versed in his subject. We found ourselves immensely impressed with his knowledge of the opponents' tactics, and we felt that his strategy of using civil rights laws as a foundation for our case was both shrewd and practical. But it wasn't his legal scholarship or tactical generalship that put smiles on the faces of those who left the Saturday morning meeting. It was Clint Bolick's air of confidence that set our minds at ease and gave us hope: perhaps this David could emerge victorious even against the union and educracy Goliaths. Clint Bolick was a godsend.

THE CHALLENGES CONTINUE

The opposition's next salvo came not in the form of a legal challenge but in an unprecedented requirement to the six schools that had inquired about participating in the choice program. Grover stipulated that as a prerequisite to choice participation, each school would have to sign an extensive array of regulatory requirements unprecedented in the state: special staff for orthopedic disabilities, medical services for diagnosis and evaluation of mentally challenged children, and psychological services. The eight-page-long list of requirements also included disabled access, including elevators and transport vehicles. The fact that no public school could meet the requirements—and indeed that few public schools accommodated *all* special needs children—didn't concern Grover.

School administrators were baffled and incensed by the requirements. Refusing to sign the letters of participation would eliminate their schools from participation in the program, but agreeing would put them under the thumb of the state. A meeting to discuss the matter left most schools and activists as confused as before. The only path appeared to be a court challenge, which might open a Pandora's box of litigation.

Soon those deliberations were moot, however, because on Friday, June 1, a coalition of public teachers and administrators filed suit to enjoin the choice initiative on the grounds that it was unconstitutional. The Wisconsin Education Association, Felmers Chaney, Lauri Wynn, the Wisconsin Federation of Teachers, and the Administrators and Supervisors Council of Milwaukee (an organization representing school principals) argued that school choice inappropriately directed state money to schools that didn't have to meet state educational standards. They also charged that school choice was unconstitutional because it diverted money to private schools in violation of "public-purpose doctrine."[9]

Chaney held that the choice initiative violated the basic tenets of the NAACP "by fostering segregation and [did] nothing to improve the quality of education for the sixty-four thousand African Americans who will remain in the public school system."[10] He also avowed that the program would discriminate against some ethnic groups and thus was in violation of the NAACP's goal of an integrated society. The ludicrous argument was obviously employed to offset the racial overtones of the choice opposition. MTEA officials were cognizant that their opposition to school choice would unmask the union as being anti-Black and antipoor, and the NAACP—or Chaney and Wynn—was needed to defuse that stigma. Grover, State Treasurer Charlie Smith, and MPS were named defendants in the suit. MPS was involved in order to tap into city funds to finance the lawsuit, since the city attorney's office was the legal counsel for the board.

Literally within moments of hearing of the lawsuit, Williams gave Bolick and his team the go-ahead to cross the t's and dot the i's on legal documents they had been preparing for several months.

At one of our weekly meetings a number of angry Black parents called for a boycott of the NAACP. "They sure don't represent *us*. They're an embarrassment to Black people," one angry mother charged. "Ain't nothing but water carriers for White bigots," she continued in a tearful and angry tirade that drew nods and cheers. "To hell with that integration shit, excuse my French. For Chaney and them to say Black people can't educate Black people, or anything Black is bad is an insult to all Black people. We need to send a message . . . they don't represent us."

Williams moved quickly to calm the incensed soldiers, asserting not only that we didn't need another distraction but also that "we shouldn't give White folks the satisfaction of seeing Black people fighting each other in public. The NAACP is wrong, but the organization still has done too much for Black people to attack them like that." She told parents who wanted to send a message to the NAACP to withdraw their membership or contact board members. Eventually, Williams's wisdom prevailed, although several parents and supporters did denounce the NAACP on radio talk shows and at various community forums. It was obvious that the Black community was splintered, and it would not be civil rights business as usual in Milwaukee.

We had passed this way before. Ironically, the NAACP had consistently been at odds with parents and more progressive and militant Black leadership over the issue of reforms. But Williams was correct in another respect: obviously the tactic of the MTEA was to divide and thus to conquer, and Black groups fighting each other publicly only served to benefit the union. Moreover, while we vehemently disagreed with the NAACP on this issue, we couldn't forget that the association

Divido conquer again

had fought battles for Black folks when other groups and organizations had turned their backs.

For now, the legal battle was on. On June 5, 1990, Bolick, representing a group of eight African-American parents, filed a countersuit. As nearly everyone wanted to be named in the suit, guaranteeing their places in history, the parents were chosen by lottery. During a telephone strategy session several days later, it was suggested that parents call for a communitywide prayer vigil. "Let's call on God to do for us what He did for Moses and the Jews. Dear God, look upon us as you did the Israelites in Egypt. Let Polly be your Moses . . . provide for our children." This suggestion was considered for several minutes, and then one parent proposed that we stage a march from Milwaukee to Madison to impress on the Supreme Court our strong sentiments regarding school choice.

However, none of these expedients proved necessary: the state supreme court dismissed the teachers union's request for an injunction to halt the new parental choice initiative. The court ruled that the public interest would best be served if the program continued as the lawsuit was heard, in effect giving the private schools at least a one-semester reprieve. Before the *Journal's* and *Sentinel's* ink dried on their respective feature stories, Bolick filed suit against State Superintendent of Public Instruction Herbert Grover.

Most of us wanted to hold a community party to mark the significant achievement. Williams had other plans, however—using the momentum to strike back immediately at Grover, whose callous disregard for the law was only equaled by his flagrant and malicious attempts to circumvent the registration process.

"We ain't got time to celebrate," Williams told us at a briefing. "Time is running out. If we can't clear up this mess that Grover has put on us, choice ain't gonna' happen."

Our suit charged that Grover illegally undermined the participation of six private schools by attempting to force them to sign an extensive array of regulations. Bolick asserted that Grover had no legal grounds to force the schools to sign these requirements, and in addition to requesting that the court expand the registration deadlines, he called for a revised listing of eligible schools that would include those that had refused to sign the imposed requirements.

A July 25 court date was set for the most important educational initiative in state history. Although the lawsuit pitted a group of poor Black and minority parents against the combined power and influence of the State Department of Public Instruction, the state teachers and administrators unions, and the NAACP, we felt that we had them outnumbered.

Faubas at the door first came in 1990 over Grover

Soon Herbert Grover, the educrat's educrat, was reeling from a June 27, 1990, *Wall Street Journal* editorial that painted him with a highly critical brush.[11] The editorial compared Grover's attempts to stop poor children from entering private schools to the efforts of Arkansas Governor Orval Faubus, who called out the National Guard in 1957 to stop Black children from attending an all-White school, and of George Wallace, the racist governor of Alabama who stood in the schoolhouse door to block the entrance of Black children, declaring "No integration today, tomorrow, *ever*." The editorial played the race card against the so-called liberal, using some of the same epithets I had invoked months before when referring to State Representative Barbara Notestein. Judging from Grover's reaction, he didn't like being called a racist any more than Notestein did. Pulling the cover off apparently hurts.

"This isn't fair, is it?" Grover complained in a June 29, 1990, *Milwaukee Journal* article circulated by the Associated Press. "I'm just trying to do my duty as I see it."[12]

Grover tried to turn the tables, claiming that under choice legislation a right-wing group such as Posse Comitatus could get public financing for a school. Choice did not address what he saw to be the fundamental needs of educational reform. He didn't explain, however, what those mysterious needs were and how they would be carried out. Nor did he comment on how and why Milwaukee's public education system was allowed to deteriorate so drastically under his watch. Constitutionally, the state is mandated to ensure that all children receive a good education. And as state superintendent of public instruction, he was the constitutional gatekeeper.

OVERCOMING OPPOSITION

The roller coaster took another turn around the track as arguments before Dane County Circuit Judge Susan Steingass began on a warm July morning in Madison. Patrick McDonnell, Milwaukee assistant city attorney, pulled a rabbit from a worn-out hat when he argued that school choice would make the MPS system more segregated. "What this legislation does is ignore twenty-five years of history of desegregating Milwaukee public schools," McDonnell said, asserting that the exodus of Black students would further harm desegregation statistics.

"How he could form his lips to utter those words?" was one of the many comments from the gallery, which nearly overflowed with parents and press. "I don't know how he said that with a straight face," another Black woman said, fidgeting in her seat.

McDonnell's assertion was not only illogical but also dishonest. The Milwaukee Public School system continued to be segregated by virtue of the absence of White families who either fled the system for private schools or the suburbs or who occupied a disproportionate number of seats in specialty schools. "Make the White kids come back to neighborhood schools," one angry mother declared while in the background McDonnell's comments reverberated. "School choice will help integration 'cause the more Black students to leave the system, the smaller the number you got to integrate. You don't need to be a genius to figure that out. I just hope justice isn't blind and can see through these lies," the woman said.

Following McDonnell, Robert Friebert, representing the NAACP, came up with a similarly specious argument that the civil rights group opposed choice because it failed to provide a system of monitoring of students' progress. "You can't have the public funds without the public controls," he declared to moans from the gallery.

"So who's monitoring the failure at MPS?" one mother asked loudly.

A short time later, choice supporters' frowns turned to smiles and a few whispered amens as Bolick masterfully ripped apart every argument set forth by the defenders of the status quo. In an impassioned plea to the stern-faced Judge Steingass, Bolick described school choice as an educational opportunity for the state's largest and most troubled school district. School choice was created by parents for parents and would involve them in the process that would determine failure or success. Parents, asserted Bolick, know best what is good for their children. They are the best judges—far better judges than educrats, bureaucrats, or politicians. The state's responsibility under the constitution is to educate children. If one system is failing them, how can anyone deny them the chance to get a quality education elsewhere?

Changing his focus to Grover and his misguided, illegal efforts to block choice through mean-spirited mandates, Bolick said, "Mr. Grover, in his zeal to destroy this program, has sentenced this program to death by bureaucratic strangulation."

It takes about an hour and twenty minutes to get from Madison to Milwaukee. It can seem like an eternity if you're carrying bad news. On this day, however, the return trip went quickly, as there was a general sense that things had worked to the favor of the choice families. Bolick's presentation was expertly handled, and as Zakiya Courtney was to say later, "We made an excellent choice in bringing him in. That White man is good. He made [our opponents] look like the hypocrites they are."

After more than a month of suspense, on August 22 the State Court of Appeals unanimously rejected a key motion by the plaintiffs. A hearing was scheduled for the following week to examine the constitutionality of the program.

The first week of school under choice was uneventful in most respects, except for the throngs of television cameras and reporters. About 350 students signed up for the program—not including the four hundred who would have participated had it not been for the eleventh-hour amendment that barred those already in private schools from registering in the program. Fortunately, Williams's requests to the Bradley Foundation and other groups had been heard, and scholarships were offered to the parents affected by the amendment. None were turned away.

In many respects, the first week of the post–school choice era concluded with a collective sigh of relief. True, we had achieved a major victory in the educational reform war. School choice was a major piece of the puzzle and reaching this point was a monumental achievement. But we also recognized that the world was seemingly against us. We had outstrategized and outmaneuvered the opponents thus far, but there would obviously be many legal and other hurdles ahead. And we had to face a powerful army—not just the teachers union, educrats, and assorted bigots intent on maintaining the status quo, but also the White media, which sought not only to derail our Freedom Train but also to make us look like criminals (or at least misguided ingrates) in the process. Against that impressive army stood parents, a few allies, and one newspaper—the MCJ.

It would prove to be enough.

PLEADING OUR OWN CAUSE

Education being an object of the highest importance to the welfare of society, we shall endeavor to present just and adequate views of it, and to urge upon our brethren the necessity and expediency of training their children, while young, to habits of industry and thus forming them for becoming useful members of society. It is surely time that we should awake from this lethargy of years, and make a concentrated effort to the education of our youth. We form a spoke in the human wheel, and it is necessary that we should understand our dependence on the different parts, and theirs on us, in order to perform our part with propriety.

—SAMUEL CORNISH AND JOHN B. RUSSWURM

In many respects, the campaign for parental school choice defined the *Milwaukee Community Journal*.

On the one hand, we embraced the concept of vouchers as an educational option for low-income families denied the opportunity of quality education. On the other hand, the crusade for school choice was a fundamental civil rights issue—one that redefined the Black agenda, refocusing our attention from failed assimilation and school board antipathy to Black self-determination and community building. School choice empowered the have-nots while striking a blow at the Establishment. Potentially, this one small battle for educational equality could shift the power pendulum in the favor of African Americans.

I'm not among Black conservative Alan Keyes followers. But there's a passage in his eye-opening book *Masters of the Dream* that expresses one of my basic tenets: "The struggle of liberation is not just a struggle to be free of the master. The aim is to be your own master."[1] That's what school choice symbolized for those of us involved in the struggle: an opportunity to break the shackles of educational mediocrity, what I call the conspiracy to mis- or undereducate Black children.

School choice provided the *Milwaukee Community Journal* with the perfect platform from which to agitate for change. This was our mission, our quest, and our responsibility.

Our coverage of the school choice crusade epitomized what the Black press is supposed to be about—its core reason for being. America's Black press was created to advocate on behalf of and provide leadership to Black America. The Black press was born out of a need for a voice to champion Black causes, a weapon in the war for equality and justice. The Black press provides balance and is the only vehicle through which our opinions are not filtered or (mis)interpreted.

The first Black newspaper was introduced in New York in 1826 because Africans on these shores—both free and enslaved—needed an uncensored voice to "speak our own cause," to rally our forces, and from which to signal revolt. However, by the mid-1970s, Milwaukee's Black press had become stagnant, uninspired. Worse yet, its owners were thinking only of business instead of advocacy. True, the Black media is a business—one of America's oldest. But it is also an arm of the Civil Rights movement, a fact that can be obscured by dollar signs. It was clear that another voice was needed to shake up the system.

Freeway

Black Milwaukee was politically, socially and economically impotent. The city's program of urban renewal was devastating Black businesses. School desegregation was destroying our neighborhood structures as the quality of education continued its downward spiral. Police brutality and institutional racism had the city near the point of racial explosion. The local Black press filled its pages with depressing accounts of injustice and social anarchy, but it didn't provide leadership. In some respects it had given up and accepted the status quo. It had lost its energy and zest. Milwaukee needed new ideas and new philosophies. The *Milwaukee Community Journal* was founded in 1976 to fill that void.

With school choice, the MCJ assumed its most important responsibility, providing an alternative forum for the Black masses. It was obvious that neither the White media nor the so-called liberal press would suffice. They were not content to editorialize against school choice; instead, they sought to sabotage it by misquoting Black leaders and refusing to print supporters' side of the story. This state of things made the MCJ's role all the more crucial—and, as we were to discover, also made us a target.

"WE CAN, WE WILL, WE MUST"

The *Milwaukee Community Journal's* owner and publisher Patricia O'Flynn Thomas fought to open the doors of educational opportunity for Black children first as a

Milwaukee public school teacher, then as a parent with children in the system, and finally as a civil rights activist and newspaper crusader with her husband Robert Thomas, a noted Black business and community leader.

At the root of Patricia Thomas's education agenda were the seeds of self-determination instilled in her as a poor child growing up in the physically decrepit and fiscally bankrupt city of East St. Louis, Illinois. Thomas's mother pushed and prodded her children to excel in spite of the obstacles that arose from their socio-economic status. Early on, Thomas adopted a motto describing her personal philosophy: "We can, we will, we must."

She used this expression to motivate herself through the substandard public school offerings of East St. Louis and to achieve a scholarship to Marquette University. She later instilled that philosophy in her public school students and used it in many stages of her life as a business anthem and civil rights maxim. The motto became the foundation behind the *Soul City Shopper,* her advocacy news shopper that brought together businesses and activists around issues vital to Milwaukee's Negro community in the 1960s. "We can, we will, we must" eventually became Thomas's rallying cry as copublisher of the *Milwaukee Star Times* and finally as publisher of the *Milwaukee Community Journal,* which by 1989 was the state's largest-circulated African-American publication.

A product of the '50s and '60s, Patricia Thomas was an advocate for multiculturalism under the flag of desegregation, seeing it not only as a way to equalize funding and resources but also as a way to bridge the racial divide. As she once put it, the only way to neutralize racial prejudice was to stare it in the eye and defuse it with facts, logic, and a human face. Along the same lines, desegregation often provided opportunities for friendships that put African Americans in contact with the power base. As a result of their experiences at Marquette University, Patricia Thomas and then-husband Robert were able to forge lifelong friendships with individuals who climbed the business and political ladders, including prominent business leaders and political leaders such as County Executive Tom Ament and E. Michael McCann, the Milwaukee County district attorney. She later called upon those contacts to help her tackle racial injustice.

Although frustrated by the Milwaukee Public School system's methodology, Thomas shared with many a guardedly optimistic view of school desegregation. She felt that despite its flaws, public education was an important tool that could prejudice and racism or at least afford African Americans an equal opportunity. While acknowledging my belief that "you can't legislate integration," she would add, "You can achieve that ideal state through interpersonal dialogue and friendships forged in desegregated school settings."

So faithful was Thomas to the concept of public education that she endorsed her oldest son's desire to leave what was then considered the county's most prestigious private school for a public high school. The fact he emerged a doctor a decade later was not only testament to public education's potential strength, but was also a victory for the thousands—herself included—fighting to tear down the walls of segregation and fiscal inequities in Milwaukee. For parents like Robert and Patricia Thomas, the system could work—as the battle for school choice was being waged, her oldest son, Terrance, was undergoing his residency in Michigan, and her youngest son, Todd (a.k.a. Speech), also a graduate of a Milwaukee public school, was enrolled at the University of Wisconsin. Todd was also working on his musical career as a member of the rap group Arrested Development.

A classic civil rights leader, Thomas recognized early on that the battle for equality and justice in Milwaukee required flanking actions against biased public institutions. She coupled this strategy with community building and support for Black businesses and institutions. The church and education system made up the other parts of strong community foundation, each playing important roles in the advancement of the civil rights agenda.

Thomas's editorial philosophy called for accentuating the positives of Black life while directing criticism where needed. The *MCJ* was quick to praise, but equally quick to criticize Black Milwaukeeans for neglecting to vote, tolerating antisocial behavior, or remaining silent about self-destructive behavior ranging from teen pregnancy to domestic abuse. Thomas made certain to incorporate in our publication sections on youth and student achievement, business development, and progressive entertainment.

We showcased positive stories about the achievements of community residents, pearls of wisdom from the elderly, and cultural links with our Motherland, Africa, long before it was fashionable. Under Thomas's leadership, we covered issues such as South African apartheid and cultural empowerment through campaigns such as Kwanzaa. That coverage was balanced by protest journalism that challenged traditional hindrances to Black progress, including Milwaukee Public Schools and its board and administrators whose policies stifled the potential and aspirations of our children.

Though teachers and administrators were often the targets of our wrath, we also took to task apathetic parents. We both condemned irrelevant curricula and criticized disruptive students. We lambasted insensitive and racist teachers and aides and also took on political leaders who complained but didn't seek legislative changes to improve opportunities for children.

Although I was given near-total autonomy as editor, Thomas was actively involved in editorial meetings and would mandate certain slants or stories, occasionally writing an editorial or column. For the most part, she trusted my judgment, although my views at the time could tend toward the radical. My attacks could be merciless and—through my national award-winning column, *Signifyin'*—personal if warranted.

In many respects, Thomas and I complemented each other philosophically. Many in the community noted that I followed the philosophy of Marcus Garvey and Malcolm X while Thomas adhered to the tenets of Dr. Martin Luther King Jr. and A. Phillip Randolph—which always made for an interesting philosophical mix. Not that Thomas opposed self-determination, Black independent schools, or direct action with racist police or hate groups like the Nazi Party or the KKK, both of whom had branches in Milwaukee. Thomas just felt that the community was best served when some people threw rocks at the castle walls while others, like her, tried to tear them down from the inside.

No issue better illustrated our philosophical differences and mutual goals than Milwaukee school desegregation. Thomas knew I didn't support the program as it was structured, nor did I advocate cultural assimilation as a cure-all for Black injustice. I believed in equalization of funding and resources, community control of the schools (site-based management), and establishment of an African-centered curriculum in institutions that were predominantly African American. I didn't have a problem with busing, as long as it was voluntary and equitable and there was something significant at the end of the ride. Despite my refusal to support integration, I did not necessarily oppose it, as long as it was not premised on assimilation. I actively supported specialty and magnet schools and believed in multiculturalism.

Twenty years earlier, George and Sideena Holt, my parents, had participated in protests to halt intact busing, including a campaign during which they physically placed their bodies under buses to dramatize the racism inherent in the practice. They would later say that they were not engaged in that campaign because they wanted me and my siblings to sit next to White children under a forced "integrated" setting, but because they were protesting the system of educational apartheid and were attempting to force the school board to allocate greater resources to Central City schools and to construct new schools in the Black community to alleviate overcrowding. They were not then, nor are they today, opposed to integration. As a minister, my mother advocates universal brotherhood. But she also promotes racial diversity and preaches that African culture is no less blessed than European culture (Africans may in fact be the chosen people of God, by virtue of their being the first and most influential people in Christian history).

Thomas, on the other hand, was an early proponent of multiculturalism and as such felt that desegregation was a means to an end. Nonetheless, she also stressed that while we should fight to make desegregation work, the real focus should be on ensuring that Black children attending public schools receive the best education possible. Busing was a necessary evil given the demographics and concessions made prior to the court ruling. Moreover, there were tangible benefits that came even with the obvious inequities. At the same time, it was agreed that the process was biased and unfair, and it was questionable whether the benefits of desegregation were worth the sacrifices.

I had my followers and tapped into my relationships within the grassroots community, where I felt most comfortable. Mrs. Thomas moved within her more upscale and middle-class circle of Black professionals and politicians. Often our paths and agendas crossed. Even when they didn't, it wasn't a major setback because we realized long ago that while we could be on different trains, we were essentially on the same track. And that track ran right through the Milwaukee Public Schools railroad station.

So it wasn't surprising when the *Milwaukee Community Journal,* like its predecessor the *Milwaukee Star Times,* was at the cutting edge of the education reform movement, often taking unpopular positions to stimulate thought, provoke discussion, and launch a new agenda. The *MCJ* never gave the educracy a day's rest, especially regarding the desegregation fiasco.

The desegregation plan orchestrated by McMurrin and Bennett and their team of educrats provided optimal opportunities for White families with the least inconvenience. That the process could also acquire state and federal integration dollars that could be diverted to noneducational areas was icing on the cake. Those goals were achieved by closing schools in Black neighborhoods or converting them into citywide specialties and magnets. The lottery selection process to determine placement was set up to ensure that Black children would be bused from their neighborhoods and community resources, while White children were bused only if it enhanced their educational aspirations. This scheme allowed MPS to tap into a bottomless pit of state resources to feed the MPS monster at a rate second only to the property-tax levy. Busing became, as we at the *MCJ* called it, big business. Like junkies, it seemed, MPS administrators and the board would do anything to get a monetary fix.

Years later, the U.S. Commission on Civil Rights called the desegregation process a cruel hoax on Black people and a failed and misguided attempt to provide quality education.[2] The desegregation process sparked a great number of institutional problems that adversely affected Black children. Suspension rates skyrocketed. Racial confrontations exploded inside and outside the schools. Clashes over quotas imposed by the school board and teachers union limited the number of

Black teachers acceptable at each school. There were Black protests over preferences given to White children attending specialty and magnet schools and the refusal of many schools to alter culturally biased and historically incorrect curricula, including history books that painted the picture of happy-go-lucky African slaves.

With so much ammunition, rarely a week passed that education issues did not grace the front page of the *MCJ*, supplanting our crusades against institutional racism, police brutality, and Black voter apathy.

CONTROVERSY—AND CONSEQUENCES

In many respects the *MCJ* was a pacesetter. My Black nationalistic philosophy, which took root during the '70s and '80s, fueled campaigns and editorials that garnered notoriety and support in the Black community but deeply angered the Establishment.

Numerous ads were lost and doors were closed in our faces because the Establishment business community refused to advertise in the paper. More often than not, punishment came in the form of unofficial boycotts. City and county government officials used the strategy to ostracize the *MCJ* after we questioned institutional racism or government-sanctioned bias in the allocation of public dollars and services.

The police department, under tyrannical Chief Harold Breier, was rumored to have pressured advertisers to drop out of the paper during our decade-long crusade against racial injustice and police brutality and engaged in other overt and covert forms of intimidation. The police were an occupying army in the Black community. Breier was often referred to as a Gestapo officer in many Black circles. His feelings about Black people were summed up by his unequivocal support of police officers involved in a dozen so-called accidental shootings of Black people in the mid-'70s to '80s. Any doubt as to his racism was dispelled by his comment in the *Milwaukee Sentinel* that "school desegregation will do nothing but bus crime around the city."[3]

Against this backdrop, Patricia Thomas toiled and struggled, advocating on behalf of the Black community while trying to maintain a business that employed a dozen people. It was not an easy task, and there were many personal and economic sacrifices. But Thomas never deviated from the path or succumbed to the pressure, which included threats against her and her family, intimidation by Breier, and economic boycotts of the *MCJ*.

Thomas's sacrifices were premised on hope for an equitable and bias-free society, and education was and would always be the building block for Black success in society. In every city—even in the most racist environments—there would be pockets of excellence and dedicated teachers who empowered Black children, breaking cycles of poverty and grooming future leaders for the war against injustice. As Thomas once noted, nearly 45 percent of all Black professionals have jobs in the public arena—and teachers are at the head of the list.

The task before the MCJ was clear: to accentuate the positives while attacking the negatives. Our job at the MCJ was to prod politicians and to encourage parents to become active. We would showcase private schools as models to be emulated, and if all else failed, as we thought at various times it did, Thomas begrudgingly supported our call for an independent school district. But she made clear her refusal to give up on MPS, school desegregation, or the efforts by parents and politicians to bring about reforms—and she was hesitant about the campaign for parental school choice. Like many Black middle-class and traditional civil rights leaders, she initially feared the choice movement would lead to the abandonment of the public school system or the loss of jobs or seniority by Black teachers and administrators. Probably more than any other ethnic group, Black Americans had long viewed the public school system as a springboard to inclusion in the American melting pot; school choice, the rhetoric went, threatened that potential.

Not surprisingly, Thomas's fears about school choice were echoed by a small number of influential Black power brokers, almost all of them middle- and upper-middle-class professionals. To them, there were only Black and White, Democrat and Republican, liberal and conservative. Many criticized Polly Williams for blurring the ideological lines when she forged an alliance with Republicans to advance school choice. These influential Black professionals viewed choice as a Republican ploy to undermine public education, even though most Black students were underacheiving, if not failing outright. Most of them didn't see the hypocrisy in their opposition: they themselves sent their children to private schools—many to University School, the premiere private school in the state.

It could be said that too many members of Milwaukee's Black middle-class community had gotten comfortable and had forgotten the African adage "I am because we are." Like most urban communities, Milwaukee had a well-defined Black caste system that pitted middle-class African Americans against low-income African Americans, in part because the Black middle class disproportionately found its employment in the public sector and felt threatened by movements like school choice. Many of Thomas's peers were unwavering supporters of the NAACP, and some were members of a quasi-political group called the Milwaukee African American Council. The group never took a public position on school choice, probably out of fear of the backlash such a stance would elicit from grassroots Black activists, but did work behind the scenes against the measure in a variety of ways, including pressuring Thomas.

Fear would not have impeded Thomas, a principled woman who was known to take unpopular positions she felt strongly about. She supported me even when her support strained friendships or cost her advertising revenues. On more than a few occasions she jeopardized friendships over my editorials and commentaries, particularly those in which I lambasted Black politicians for their inactivity or silence on certain issues. For instance when I wrote a *Signifyin'* column charging that a Black county supervisor was asleep at the wheel as her colleagues waged attacks against the Black community, she demanded that I be fired and threatened to sue the paper if I wasn't.

The article, entitled "All My Chillin's," was a soap opera parody in which I took the city's Black politicians to task for various sins ranging from backstabbing and adultery to inaccessibility, arrogance, and, in one case, Uncle Tomism. In each instance I used actual events to make my point, which didn't sit too well with the targets of my wrath.

Thomas refused to apologize, much less fire me. But her support cost the newspaper dearly. I later learned that the supervisor had a hand in killing financial support for the paper's annual Black Expo, a three-day entertainment and information exhibition that included nationally recognized entertainers, education and information booths, entrepreneurial workshops, and cultural presentations. The supervisor also reportedly pressured various county departments to exclude the *MCJ* from its advertising placements, even if the programs targeted the Black community.

I should have predicted a similar commotion over school choice. In my discussions with Thomas, I focused on the benefit of the program to the thousand or so Black students who could avail themselves of private school education and force the public school system to address its deficits. School choice, I told Thomas, would be the lead salvo in the war to change public education for the better. Other programs and initiatives would follow and through them we would turn this nightmare into the vision that so many people had fought for.

If those arguments didn't sway her, the statistics I constantly brought to her attention surely did: fewer than half of the Black children attending MPS would ever graduate; the collective grade point average for Black children since the start of desegregation had dropped and was now at an all-time low of 1.6; suspension and expulsion rates were at an all-time high; and reading and math scores had plummeted.

"We're losing an entire generation of Black children because the system doesn't work in our best interest," I often told Thomas. "You know better than most, because you've been there."

Thomas grudgingly agreed with me and withstood the criticism of friends over the school choice issue and our unprecedented—and often solitary—support for it.

MCJ VS. MTEA

The MCJ's weekly meetings were its lifeblood. During these meetings our editorial agenda was set, revenues were discussed, and our hunger for justice was reinforced. But there was distressing news at a fall 1991 meeting that would forever change the paper's financial base as well as its relationship with so-called allies in the war for equal rights.

Karl Evans, the MCJ's advertising manager, brought depressingly bad news that I could only hope would not soften the publisher's fragile support for parental school choice: key businesses were apparently being pressured by unknown entities to withdraw their advertising because of the newspaper's advocacy for parental school choice. Evans's weekly report would not help my case—not at all.

As the advertising manager of a Black newspaper, Evans had heard every excuse under the sun from companies that did not want to advertise in the Black press, the two paramount reasons being ignorance and prejudice. The latest addition to the excuse list, however, caught him off guard.

These advertisers eventually admitted that their refusal had to do with the paper's "anti-union positioning," which is a misnomer for "supporting school choice." The irony of a nonunion business withdrawing advertising because of a newspaper's supposed anti-union position was just too ridiculous to comprehend.

"They said they wouldn't advertise because of our support of school choice," Evans told me, frustration written on his face. "That's the second one in less than a month," he continued, noting that the first client was a longtime advertiser who refused to renew its contract.

"It's obvious this isn't a coincidence, because both of those who dropped out used some of the same terminology. It was almost like they were reading from a script. The question is, who is behind this?"

The question was rhetorical; we both knew, or at least strongly suspected the answer: the teachers union.

We were not unfamiliar with this tactic. In fact, it was a situation most Black papers, or at least those with a strong editorial philosophy, had faced thousands of times. And the MCJ fit that profile. For example, one of the city's major banks refused to advertise with us—even though in the Central City our circulation was stronger than the city's dailies—because we criticized the financial institution for selling Krugerrands, the South African gold coin, during the height of the anti-apartheid movement. Ironically, the bank's refusal to advertise was an economic sanction, exactly the strategy we supported in South Africa. However, this tactic didn't work. We refused to modify our views.

Several years earlier, it was rumored that a Jewish organization had pressured a financial institution into pulling away from advertising with us because of favorable press we gave to the Nation of Islam and its leader, Minister Louis Farrakhan. We weren't high on the lists of friends of Realtors, insurance agents, or mortgage companies after several exposés about redlining, discriminatory lending practices, and disparities in costs for African Americans and other Central City residents. But as the saying goes, what doesn't kill you makes you stronger, and each of these rejections strengthened our resolve and solidified our status in the African-American community. The *Milwaukee Community Journal* was recognized as not only the fiercest fighter for the downtrodden and for Black Americans but also as the people's voice.

In many respects, the unofficial boycott and intimidation of our advertisers by the teachers union was to be expected, though we didn't have any idea of the extent to which our financial situation would be affected. To our dismay, our revenue dropped significantly. I could only hold my breath in fear that the dip in revenues—which for a small business was significant—would not chip away at Thomas's tacit support for choice.

Strong, determined, and spiritually grounded, Thomas is constantly tested, but rarely wavers. She has strong maternal feelings—not just for her own two sons, but for every member of her adopted MCJ family. She is the lioness who protects, provides for, and nudges forward her cubs. For example, even in the rough times, she always made sure we were paid, whether that meant tapping MCJ savings or using her own personal resources. And so her support for choice did not waver: in fact, the MTEA attacks apparently strengthened her resolve to push the measure forward and to question the rationale behind the union's opposition in the face of such abysmal achievement statistics on the part of Black students.

Thomas suggested that we advance an even stronger case for school choice, putting a human face to the initiative, and dispelling myths about its taking money from MPS. She also felt that we should examine the initiative's support base by conducting a survey of our Black readership. At her suggestion, we began looking at Black independent schools as viable alternatives, contrasting their successes to the poor performance of public schools. Thomas also mandated that we look more closely at how school choice could serve as a vehicle to strengthen single-parent households—to fill the void often created by the absence of a father—and encouraged us to tap into our connections with the MTEA to get a better feel for their campaign against us.

I don't know if Patricia Thomas saw herself facing the same dilemma as John Russwurm or Samuel Cornish, founders of the Black press in 1826, who declared when confronted by similar circumstances that "we wish to plead our own cause . . . from the pulpit to the podium, for too long have others spoken for us. . . . "[4] But amid repeated financial and verbal attacks, it is likely a light went off in her mind questioning the lengths to which school choice opponents would go to stop a handful of children from attending private schools. The vehement and all-encompassing attacks suggested something far more ominous than routine policy disagreement.

What the union hierarchy didn't know—indeed what the government, corporations, and slaveholders a century ago never understood—was that Black people were and continue to be *family*. We may be dysfunctional, we may be in disarray, we may even be discombobulated, but we are still family, and we share a special ancestry, a common oppression, and a certain destiny. On those grounds, we understood that our paramount loyalty was not to "the man," to White friends, or even to spouses of other races. Thus we kept our eyes open while contributing to the collective pool of knowledge.

House slaves once kept the field slaves abreast of what was going on in the Big House, paving the way for revolt or escape. A generation later, janitors and junior vice presidents alike made note of policies or statements that affected the Black community and fed the information back to the line workers and the community. And Black teachers—a part of MTEA but never really a part of the system—fed us information from union officials, all of whom were White and, despite words to the contrary, many of whom held racist beliefs.

Indeed, the relationship between the union and its Black teachers had always been tenuous at best. In 1977, the union called a strike that planted a wedge between the Black and White teachers. The Black teachers, who had formed a separate caucus because of conflicts with White teachers, had been at odds with the union over issues including the union's position on desegregation, quotas on the percentage of Black staff at any given school, Black representation on the union's ruling body, and, at that time, the impact of the strike on Black children. After several closed-door meetings, many Black teachers emerged declaring their opposition to the strike because it would adversely affect Black children.

During the strike, dozens of African-American teachers crossed the picket lines, choosing the children over the union. Their actions, as expected, created a stir within the rank and file of the MTEA as exemplified by union officials' racially charged statements. If their words didn't hurt, the rocks and eggs with which Black teachers were pelted as they entered or left their assigned schools certainly did.

I watched those attacks while covering the strike at two Northside schools. I will never forget the looks of hatred and the racist epithets spewed by White teachers, who would later return to the classroom to teach our children! Nor could I ignore the pain written on the brows of the Black teachers who were punished only for loving Black children.

The strike eventually ended, but the relationship between Black and White teachers was strained forever. Thus, Black teachers, most of whom were sympathetic to choice (a large percentage of Black teachers sent their children to private schools, including Harambee and Urban Day), fed us a steady diet of union strategies against the movement and the *MCJ*. That information lent credence to our theories about threats to advertisers as well as efforts to discredit choice movement participants. We learned that the MTEA was meeting with politicians, including Grover, to undermine school choice.

Through editorials and public presentations, we began to put the MTEA on the defensive, questioning the organization's motives and noting its history of neglect of, if not open hostility toward, quality education for Black children. The facts spoke for themselves: The MTEA had undermined desegregation, viciously fought all attempts to institute site-based management, battled to maintain quotas on the number and percentage of Black teachers at any given school, and condoned tenure of racist and unquestionably immoral teachers. The MTEA endorsed a seniority system that allowed the best teachers to avoid teaching in schools with high minority representations. The union also challenged and questioned African-centered curricula, including a proposal authored by a group of Black professionals to implement an African-immersion specialty for Black males.

Against such a track record, the MTEA was put in the position of defending the indefensible. Because of its war against school choice and the lunacy of its accusations, the MTEA even had to ward off charges of racism.

During a Central City forum on education reform in spring 1991, an audience exchange pitted a union member against a pro-choice parent. The union spokesperson was eaten alive. His attempts to explain how "choice will steal money" from MPS was laughable; he realized he had put his foot in his mouth when someone in the audience asked if he had a similar belief about Chapter 220 or contracts MPS had with private schools to educate at-risk students. For the tired old refrain that "choice will only focus on a handful of students, and thus is no solution," he was similarly attacked. One parent asked sardonically, "Specialty schools only serve a handful of children—should we drop them? If my house is burning and I only have time to save some of the children, should I not make the effort because I can't save them all?"

The union member went home angry, but with a new understanding of the depth of Black support for choice and the hostility and disrespect for MPS and the abysmal job White teachers were doing in the classroom.

A FORUM FOR EDUCATORS

While our publication engaged in its war of words over choice, we invited Black teachers to express their views on how best to educate Black children. One of the most prophetic voices to come out of that campaign was Taki Raton, an MPS teacher who made no bones about his disenchantment with White teachers who were "intentionally miseducating Black children; setting them up for failure and infusing them with low self-esteem."

Raton was a regional director of an African-antiquity study group and advocated the infusion of African-centered education in Milwaukee public schools. The absence of such a curriculum implied to him that the system was controlled by White supremacists whose primary goal was to miseducate Black children or maintain the status quo system of Black failure. Public education in Milwaukee was destined to fail Black children for two reasons, he was fond of saying. The first was that White teachers taught a false history, giving credit for inventions to Europeans who stole them from Africans. The best way to inspire Black children is to give them a sense of identity, a foundation of self-worth, and a knowledge of true history. Second, MPS failed Black children because it was set up to fail Black children. Its purpose was to fuel White supremacy, to ingrain low self-esteem in Black children, and to provide students with poor education in order to limit them to service-industry and menial jobs.

Eventually, Raton became a household name in Milwaukee's Black community—a hero to Black parents and a threat to the status quo. He constantly found himself on the hot seat and eventually lost his job. But the seed he planted helped shape policy regarding African-centered education and the need for more Black teachers empathetic to Black culture. Raton's aggressive attacks paved the way for others, such as former MPS parent liaison Muhammad Sabir and Milwaukee Metropolitan Alliance of Black School Educators President Ola Benson who, in more subtle ways, questioned the integrity and agenda of the MTEA.

Sabir and Benson found receptive audiences wherever they went because they prioritized the needs of the parents and students over the system and the union. Sabir, an Ahmadiyya Muslim (an Islamic sect credited with helping to develop Marcus Garvey's nationalistic movement), left his secure job as a parent liaison and returned to college to acquire teaching certification after engaging in a series of confrontations with teachers who were either insensitive or patronizing toward parents. He gave up money and prestige to become a teacher, to ensure first-hand that Black students were educated properly. He would eventually expand his efforts to his Northside Karate School, where he taught Black children self-discipline, self-respect, and self-defense and provided them with a thirst for educational excellence.

With Raton, Benson, and Sabir in action, the *MCJ* never had to struggle to find voices of criticism of the MTEA from within its own ranks. It soon became obvious, however, that the union's counteroffensive was taking its toll in advertising revenues, even as our subscription base continued to climb. The sad truth is that one does not offset the other—advertising, not subscriptions, is the lifeblood of newspapers.

What made matters worse was that the union had apparently solicited other groups to join them in their boycott of the *MCJ*. Their disingenuous strategy diverted advertisements to either the *Milwaukee Courier* or the *Milwaukee Times*—the city's other two Black newspapers—to kill criticism that the advertisers were abandoning the Black community. That strategy had the indirect effect of silencing the other Black papers, which couldn't afford to lose revenues and had publicly stated their ambivalence to school choice. That left us with the choice of either taming the expression of our views or struggling through a period that could lead to our collapse.

The answer came during a staff meeting when Patricia Thomas boldly told a sales representative, in effect, "Screw 'em. We will not compromise our integrity and sense of purpose for advertising. We will not be blackmailed, and we will not retreat from threats."

The MTEA had committed a cardinal sin: it had angered a Black woman, a mother, a lioness. And Lord knows there is no stronger force, no more tenacious being, no fiercer and more resourceful entity than a Black woman who feels you have harmed or hindered her children.

FRIEND OR FOE: THE WHITE MEDIA

The new year—1990—seemed an appropriate occasion to catapult the community's consciousness about school choice, and there was seemingly no opportunity that escaped the attention of the growing army of choice supporters, which I dubbed "Polly's Parent Platoon."

That campaign was orchestrated from Williams's office, which had put into place an *ad hoc* speakers' bureau, jointly coordinated by Williams and her aide, Larry Harwell. Urban Day School parent liaison Zakiya Courtney and principal Virginia Stamper, Harambee Community School's School Board President Tommie

Alexander and Principal Sister Callista Robinson were consistently called upon to speak at or attend various forums to tout parental school choice as well as to maintain their duties as chief spokespersons for media interviews.

A general rule of thumb was to check with Williams's office when interview requests were made. That procedure was put in place after it became obvious that many of the local journalists were not looking for insight, but for negative, sensationalistic angles. Although schools rarely denied interviews to reporters, they took precautions after several incidents in which reporters' actions bordered on rude or disruptive.

It was obvious that many White reporters looked down upon the "poor" Black schools—they apparently felt free to interrupt classes or thrust microphones into teachers' or children's faces at inappropriate times. They had also been misled by prejudicial city editors or union spokespersons who attacked the quality of education at community schools.

In fact, when visiting Harambee or Urban Day, many reporters expressed surprise as to how quiet and orderly were the buildings, how disciplined were the children, and how orderly and well-maintained were the facilities. Such condescending, quasi-racist comments would generally put administrators at odds. Reporters were astonished to encounter innovative teaching methods, enthusiastic children, and professional instructors. They saw Black children—often wearing uniforms—performing advanced algebra, speaking the Queen's English, and generally behaving in a manner that defied the stereotypes that much of White America accepted as the norm for poor Black children.

At Harambee, Urban Day, and Bruce Guadalupe—the primary sites for journalistic visits—reporters didn't find children with hats cocked to the side, lugging boom boxes. They found disciplined, respectful, articulate students who walked with their heads high. Unlike those in the average urban public-school setting, children in the parental choice schools were met not with metal detectors and security guards, but with high expectations, a firm hand, and enthusiastic teachers. As a result, reporters saw children who displayed the aura of confidence and pride that comes from being grounded in a cultural foundation and being allowed and encouraged to excel.

Reporters received quite an education at these schools, even though many refused to admit that something special was being offered to these products of "urban decay" and "dysfunctional families." Eventually, the schools found it necessary to dictate special procedures and limit visitations and even to put some reporters in their place when they got out of hand. Courtney was a master at putting a reporter back on his or her heels, and Sister Callista's years of working with juveniles had more than adequately prepared her for correcting the conduct of spoiled children.

For her part, Williams maintained a rating system for journalists so that schools could have an idea of whether the reporter was friend or foe and therefore, what slant an interview might take. Friend in this case didn't necessarily mean someone who supported our cause; it indicated one who approached the subject without bias. We soon learned that national reporters fit that category far more frequently than local journalists. It was obvious from day one that the supposedly liberal *Milwaukee Journal* and conservative *Milwaukee Sentinel* were opposed to Black empowerment in general and school choice in particular, and framed their articles accordingly. Even when covering a clearly positive event, both papers seemed to go out of their way to taint their coverage by infusing a negative comment from a choice opponent. Often, the papers' school choice stories led with criticism or cast headlines in such a way as to taint the event. They also constantly misled the public with inaccurate information about Black concerns, political platforms, and cultural customs.

Which is where I came in.

While we in the school choice army were occasionally able to plant an article in the *Milwaukee Courier* or the *Milwaukee Times*, neither paper would endorse our movement. The MTEA also planted stories in the *Courier* and reportedly encouraged Black teachers to do likewise. For the most part, however, the *Courier* remained neutral. The *Milwaukee Times*, on the other hand, refused to describe itself as a black newspaper, although its publisher was the former managing editor of the *Milwaukee Community Journal*. Instead, the *Times* stood fast in the middle of the road, swaying more often to the beat of the NAACP and MTEA than to the harmonies of the Black masses. The *Times's* publisher Nathan Conyers, aside from political ambitions that required the aid of the MTEA, benefited financially from the teachers union, MPS, and the NAACP and wasn't willing to risk losing his golden horses. Although political realities stopped it short of openly challenging school choice, the *Times*, unlike the *Courier*, tended to lean toward the status quo stance on education.

Editorially, the *Milwaukee Times* was the weakest of the three papers, and its historic refusal to get involved in any controversial editorial issue had long since stymied any influence the paper may have had. Polly Williams and others had left the paper frustrated by Conyers's refusal to lend his voice to the movement, but for the most part were content with his position of subjective neutrality. After all, it was better than if he had openly fought choice.

The MTEA was able to use advertising dollars to advance its position in both the *Courier* and the *Times*. The MCJ, on the other hand, was ostracized at every turn, even though we never refused the MTEA space to present its position—we even encouraged it to do so. Moreover, we maintained our youth section, which generally highlighted positive stories about MPS programs and public school student activities. But then again, we were the threat, and as long as the union could influence the other papers, it thought it could sway the masses. The union was wrong.

SCHOOL CHOICE IN THE NEWS

For the MCJ, the school choice campaign was part of our mission. Indeed, the tenet of the African-American press is to advocate and define the civil rights agenda. Championing school choice was our responsibility as an instrument of the Civil Rights movement. If that meant that we were the only publication in town to support school choice—and were penalized for it—so be it. The MCJ never forgot why it was created or why the Black press was formed a century and a half ago.

Williams and Harwell had created a paper route of sorts in Madison and would circulate the MCJ every time we printed an article or editorial on school choice. Thus the MCJ became not only the voice of Black Milwaukee but also a weapon used by both political parties to advance their often-conflicting agendas. We would praise an elected official one week and chastise another the following week. Williams and Harwell would then circulate the articles, pitting legislator against legislator.

MCJ managing editor Tom Mitchell and I worked out what we called a media code system for our stories, as much to plant philosophical seeds as to dilute and redefine attacks from opponents. For example, Mitchell suggested early that we should never use the word "voucher," opting for either "choice," "school choice," or "parental school choice." The term voucher was too limiting; it conjured up images of people getting something for nothing. Choice, in addition to being confused with the abortion controversy (in which most liberals came out on the pro-choice side), implied an option that wasn't inherently bad. Parental school choice symbolized empowerment.

We also took advantage of the unique marriage between Democrats and Republicans. We made note of that situation as often as possible and pigeonholed opponents as being opposed to Black empowerment. We quoted them as often as possible so the masses could experience first-hand the hypocrisy of their agenda. We noted, for example, that most of the Black opponents of school choice were either teachers who had bought into the company line or middle-class citizens who sent their children to private schools or at least had the opportunity to make that choice.

Maintaining steady coverage on school choice was often a herculean undertaking because much of the crusade was impromptu. Supporters took advantage of church outings, community meetings, and even family reunion picnics to raise the community's consciousness about school choice and the new educational battle-field. It was no coincidence that members of the platoon were visible at dozens of community events. A general schedule of events was prepared and where possible, school choice supporters were directed to attend and promote their cause.

It didn't take much to enlist supporters—the abysmal education offered by MPS, the discriminatory nature of the busing program, and the good reputation of private schools ensured constant interest in the school choice movement. Even families without children were sympathetic—they understood the importance of the battle and the possible ramifications a movement of this type could have on other campaigns.

Although the MCJ covered only a small percentage of these events, you didn't need the media to note that choice was the talk of the town. There were choice booths at the annual Juneteenth Day Celebration (an event held each June 19th to commemorate the day when slaves in Texas learned of the Emancipation Proclamation) and at the African World Festival in August 1990. We passed out fliers at school board meetings, asking why MPS and the teachers union wanted to hold Black children hostage. We also sent letters to ministerial organizations asking them to visit a Black independent school or to consider starting their own.

The message was simple and direct: Black people must be more involved polit-ically in the education system, whether it be through the school choice movement, educational reform crusade, or parent advocacy. The ultimate goal was community control of the institutions—public or private—that affect our children.

The MCJ's role became increasingly important as it became obvious that there was a White media blackout as it related to positive stories about school choice, the unique crusade by poor Black parents, and the issue of Black empowerment and self-determination. Apparently the editorial staff of the *Milwaukee Journal* had determined to sway public opinion against school choice by watering down news events they couldn't ignore, or tainting them through the use of plants to neutral-ize our coverage.

There was one notable exception: as the various challenges to school choice awaited court scrutiny, Lynne Jung wrote a stunningly positive piece in the *Milwaukee Journal's* August 1, 1990, edition about the many families benefiting from the program. The article linked the choice debate to human faces and thus added many supporters to the campaign.

Jung's story was a departure for the *Journal*, which had been blatant in its attacks on choice and had focused much of its coverage on opposition to the pro-gram. The paper used the NAACP as a shield of sorts to mask the hypocrisy of its opposition to allowing poor Black children to attend private school. The coverage, consistent with the reporting of the *Milwaukee Sentinel,* at times bordered on unethical, even libelous. Many in Williams's army canceled their subscriptions in protest of the biased articles after repeated cries for editorial meetings to work toward balanced stories fell on deaf ears.

Williams's response throughout was politically expedient. "We have the *Community Journal,*" she said at a forum, "and that's what Black people read in the barber or beauty shop, our radio stations quote on the air, and our people take home with them from church. The daily newspapers are nothing more than extensions of the system that holds us in bondage; we didn't enter this battle thinking we could convince the propaganda arm of the status quo to champion our cause. But I bet most of those White people writing those articles, who tell us we have to be satisfied with poor educations for our children, teachers who don't care about our children or who believe they can't learn, and school board policies that teach our children to have low self-esteem, I bet these White people who condemn us for wanting to escape the plantation school system have their children in private schools."

It was against that backdrop and history of opposition that Jung's article appeared, shocking many of us and planting the idea that maybe the *Journal* was seeing the light—or at least redeeming itself for its history of biased reporting.

Jung wrote about the many parents of children failing in public schools who rejoiced at the ruling of Dane County Circuit Judge Susan Steingass that the choice program was indeed constitutional. She also put in perspective State Superintendent Herbert Grover's campaign to usurp the program: his efforts were crippling registration and scaring off potential schools. But most important were the faces she brought to the fore: the images of strong, articulate Black parents, poor and often desperate, who wanted more for their children.

School choice enabled Ronkae Kazmende, a single mother attending Alverno College, to enroll her son in Urban Day. Without choice, she would not have been able to afford the $700 tuition, not to mention money for uniforms and other necessities. Kazmende called choice a great program, noting that it would "give kids from low-income families the opportunity to attend private schools."

Then there was Janice Crochrell, who begged for the opportunity to allow the program a chance "because the parents are going to make it work." Crochrell enrolled her three children in Juanita Virgil Academy in the hope that they would receive the strong educational foundation needed to break the cycle that plagues many Black urban families. Crochrell said that in their large classes at public school, her children did not get the individual attention they needed: "Sometimes students would come in and tell the teachers what to do," she was quoted as saying. "A lot of students [in the public schools] have no respect for the teachers and no respect for other students' belongings." At Juanita Virgil her students would get more personalized attention in a disciplined atmosphere in which cultural pride and true ancestry would be valued.

"Instead of learning about Black history in February, they will have an opportunity to learn about their history all year 'round. They will be able to learn more about famous Black men and women, and hopefully, they will not be ashamed about being Black."

That's an aspect of education in a Black private school that appealed to community activist Freda Curry, who was looking at choice after an unsettling experience in the Chapter 220 suburban desegregation program. In that program her children attended a nearly all-White suburban school nearly twenty miles from their home and light years away from their proud African-American heritage. Eventually it hurt their self-esteem and distanced them from their history. Curry was hopeful that that would change when her children attended a Black private school under choice.

Jung's article also touched on the frustration of poor parents who were on waiting lists to get into the program. These included Annette Bonilla, a single mother of two who applied to four choice schools and was praying for acceptance to any of them. Determined not to send her children back to the failing public school they were attending, Bonilla viewed choice as a dream come true for her daughters because it offered them a better environment and a quality education.

Of course, such positive coverage was a real anomaly. The *Milwaukee Journal's* and *Sentinel's* coverage of the Black Women's Network Conference provided insight into the typical reporting bias. Both papers covered the conference and quoted Governor Thompson, although neither adequately reflected the enthusiasm of the participants or the significance of their support.

The MCJ, on the other hand, more than filled the void, providing front-page stories with photographs to match. It was obvious from the disparities in coverage that we would be forced to go it alone in keeping grassroots folks informed of the events that would shape this debate. One of our primary strategies was to use comments from school choice antagonists Felmers Chaney, president of the Milwaukee Branch NAACP, and Lauri Wynn, former Black president of the state teachers union and NAACP education czar. The newspaper's task was to neutralize Chaney and Wynn not through character assassination or personal attacks, but by questioning their motives, highlighting their contradictions, and challenging their leadership, at least on this issue. We decided to publish their statements verbatim whenever possible and to let the people decide. It would soon come to light that their opposition to school choice was weak, condescending, and hypocritical. As I personally liked both Chaney and Wynn, it was not easy to attack them, but putting them on trial was essential in order to show the public the contradictions inherent in the NAACP's opposition to school choice.

When I interviewed Felmers Chaney in June 1990 for an *MCJ* article, I asked him why he opposed choice.

"Because it will lead to more segregation," he responded.

"How so?" I asked

"Number one, the program is only set up for Black children. And number two, the private schools are all segregated now and will be more so when all these children leave MPS."

I countered that school choice was not only for Black children; it was income-based and thus any family—Black, White, Yellow or Brown—who met the poverty guidelines could participate. Second, choice would not lead to more segregation. In fact, the opposite would occur because the program could theoretically increase the number of Black students leaving MPS, which enhanced opportunities to meet the court-ordered desegregation goals. Lastly, most of the private schools—and I named several, including Highland Community School, Messmer High School, and even the University School (an upscale private academy that refused to participate in the choice program)—were *integrated*, unlike public schools, which were *desegregated*.

"Have you ever been to any of these schools to look at the quality programs there, or to talk with the parents?" I asked Chaney.

"No," he replied in his blunt, matter-of-fact manner, "but I don't have to. Anything all Black is all bad." [5]

That comment didn't have to be printed in bold type to reverberate throughout the Black community. It angered Black nationalists, parents, and supporters of Black institutions. We were to learn that it also put many Black members of the NAACP in a precarious position. Two board members called me within days of the article to distance themselves from the comments. One took me to task for setting up Chaney. I responded by noting that I respected Chaney, but his opposition made no sense and people had to know of his ignorance about the initiative. I told the board member that the NAACP was being used as a racial screen to offset criticism of the MTEA's position.

Chaney's statements were ignored by the White media, as was the fact that Wynn was a former—and the only—black president of the state teachers union, the same body that had declared school choice to be its No. 1 enemy.

CONFRONTATIONS

One of the ironies to emerge out of the war for empowerment was that even though Black folks could and did chastise and lambaste Chaney and Wynn for their positions, in all but a few instances, their criticism was levied behind closed doors—and only rarely before White people. It was a family fight, Williams would often say, and unless it became necessary to pull out all of the stops, "we ain't gonna' put on a show for White people. [Chaney and Wynn] are on opposite sides of this issue, but that doesn't mean they are our enemies and we can't work together on many other issues."

Williams told us not to back down from unavoidable debate or public confrontation, but encouraged us to follow two ironclad rules: when possible, let the fight be gender-focused—Black woman against Black woman, Black man against Black man—and second, don't put on a show for the White media; don't fall into their divide-and-conquer snare.

There was one occasion when I violated that strategy—and it cost me. Following a press conference in mid-1990 at a Northside school to announce a new MPS program, Lauri Wynn decided to use the opportunity to discuss school choice with a half-dozen print and broadcast reporters. It was a familiar scene, with the self-righteous reporters from the *Milwaukee Journal* and *Sentinel* intent on leaving with something negative about school choice—I had witnessed it so many times in the past several months that it almost seemed scripted.

With reporter's notebook in hand, I assumed my familiar position on the outskirts of the circle of reporters, more to observe the antichoice reporters' enthusiasm than to gather any useful news. But my intentions soon changed after listening to three or four biased questions and an equal number of stock responses from Wynn about the evils of school choice and the naïveté of Black parents who considered participating in the right-wing conspiracy. Finally, when Wynn said something negative about Urban Day, I lost my patience and aggressively fought my way through the throng of reporters to face her. Without thinking, I blurted out, "Excuse me, Mrs. Wynn: if Urban Day is such a bad school, why did an educated woman like yourself send your children there?"

The sarcastic tone of my voice, as much the nature of my question, caught everyone off guard, and all attention shifted to me before returning to Wynn, who wore an expression of both fury and embarrassment.

"Let me rephrase the question," I said more calmly. "Are you saying Urban Day provides its students with a poor education?"

Regrouping herself, Wynn finally fired back, "That's not what I said. But yes, it wasn't what I thought it would be."

As all eyes turned back to me, I quickly responded, "If that's the case, and I'm sure there are plenty of teachers and parents who take issue with your assessment, why would an educated public school teacher send her children to such an inferior school? And also, if MPS is so great, why wouldn't you automatically send your children to schools where you teach?"

Wynn retorted, "It was a choice on my part that didn't work out, and after finding out what took place there, I took my children out after a couple of semesters."

Unsatisfied and unwilling to let Wynn off the hook, I rephrased the first question. After she wriggled and evaded through yet another unsatisfactory answer, I fired off, "What does it say, either way you look at it, that you looked outside the public schools where you worked for an education for your children? And secondly, why is it so much of a crime for poor Black parents to have the same opportunities that you had?"

Before she could answer, and in an obvious attempt to run interference, a White reporter interceded, asking Wynn to respond to a question about the position of the national branch of the NAACP. His affront to my question prompted me to raise my voice and challenge his timing.

"Excuse me sir, I have a question pending," I spat at him, forcing him to back down.

"Are you going to answer my questions, Mrs. Wynn?"

"Well, it's obvious who you're working for," she retorted.

"And who would that be, other than Black people and not missionaries and others who want to keep Black people trapped in substandard education . . ."

Before I could complete my tirade, a Black photographer pulled me away.

"Who is he working for, Mrs. Wynn?" one of the reporters asked her as she turned away from me and my line of questioning.

I didn't hear her answer because I moved away from the circle and the horde of reporters, several of whom were now pushing microphones in front of my face. The Black photographer whispered to me that I was giving the White reporters "what they want: two Black people fighting. Don't get caught up in that," he said.

The experience taught me several lessons, particularly after absorbing the White media's account of what happened. The slant, as usual, was against school choice and I was portrayed as being an anarchist and militant—which are code words to White America—in an attempt to undermine and discredit me and the movement. It was a tactic as old as the quest for Black equality and one which the

White media used successfully in its attempt to divide and conquer Black America and to poison the minds of progressive Whites. The *Journal* and *Sentinel*, although supposedly holding opposing editorial philosophies (the *Journal* was painted as the liberal paper, while the *Sentinel* was supposedly conservative) were like the Democratic and Republican Parties when it came to Black people; essentially, different wings of the same bird. Both papers, just like both political parties, wanted first and foremost to maintain White control. The best way to achieve that goal was to maintain the status quo—not to let the slaves escape the plantation. School choice not only empowered Black parents, it could weaken the chains that held us captive.

The key for those of us who understood the power of propaganda and the manipulation of the media was not to fall prey to adversarial tactics, but to focus our energies on educating our own. And thus far, given the level of support school choice had garnered in the African-American community, our media—at least the MCJ—was enough to turn the tide.

As well as we could figure it, the *Journal* and *Sentinel* were the propaganda arm of what we generally referred to as "The Status Quo," but more appropriately should have been called "The Establishment Press." Both papers, and to a lesser degree the broadcast media, served the express purpose of maintaining a standard of life that kept select people trapped in an abyss of second-class citizenship. It wasn't about race as much as it was about class—the haves versus the have-nots—and the primary intent was to keep as much of the resources—that is, quality-of-life benefits and money—in the hands of the haves. Maintaining that equilibrium meant there would forever be an underclass to serve the haves, to assume predetermined menial jobs as well as to provide employment opportunities and contracts for them in social services and criminal justice. Those jobs would flourish because limited opportunities and cultural dysfunction always result in social chaos.

This conspiracy theory may sound farfetched, but it would explain not only the resistance to school choice by entities that should embrace it but also the attempts to undermine what essentially are constitutional tenets. Black America has long pondered this dichotomy as it has tried to understand the hypocrisy of Thomas Jefferson and George Washington, who on the one hand advocated a revolution premised on the equality of man, but on the other returned home to plantations serviced and sustained by African captives whom they considered subhuman. (Allowing slaves certain rights within the confines of their prisons does not erase this contradiction.)

Every time a liberty or right is secured, it takes away power from the status quo. Men fought so hard to deny women the vote because they wanted to maintain their power base. The same is true in the case of Black Americans and the vote, job opportunities, and even open housing.

The battle over school choice is rooted in the conspiracy to maintain the status quo—to maintain the power base of the Establishment and its cronies. How else could one explain the hypocrisy of the resistance of the teachers, the middle class, and the Democrats to school choice? Granting poor families the right to attend better schools not only reduces the seats reserved for middle-class children, but potentially means there will be a larger employment pool competing for a decreasing number of jobs in a technologically advanced society.

If you take this theory to its natural conclusion, you can then understand the role of the media. If it is indeed the propaganda arm of the Establishment, everything else falls in place. That's why a liberal newspaper like the *Milwaukee Journal* could justify denying poor people a right that would break the cycle of poverty, supposedly a central tenet of the liberal agenda. The *Milwaukee Journal's* support for desegregation makes sense if the newspaper meant to delay the inevitable, to ensure that disenfranchised "slaves" would continue to chase an elusive dream.

The *Sentinel*, Milwaukee's second-largest daily newspaper, could also oppose choice even though it was considered to have a conservative editorial philosophy as evidenced by its support for Republican causes. The *Sentinel* readily acknowledged the failings of the public school, yet turned its back on those failings because its focus, like the *Journal's*, was to maintain the status quo. School choice could break the chains, promoting market-grounded strategies and public-school accountability. Above all else, it would solve the problem of an ill-prepared workforce.

After a political forum in Washington, D.C., in May 1990, a press conference with national media put to rest any questions about media bias—and our determination to overcome it.

The meeting with political figures went smoothly; they quizzed Williams and I more about political ramifications than about the substance of the legislation. Would Black Americans embrace choice legislation sponsored by Republicans? Could an allegiance similar to what was forged in Madison be duplicated elsewhere in the country? Would Black Democrats buck the status quo in response to an undercurrent of support from the Black community for school choice? Could a distinction be made between supporting school choice and being anti–public school? Would the Black community support a religious school choice measure?

For the most part, our answers were theoretical at best. Though we could venture to speak for parents in Milwaukee based upon years of forums, focus groups, and voting patterns, it was obvious that the political mechanism, level of cultural sophistication, and degree of nationalistic philosophy varied from city to city, state to state. The only consistent factor, apparently, was that public education was not adequately serving minority and poor children and that teachers unions, educrats, and poverty pimps had a vested interest in maintaining the status quo. Poverty is America's second largest industry, employing more White Americans than the auto, steel, and construction industries combined. From prisons to welfare case-workers (now Welfare to Work programmers) to social workers, the poverty industry has its tentacles everywhere. It should not go without saying that most of the dollars generated by that industry end up in suburbia, further stifling a pragmatic remedy to the Black economic crisis.

When asked, I asserted that opposition to school choice was a conspiracy to maintain an underclass. I also noted that the Milwaukee Parental School Choice initiative passed because it was the product of a grassroots crusade; it was a *bottom-up* solution. It was no coincidence that choice legislation offered by both the governor and MPS had been shot down, while ours was enacted.

What the politicians and policy makers left the meeting with is anyone's guess. Williams was probably guarded in her answers, and I was downright paranoid. Besides worrying that they would abuse the information, we knew that it was a historical fact that political friendships and allegiances of any stripe between White and Black Americans were tenuous agreements at best. More often than not, we have found that Whites in power want to lead, to circumvent, and even to corrupt, when it benefits them. There can be and will continue to be opportunities for mutually beneficial coalitions and our agendas will at times overlap, but when it gets down to the nitty-gritty, they will protect theirs and we should protect ours.

The meeting with politicians and policy makers was child's play compared to what awaited us in the conference room. Two dozen assembled media—my colleagues, I thought—were poised not to solicit information and a quote to highlight an article on our affairs of the past six months, but to prey upon us like buzzards. Save for one or two who sought fodder for a balanced story, the reporters seemed intent on discrediting us.

The very first question reeked of slander: "There are some who call you pawns of the conservative right. How do you respond to that charge?" The White reporter's open hostility was such that a veteran like Williams was quick to don her armor and to ask me to accompany her to the podium—partially for psychological support, partially for physical protection.

"I beg your pardon," Williams fired back at the reporter. "Let me set the record straight from the onset. We ain't the pawns of nobody. Are you implying Black people can't think for ourselves, or we don't know what's good for us?"

The reporter, somewhat taken aback, collected himself enough to suggest that maybe we had misunderstood his question.

Apparently White journalists have a problem with standard English, said Williams. "No matter how you clothe what you're saying, it's still implying Black people don't know what's good for us. Let me put it another way. We have an agenda, one that we know is good for us. Whoever wants to work with us is our friend for the time being. Tomorrow is another matter.

"Now, if you're saying all Democrats are liberals and supportive of whatever Black people want, and all Republicans are evil and racists . . . if that's what you're saying, I'll respond. But I need to know what you're saying."

After ten minutes of sparring over the dead-end issue, the reporter ultimately relented, but not before declaring that Black people who strayed from the status quo were fools who were biting the hand that fed them.

The next couple of questions were civil. A foreign journalist went so far as to inquire about the children who could benefit from the opportunities presented under choice. But then it was back to business as usual. This attack came from a Milwaukee reporter, who asked about the "unholy allegiance."

By now even I was fed up, and when Williams took a deep breath out of frustration and anger, I nudged her to the side and said, "Our people are drowning in a sea of mediocrity and apathy. To be honest, we don't care who throws us a lifeline. Where do your children go to school—is it MPS?"

A baffled look crossed the reporter's face. When he began, "I'm not the subject of this article . . . " I quickly cut him off.

"Does that mean your children go to public schools? Or maybe you have some control of the schools? For most Black people, we don't; all we have is a history of neglect. We have been spitting into the strong wind for three decades. All we're asking for is an option for a small group of kids. Is that too much?

"The Milwaukee Public Schools are known for their specialties, which are schools created to address specific needs or deficits. Look at choice as specialties for children otherwise failed by MPS."

The hour-long news conference took on a life of its own. Williams and I alternately defended Black people's rights to self-determination, poor people's rights to choose alternative educational options for their children, and the Black community's collective intelligence and ability to determine who and what could advance our own agenda and when it could be done. It was more a philosophical debate than a news conference; apparently only a handful of reporters were interested in our story. None of the reporters in attendance were members of a minority. According to our impromptu poll, only three had children.

The reporters from the *Milwaukee Journal* and *Sentinel* were adamant in their opposition to choice—so much so that a reporter from another newspaper posed a question about the impartiality of the Milwaukee media. The *Journal* and *Sentinel* made no pretense of objectivity and at one point provoked an exasperated Williams into rebuking a reporter.

"For the record, I'm a Democrat, but I'm Black first," she said deliberately. "My allegiance is to my people, and my agenda is the welfare of my people. There are many Democrats supporting our legislation. It is bipartisan legislation. But I will tell you this, there are just as many racists in the Democratic Party as there are in the Republican Party. Racism is not restricted to a particular party. George Wallace was a racist, and he was a Democrat.

"Black people ain't stupid. We will work with whomever wants to work with us. We are not anti–public schools; we are pro–black people. If you think we are betraying something by putting ourselves first, then you're either a fool or a racist."

Ironically, the news conference ended on a positive note—a White reporter applauded Black parents for dispelling stereotypes that they don't care about their children. "I think it's immensely important to note that these poor, sometimes inarticulate mothers and fathers are stepping to the forefront on behalf of their children," the reporter said. "My question is why so many people don't see the worth in what you're doing? Why are the teachers union and some Democrats trying so hard to discredit what is such an admirable effort, a campaign that is as much about civil rights and economic disparities as any witnessed since *Brown* v. *The Board of Education?*"

Williams and I smiled at each other.

"That's a good question," said Williams. "*You* know the answer. The point is whether *they* do," Williams said, pointing at the small group of *Journal* and *Sentinel* reporters who had led the attack. "Why don't you ask them?"

CHAPTER
7

SAME TRACK, DIFFERENT TRAINS

*Real education means to inspire people to live more abun-
dantly, to learn to begin with life as they find it and make it
better.*

—CARTER G. WOODSON

The crusade by Black parents to enact a school choice program in Wisconsin served the dual purpose of empowering low-income families with educational options denied them by their economic status and bringing to the national stage the debate over the direction of the Civil Rights movement. School choice brought together those of different philosophies, needs, and economic backgrounds in a common cause. Working side by side were low-income mothers for whom substandard education was the norm; powerful foundation heads intent on altering the status quo; Democratic Party liberals; conservative Republicans, Black Nationalists and Pan-Africanists intent on infusing America's oppressed with the powerful tool of cultural enlightenment and a value system grounded in self-determination; and progressives committed to correcting a civil rights injustice. Together, White, Black, rich and poor sought to take on a powerful union and entrenched bureaucracy, to right a grievous wrong, and to jumpstart an educational reform movement that they each hoped would give America's have-nots the opportunity to break the cycle of poverty. Together, they put America's failing public school system on trial.

The school choice campaign opened a veritable Pandora's box of education policy questions ranging from the unwillingness of the MSB to embrace proven educational innovations in order to address the educational deficit forced upon Black students, to its antipathy toward decades of parental cries for meaningful involvement in the system. From protests to prayer vigils, boycotts to lawsuits, the Black community had employed dozens of tactics to prod the school board to institute change, but to no avail. At best, the Black community was offered place-bos along the lines of school desegregation.

Eventually, African Americans in Milwaukee came to accept two staggering realities: The education Establishment—the school board and the MTEA—would not be moved. As the casualties mounted, it became painfully obvious that the board, teachers, and staff were all pawns or purveyors of the Establishment.

It also became clear that the Black leadership strategy of assimilation as a cure-all had ill-served the masses. Figures released by Governor Anthony Earl's Special Task Force on Education showed a significant increase in Black students' dropout and suspension rates and an overall drop in academic achievement by Black students during the ten-year period immediately following desegregation.[1] Weigh those failings against the harm to Black community structures as well as the economic instability caused by an uneducated—and thus unemployed—workforce, and the devastation was immeasurable.

From that reality emerged a new course, new leadership, and a renewed commitment and resolve. This time, instead of spitting into the political wind, the Black community turned to empowerment. Instead of begging for an opportunity to eat at the Massa's table, to accept a few crumbs and promises of a reward in some distant future, the Black masses moved to create their own schools and control the institutions within their community.

The educational reform movement thus moved from a position of begging to one of demanding. The new strategy called for decentralization, site-based management, and African-centered curricula taught by teachers with a vested interest in the welfare of the children. That strategy, which at first called for the creation of an independent Black school district, evolved into the school choice campaign as we knew it. The new vision called for what Howard Fuller referred to as a system of schools to provide a variety of options for Milwaukee's children of all races, incomes and social statuses. In this new design, private schools would join partnerships, specialties, charters, and general-education institutes in offering options to parents. Each school would have to compete for students—which meant improving its offerings or standing the chance of being closed. This healthy competition would benefit both schools and families.

Of course, in order for this vision to be realized, *all* parents must be able to avail themselves of *every* option. How would they manage to do so with the George Wallaces of the teachers union and educracy blocking the door of educational opportunity?

The school choice battle is part of a civil rights war that seeks to make all parents equal irrespective of race or socioeconomic status. Middle-class white parents and poor Hispanic and Black parents share a common interest in seeking out the best educational opportunities and options for their children. Yet income becomes the determining factor in a dual system that, by denying the poor, robs America of the unique contributions and service of millions of children. If America is to be a true melting pot (or, more truthfully, a Caesar salad), there must be a level playing field. That is not to say that all private institutions should admit anyone regardless of their ability to pay: that is unfair to those who have worked hard and sacrificed or who possess special talents or abilities. But when the fundamental right to a quality education is denied through the public venue, there should be options. Indeed, the state of Wisconsin has the primary responsibility to educate all children and to provide them with alternatives when the status quo does not fit or satisfy their basic needs. That is the law—although a law that has not been honored. And when a basic constitutional right is denied, it is incumbent upon those victimized to seek redress. That's where school choice comes in.

School choice is purely voluntary for parents and the schools, thus it epitomizes a fundamental democratic concept that benefits everyone. Public schools benefit through the reduction of student numbers, which lowers the systemwide pupil/teacher ratio, and also through the creation of innovative and attractive programs to compete with the private schools. The public school system also benefits financially in that while it loses state aid based upon a student population, it maintains the local property tax allocation, even though choice students are no longer in the system.

Parents happy with their children's education have no desire to seek options, but those who are not satisfied can avail themselves of a plethora of private school offerings. Conversely, private schools that don't wish to participate in the school choice program (such as the elitist University School) are not forced to, and thus are able to maintain their autonomy. And lastly, the public benefits when more children are educated.

VISIONS OF SCHOOL CHOICE

Those of us who fought the grand battle to enact a school choice program in Milwaukee had different visions—albeit overlapping aims. And it was to be expected that the Establishment would use all of its resources to derail our movement. To them, our movement posed a serious threat to the educational plantation and, if successful, could also spur other campaigns. Urban Day business manager Sister Virgine and principal Virginia Stamper[2] looked at building the school's support base, providing low-income parents on the fringe with economic assistance, and redirecting Black tax dollars from a self-serving monopoly to an environment in which high expectations were matched by positive, supportive mechanisms.

Zakiya Courtney, Urban Day school parent liaison and parental involvement coordinator, had similar beliefs, although she was also on a quest to expose as many African-American children as possible to an African-centered framework. Courtney looked beyond Urban Day and saw a dozen Black independent schools staffed by dedicated teachers who taught children not just *how* to count, but *why*. She envisioned Black children armed with a sense of self and a worldview that not only would enable them to meet their academic and career goals but also would instill in them a commitment to return to their communities to lead others.

"Empowerment comes from a knowledge of who you are," Courtney was fond of saying. The richness of the African culture provided a strong educational foundation and developed personal strengths that could benefit the children for the rest of their lives.

Harambee School Board President Tommie Alexander and I shared Courtney's vision, but we also thought in nationalistic terms of a second school system designed and controlled by Black people. We took seriously the meaning of the Swahili word *Harambee* ("pulling together") and saw our school as the foundation for community empowerment. Harambee Community School, governed by community families for community children, is the prime example not only of site-based management but also of self-governance and self-actualization. It is, in many respects, a *public* school that proves conclusively that commitment and nurturing and high expectations can offset the disadvantages of inferior financial resources. It also provides clear evidence of what can be accomplished through community cooperation. Harambee is a community school supported by an otherwise impoverished and sometimes seemingly apathetic community—a school that understands its mission and potential to create a better tomorrow for our children. The Harambee concept and its achievements—94 percent of its students graduate from high school and 78 percent go on to an institution of higher learning—are the direct by-product of citizen involvement. Harambee is supported by citizens whose only affiliation with the school is their fundamental understanding that, as in days before school desegregation, the neighborhood school was the foundation and center of community activity and pride. At Harambee we were grooming *soldiers*: articulate, resourceful, and culturally grounded individuals who would become the next generation of community-conscious businessmen, politicians, and civil servants.

We envisioned a system of private schools that would become specialties of a sort, reeducating public school students, grooming from birth Black and Brown children who would eventually assume leadership roles—a modernization of W. E. B. DuBois's Talented Tenth concept (10 percent of the Black populace must be groomed for leadership roles), with a nationalistic bent. In our ambitious scheme, we would use school choice as a catalyst to transform the Black community from a position of subservience and mediocrity to one of vitality and strength. We sought to undermine the Establishment conspiracy, reversing two decades of cultural dependency and decay. Most of the nation's two hundred Black independent schools shared Harambee's mission to provide a blueprint for a new community.

Harambee Community School was a prime example of site-based management in action. What was occurring at Harambee could be duplicated within the public school arena if parents and community visionaries could somehow wrestle schools away from the educracy. Along with decentralization (a process Fuller had put in place while superintendent), which would allow individual schools greater autonomy and would remove some of the bureaucracy that hinders effective teaching, site-based management would allow for greater parental involvement not just in curriculum, but in the hiring and firing of teachers as well.

Naturally, the teachers union opposed the concept; representatives went so far as to suggest that parents are not qualified to have input in the educational process. But the success of Harambee, Urban Day, Bruce Guadalupe and dozens of other independent and community-based schools proved them wrong. Having successfully educated poor children for two decades, Alexander and I refused to accept the excuses of the public school educrats. If we could do it on a shoestring budget, with bill collectors forever at our door, within the confines of an aging (although immaculately clean) building, and with teachers who are paid approximately *half* of what the public school offered, then they surely could. Let them explain to the world our successes and their failures. And when right finally prevailed over evil, the injustices and inequities of the past would be corrected.

Polly Williams's vision was the most ambitious of all. She wanted to expose and force the public school system into accountability, but she was also guided by a belief that the public school system as it was structured would never serve the interests of Black and poor people. As a result, Williams saw as her mission the creation of a separate Black public school district that would complement a private consortium of nonsectarian and parochial schools. An unwavering advocate of Black independent schools, Williams saw community control of institutions—public or private—as the ultimate goal.

If the North Division Plan had strained Williams's relationship with her party, school choice was the straw that broke the camel's back. The battle wasn't over just a handful of kids being allowed to follow White children to private schools. School choice challenged the root hypocrisy of the public education system in Wisconsin and throughout the country, a system that intentionally failed Black and minority children, then masked that failure with code cloth like "at risk" or "poverty." The public school system epitomized the Democratic Party's failed leadership and underscored the link between the party and the union, which controlled the party through major contributions and political muscle.

Black children, said Williams, were cattle, herded around from gate to gate under the watchful eye of the land barons who profited from Black misery and suffering. "They have never demonstrated that they care for our children; if they did, they would educate them. This is a moneymaker for them, from the millions they get from busing our children to nowhere, to the social worker they put in the schools to say most of our children are at risk or hyperactive (and should be medically sedated) or educationally deficient. They label what they can't control and get rich off us. Many of these teachers don't believe our children can learn. Some of them are just out-and-out racist. There are many good committed teachers in MPS, but they fall prey to the system.

"Meanwhile, while everybody is covering up the failure or blaming the victims, thousands of Black children, the majority in the Milwaukee public schools, are failing," Williams said. "That pisses me off to the boiling point. Everybody has their damn excuses when the bottom line is [they] don't really care. It has to be that, because the alternative is that [they] are intentionally destroying my babies."

The North Division Plan was designed to prove what could be done if caring people—*black people*—were in charge. School choice allows a few children to escape to private schools knowing full well that the world will watch what happens to them. The end result will be the same: when those children excel in the private schools, people will begin asking, "Why can't MPS educate them?" Heads will roll, and reforms will follow. Choice would spark the revolution.

Williams's other reason for pushing choice was as simple as it was profound: "How can they all send their children to private schools and then tell us we can't send ours? How can they justify blocking the doors, telling poor parents it's MPS or nothing, just because they are poor? It's about right and wrong; it's about civil rights. What's good for the goose is good for the gander."

To say that Williams is passionate about children in general, and their education in particular, would be an understatement. The issue energizes her, defines her, capsulates her. The opposition to her career-long quest for Black empowerment through education, for equality of opportunity, for the basic fundamental opportunities that White America enjoyed and took for granted, could never pierce her ironclad armor of righteousness.

For Williams, school choice wasn't just an issue, it was the core battle on which the war for Black opportunity rested. And she grew stronger with each attack aimed at her and her supporters. I have no doubt that Williams would be willing to die for Black America if she thought it would advance the agenda she felt so strongly about.

At one of our weekly strategy and information meetings, someone suggested that school choice was a form of educational affirmative action. Though the statement seemed ambiguous at the time, in retrospect it makes sense. Like affirmative action, school choice remedied past injustices and leveled the academic playing field; it was up to the individual to take advantage of the new opportunity. School choice was never intended to *replace* the public school system, as critics erroneously charged; it was meant to compliment it, to provide another option for parents. Choice schools, for all intents and purposes, are specialty schools, providing specialized education in particular environments.

Politically, the school choice crusade underscored Black America's shift away from hopes of assimilation or some kind of sudden moral transformation by those who kept their boots on the necks of Black America. The school choice movement raised questions about who should set the Black agenda and who should speak for Black America. It was not about integration over segregation, but handouts versus a hand up. It was about dependency on the system versus self-empowerment and self-sufficiency. Black Americans have been duped into thinking others know what is best for them. But the essence of America—one of the core principles behind democracy and the Bill of Rights—is equality irrespective of financial wherewithal. This principle guarantees freedom of choice.

The first phase of the Civil Rights movement dealt with civil liberty and equal opportunity. It knocked down many barriers, but left us economically and culturally impotent—an unacceptable price. The civil rights strategy of King, Randolph, Abernathy, and others ran its course. These talented leaders never fully achieved their stated goals because they were dependent upon a change in America's moral fiber. That transition was herculean enough, but as we have since learned, the moral imperative as espoused by the civil rights traditionalists of the '60s and '70s was also co-opted by their civil rights allies—individuals and organizations—with a vested interest in using us as pawns either to advance their own interests or to control the speed and essence of change. Thirty years after the height of the Civil Rights movement, Black people had no more power than before. We could eat at the lunch counter—but couldn't afford to pay for our food.

The second phase of Civil Rights must deal with empowerment, economic stability, and cultural development.

GOING NATIONAL: REAL PEOPLE, REAL CHOICES

In summer 1992, the White House extended an invitation to the school choice army to discuss the movement in a public setting. This forum would coincide with the unveiling of a proposal loosely modeled on our school choice legislation. The suddenness of the invitation caught us off guard and was made even more difficult when Polly Williams announced she had a conflicting engagement and couldn't make the trip.

It was decided to put together a group of a half-dozen people to accompany Thompson and Mayor Norquist to Washington, D.C., Along with Zakiya Courtney and Messmer High School Principal Brother Bob Smith, I was asked to participate. Three parents were also selected from a list of volunteers. It was time to take our campaign to the national stage, before an international audience—with the president of the United States as emcee.

Choice parents David and Connie Frazier and Janette Williams would accompany Courtney, Brother Bob, and me. Though each of us brought a different philosophy and worldview to the table, we shared a strong belief in school choice and were willing and eager to take our respective stories to the national media.

The Fraziers would later be described by an East Coast reporter as the perfect American couple—with one exception, that is. While attractive, articulate, and epitomizing the positive aspects of a strong Black nuclear family, they were unable to live out the American dream. Though both of them were working and were quick to note that they were enjoying a comfortable lifestyle, they were nonetheless at the low end of the economic scale, which restricted their options both in housing and in educational opportunities for their children. And for the Fraziers, the latter was more important than the former.

For the better part of the last two years, the Fraziers told us, they had engaged in an ongoing battle over the poor education offered to their son. They refused to accept what they viewed as condescending comments from their son's teacher and the patronizing attitude of the school administration. Unlike the many low-income parents who were intimidated by educrats, the Fraziers were ostracized because they refused to accept the status quo and were vocal and articulate in their demands for accountability. It was obvious to the Fraziers that their children would never reach their full potential in a setting where teachers did not have high expectations for them and where their parental input was ignored. Theirs was a story too often heard in the Central City: though they were active in their community, church, and school, their children were not achieving.

After fruitless confrontations with teachers and administrators to fight an effort to isolate their son in a special education program for at-risk children, the Fraziers encountered the straw that broke the proverbial camel's back: their son's teacher attempted to hold him back because she felt he had an attitude and didn't read up to par. On the advice of a family friend, the Fraziers investigated the Parental School Choice Program, and after interviews with Courtney, transferred their son to Urban Day.

Not so strangely, under the tutelage of more caring and ethnically attuned teachers, their son underwent an immediate transformation. His "attitude," which Urban Day teachers assessed as being shy and reserved, evaporated. More important, his reading problem mysteriously disappeared and within a few short months, he was excelling in every subject.

School choice and Urban Day were a godsend, Connie Frazier said during a dinner get-together. Something is seriously wrong with a public school system that punishes Black parents for caring about their children or questioning teaching styles, she said. And something is wrong with administrators who support teachers without investigating parents' charges. Her husband David agreed, saying that if the choice program were killed in the courts, he would get three full-time jobs if he had to in order to enable the family to keep their children in private schools. There was nothing more important in his life than paving a way for his children, giving them a strong spiritual foundation and a strong education so that they could reach their potential.

Janette Williams was an equally interesting case—a single mother struggling to survive, but willing to sacrifice and go without in order to provide her son and daughter with the advantages she never had.

Her son, too, was failing in public school. Her experiences with his teachers and the school bureaucracy had left her bitter, and she was convinced that an alternative had to be found.

Even with the attentive mothering and moral foundation Janette Williams provided to her children, they were still exposed to the daily realities of life as a Black child in urban America: poverty that breeds despair, hopelessness, frustration, stress, and low self-esteem. A product of the streets where she now lived with her children, Janette Williams was strongly cognizant that the odds were stacked against her family. Having a low income was bad enough, but being a low-income single mother was a double strike against her. One either had to take advantage of welfare with its limitations and stigmas or struggle to survive with two, sometimes three, low-paying jobs. Working so many hours all but ensured that the streets were her children's part-time caretakers, and the streets could be an unfit parent indeed. Poverty is like crack cocaine in many respects. Its effects—particularly the culture it breeds—are seemingly stronger than the maternal, spiritual, and moral instinct combined.

More often than not, the victims are the offspring of single-parent households. Some might suggest that you need two-parent households to counteract the ravages of poverty. While that's an overly simplistic assessment, it is basically true—but not necessarily because of the added income. The Black nuclear family provides an intrinsic balance that single-parent households cannot.

I believe that one of the causes of social anarchy in the Black community is the absence of Black men in the household. A man, preferably a husband, in the household can provide security and a strong arm, and is a role model and standard-bearer. With no positive male role model (a source of wisdom and strength), with no male wage earner (no matter what his job) to emulate, the Black male child, especially, is left to rely on other models to pattern himself after. The streets become his uncle, gangs and sports athletes his role models, gangsta' rap lyrics his source of wisdom.

In West African culture, which predates European civilization, women guided boys through adolescence, after which the fathers took them forward in a rite of passage. The men taught the boys the nuances and responsibilities of manhood. There was wisdom in that process, which has been carried on through the centuries. Its absence today, as a result of societal and cultural breakdown, is detrimental to the community.

Judicious single mothers like Janette Williams understand that fact, and recognize that no matter how hard they try, they cannot assume the responsibility or take on the defining, nurturing role of men. Many single mothers will thus seek out extended family members or big brothers to fill the void. School choice also offers an option in that the communal environment of the Black independent schools provides a form of extended family.

Those who are fortunate enough to have strong family networks, religious foundations, or special talents often survive and prosper. But many can't overcome the odds, and like crabs in a barrel, want to pull others down with them. This tendency manifests itself in devaluation of education—where those students who at least try to excel are accused by their peers of trying to act White. Janette Williams understood that dichotomy and was cognizant that without a full-time father in her home, she had to build a shield around her son to shelter him and protect him from the effects of poverty, gang membership, drugs, and violence.

Education, sports, church, and strong extended family networks would hopefully fill the void that an absentee father produces; Williams chose to instill her son with overlapping layers of each in the hope that if one peeled away, there would be others in place to protect him. Thus, when problems occurred in the public-school setting, she quickly turned to the program she had read about and enrolled her son in a Black independent school. There, she felt, he would not only receive the education he needed but would receive it in a supportive communal atmosphere.

Williams quickly became the darling of the media during the trip to Washington, D.C., because of her communication skills and bubbly personality. A journalist's dream, she wouldn't shy away from any question and had an ease before the cameras that guaranteed an interesting interview.

With a charming smile and personality to match, Williams seemingly had reporters eating out of her hand. Reporters also learned that she defied typecasting—if they were looking for an inarticulate single mother, they were looking in the wrong place. Those who thought they could exploit her were quickly disappointed.

For Urban Day School parent liaison and parental involvement coordinator Zakiya Courtney, the school choice movement provided a mechanism through which low-income families, disenchanted with the public school system or in search of a more culturally grounded foundation for their children, could follow in her footsteps.

Several years earlier, the well-known community activist had made the decision to enroll her four children in Urban Day after a series of confrontations with the public school system left her emotionally drained. Her oldest son had been transferred to thirteen different schools before the seventh grade. In part because of his special needs and her high expectations, Courtney found herself riding a systemwide merry-go-round in search of a curriculum and setting that would enable the boy to reach his potential.

Simultaneously, Courtney found herself in a constant battle with teachers and administrators at her daughter's elementary school over teaching methods she found questionable. Of particular distress to Courtney was the school's insistence upon using a whole letter sight system method for reading, in which the children were taught to identify whole words, instead of the more popular phonics system.

"I had a problem with that because my daughter was having problems with the alphabet, and it was obvious this system wasn't working for her," Courtney later recalled. "But they ignored what I was saying; it was as if my opinion didn't count, even though my daughter was lagging behind and not learning. After a while, I just gave up. It seemed like my oldest children were victims, and I was supposed to readily sacrifice them to this system. I made up my mind not to put my youngest through that."

Although unable to afford Urban Day, upon learning that she could work off part of the tuition, Courtney jumped at the chance and enrolled the first of her four younger children in the highly regarded private school. Her work at the school soon grew into a full-time job: she applied her community organizing skills to a position as parent liaison. This experience and the success of her children in their new school coincided with the choice movement, which she saw as an opportunity to open the doors of Urban Day and other community schools to more low-income parents.

"My concern for my own children soon grew into a job, which eventually became a passion for me. It became a cultural issue, a parental empowerment issue and ultimately a civil rights issue. Public schools work for some, but they don't work for everybody. For them there should be options," she concluded.

To me, Brother Bob Smith was the most interesting member of our group. Like Janette, he commanded attention wherever he appeared. I first met Brother Bob when he delivered the commencement address at Harambee Community School's graduation during my son's seventh-grade year. Since Harambee parents consider themselves members of an extended family, I attended the graduation ceremony to support all my "children" and to cheer them on as they entered a new period of their lives. As a board member I also felt it was important to show our support for those with whose lives we had been entrusted.

Brother Bob's address to the assembly was full of humor and truth and touched everyone's heart. He spoke of parents' and teachers' high expectations of those who attend his school, Messmer High School. He spoke of the importance of education, particularly to poor Black children, and the responsibility of those fortunate enough to attend good schools like Harambee to give something back to their families and community. Brother Bob told the graduates they were special people, chosen for a higher purpose—a purpose they would come to realize only if given the opportunity. The school's responsibility was to provide them with the resources to carry out their destinies.

As Brother Bob concluded his speech, I elevated Messmer to a top position among the schools I would like my son Malik to attend upon graduation from Harambee. Fortunately, Malik, who had served as an usher for the graduation services, was equally impressed with Brother Bob and made known his interest in Messmer as we drove home that Saturday afternoon. This pleased me to no end.

One of the advantages of institutions like Harambee is the communal atmosphere that permeates all aspects of school life. That family concept not only ensured the school's success but also filled a void for single parents like myself. While my son's mother played an important role in his life, our divorce and my having primary custody meant that she wasn't there for him on a daily basis. Harambee helped to fill that void, and because of the extended family networking system there, Malik had more than seventy-five mothers he could—and often did—call upon when the need arose.

Without question, Harambee's communal foundation—the core essence of a Black independent school—is what separates that institution from other schools. Historically Black colleges and universities—which not coincidentally graduate more African Americans than public institutions—survive because of their nurturing environment, committed teachers (who often view themselves as extended family), and cultural compatibility. Black institutions usually have higher standards and greater expectations of students because history has shown that Black Americans must jump higher and add quicker just be to considered equal; these schools are on a mission to disprove society's prejudices and misconceptions about African Americans in general and the poor in particular. The community institutions are also set apart from the government/establishment plantation system schools because they provide students with critical thinking and analytical skills. It is important and imperative, says nationally renowned educator and African-centered curriculum proponent Asa Hilliard, that Black children know not only how to add and analyze but also when to add and analyze. At Harambee, children are instructed in these important skills—with high expectations, a goal and a mission, and an academic foundation from which to move forward in life.

Similarly, Messmer, with Brother Bob as its principal and patriarch, would continue this process and instill this cultural foundation. There are obviously good teachers, counselors, and administrators throughout the public school system. But Messmer drew the best of the best, those committed not only to the educational process but also to the betterment of the community through the children they educated and inspired. For most private school teachers, who generally receive a salary that is only 70 percent of that received by public school teachers, teaching is a love affair that transcends a vocation. They teach for the joy of it.

Brother Bob was a hands-on principal whose love for the children manifested itself in high expectations and a strict disciplinary code. He didn't accept excuses from students or parents, which helped both in the long run. And his philosophy filtered through the school, from the janitor to the business manager.

Brother Bob tolerated no disrespect. His steely stare could freeze a student in his tracks. Conversely, he would go to bat for his students, above and beyond what most administrators would do. It was not unusual to see Brother Bob sharing a joke with a student in the hallway or displaying sincere interest in the welfare of his or her family. He frequently assisted students or parents in finding jobs, provided community-service referrals, or dropped off students after a basketball game. Every member of Messmer was family to Brother Bob. For the Capuchin monk, the independence of heading a private school outside of the hindrances and restrictions of self-serving bureaucracies and educracy allowed him the freedom to be creative and innovative, to be nurturing, and to be a disciplinarian. There is no doubt that Brother Bob Smith is a unique and exceptional administrator, but he is so in part because of the freedom offered by his environment, and the faith bestowed upon him by those with the most to gain—the parents.

If Brother Bob had one weakness, it was that he was a strong Chicago Bears fan in a city that was painted in Green Bay Packers green and gold. But that was excusable, as was the biting tone that could send shivers up a chastised student's spine. A quick smile and pat on the back usually followed his scolding, allowing a disciplined student to take the criticism with the knowledge that Brother Bob really cared for his welfare.

I often wondered if the 6-foot 8-inch basketball star whom Brother Bob could bend to his will deferred out of respect or fear. Did his students know that before he moved to Milwaukee, Brother Bob was a probation officer in one of America's most violent ghettos and that he had earned great respect and admiration in that position? Did they know that Brother Bob held a second-degree Black belt in Hapkido, the Korean martial arts style used by army specialists? Brother Bob and I also shared a love for the martial arts—I hold a Black belt in Kempo Goju—and we joked about sparring on a number of occasions. About the same size and close in age, I figured I could take him, but after watching him "cultivate" some very large students, I realized that Brother Bob had weapons that transcended martial arts— weapons that gave him a unique advantage not just over me, but over every principal I had ever met.

Brother Bob may not have studied the works of civil rights leader and social scientist W. E. B. DuBois, but he obviously subscribed to his philosophy and embraced the concept of the Talented Tenth. The nephew of one of Milwaukee's most renowned philanthropists and social activists, Brother Booker Ashe, Brother Bob felt that while the wealthy and middle-class African Americans could and would avail themselves of DuBois's philosophy, his mission was to prove that *all* children, given the opportunity, tools, and setting, could swell those ranks.

For Brother Bob, Messmer's mission was intertwined with his Capuchin Order charge to empower the poor and spread the Word through deed and presence. He believed in the importance of true integration and the benefits it will bring society, and though it was obvious that Messmer would always be predominantly African American, Brother Bob went out of his way to recruit throughout the state. Equal to that goal was his quest to embrace as many low-income students as possible, although he was limited by the scholarships the school could offer or entice corporations to establish.

He often found receptive ears, and contributions, when it was learned that the poor Northside school's Black students had the highest grade point averages in the state. Messmer was able to erase the racial achievement gap that has existed for so long in the public school setting. At Messmer, the Black and White GPAs were not only identical, but higher than most schools in the region!

School choice would provide Brother Bob with a tool to help to carry out his mission. A major stumbling block, however, was the school's religious orientation. Although not affiliated with the Catholic Church, Messmer required students to take theology as a core subject. An organized annual religious retreat was offered, and each day started with a prayer. Those factors made the school overly religious in the eyes of some, including state officials who were threatened by the school's ability to educate low-income Black children.

Messmer had signed up for the choice program in early 1992 and had received preliminary approval, only to be rejected on June 2, 1992, after hundreds of parents had already sought registration information. The exclusion of Messmer, which had severed its ties to the Catholic Archdiocese a decade before and now called itself a value-based school, created an uproar throughout the low-income community. The controversy was rooted not only in how and why Messmer was excluded but also in the timing of the rejection.

It was later learned that the Department of Public Instruction had been instructed by parties unknown to do a special investigation of Messmer after initial approval to participate in the choice program. Some state bureaucrats were to say later they did not know of Messmer's "religious orientation" when the school was initially added to the list of choice school participants.

That is highly unlikely. But assuming it is true, DPI officials were quick and vicious in remedying their error.

The grounds they used were not only weak but also questionably driven by bureaucrats who feared that admission of the school would significantly enhance the credibility of the school choice movement. And Messmer's academic achievements would doubtless spark questions by Milwaukee Public Schools parents about the quality of education offered in public high schools.

To support its claim that Messmer was indeed a religious school, the DPI pointed out that the school offered a theology course, displayed several crucifixes throughout the facility, encouraged students to begin each day with a prayer, and had sought and received a grant four years prior from the DeRance Foundation, "which has funded Catholic schools in the past." The fact that the DeRance Foundation funded a variety of projects, causes and nonreligious organizations was not of consequence, although the DPI investigation highlighted the fact that the Foundation had made a grant to Partners Advancing Values in Education, an organization providing private choice scholarships in Milwaukee.

Messmer filed a lawsuit to challenge DPI's refusal to allow the school to partic- ipate. That suit drew national attention because it could open the door for an expansion of school choice into a new arena.

The DPI fiasco over the initial inclusion and then exclusion of Messmer High School illustrated the apparent ineptitude (and apparent cronyism) of the "gov- ernment" department as well as the growing realization that the choice program needed to be expanded. Not only was the choice program limited to elementary schools, but, more important, there were not enough seats in those nonsectarian institutions to accommodate demand. As it was structured, the choice program also discriminated against low-income families who wanted their children to attend religious schools.

The constitutional question raised by opponents (that including parochial schools would violate the provision of church and state) was a mute and even base- less argument to those who weren't afraid of the prospect of their children starting each day with a prayer or being exposed to religious values. Indeed, most low- income students at Catholic schools weren't Catholic—they simply appreciated the values, discipline, and commitment to excellence those schools offered. Brother Bob's mission wasn't so much to convert students to Catholicism as to tap their potential while they traveled a path adorned by basic religious values and tenets. "If that is a crime, then I'm a criminal," said Brother Bob.

A NEW BLACK CONSCIOUSNESS

The night before our visit to the White House, the members of our small choice contingent discussed the terms of battle over dinner in a downtown Washington restaurant. It was important that we not be used as pawns, one member of the del- egation said, and that our issues of educational empowerment not be overshadowed by the political side of vouchers or the ideological war between the Right and the Left, Democrat and Republican, liberal and conservative.

Chances were remote that any member of our choice team had voted for President Bush. Yet, like most Republicans who had come to the fore in recent months, he was for the moment our ally. Strange bedfellows were a characteristic of this fight. If anyone asked, most of us would probably have had negative things to say about the man Bush served under as vice president. But the current president wasn't taken in that harsh a regard. His greatest limitation was that he just didn't relate to our cause because like most White Americans, he was far removed from the realities of being Black in America.

By the standards most Black Americans use to gauge Republicans, Bush was viewed as a major improvement over his predecessor, although he continued policies established by Ronald Reagan that most African Americans surmised as being, at best, anti-Black and antipoor. To his detriment, Vice President Bush had also been silent during Reagan's tacit support for apartheid in South Africa and other foreign policies that continued century-old exploitation of developing nations.

Domestically, the Reagan trickle-down economic policy was a racially charged joke, but one no less frightening than his attacks on civil rights initiatives, including affirmative action. If America were truly a color-blind society, affirmative action would not be necessary. Evidence suggests this is not the case. The Milwaukee public schools had to be forcibly desegregated because they were not providing equal opportunities to Black children. Similarly, the Milwaukee police and fire departments were sued in the 1970s because entrenched policies discriminated against minorities and women. Both institutions were ordered to implement affirmative action hiring quotas by the federal courts to offset past discrimination. Ironically, the current Milwaukee chief of police, Arthur Jones, was the lead plaintiff in the police department suit. Reports issued by the city comptroller in each of the last four years clearly show disparities in the granting of mortgage loans to Whites and Blacks, a fact that has fueled Milwaukee's reputation as a hypersegregated city. Indeed—twenty years after the Open Housing Marches, school desegregation, and the police and fire department lawsuits—socioeconomic disparities (including a sizable gap in Black and White income), housing segregation, and a continuing high incidence of police brutality and hate crimes reaffirm the beliefs of those who say that racism is as entrenched today as it ever was.

Those issues aside, in truth there were many issues advanced by the Bush administration in which the ideological line was blurred. Choice was one of those issues, and President Bush's support helped advance our quest for Black empowerment and first-rate education.

In a larger sense, our cause was hindered by the battlegrounds on which we were forced to fight. Our campaign wasn't just a question of right or wrong; it dealt with political advantage and disadvantage. In a larger sense, it was about controlling the direction of the Civil Rights movement and about breaking the chains of political dependency and complacency that have neutralized Black political strength during the past half-century.

No one within our delegation was a card-carrying Democrat, yet most voted for that party's candidates in local and national elections. We did this not necessarily because we viewed the Democratic platform as more in tune with our agenda than the other major party, but because we believed Democrats to be more sympathetic and probably less prejudiced than their Republican counterparts.

The willingness to settle, to choose what many of us felt was the lesser of two evils, started wearing thin as the heyday of the Civil Rights movement started drawing to a close in the late 1980s. A new Black leadership and a new consciousness emerged, advocating self-determination, cooperative economics, and control of the institutions affecting our lives.

This was a philosophy rooted in Garveyism, spiced with Karenga, and stirred by Amos Wilson—nationalistic, with undercurrents of Pan-Africanism. We watched the failure of integration, the broken promises of assimilation, and the false realities of so-called political inclusion, and it was not hard to attract converts, particularly among the young and their frustrated parents, even those who didn't identify with the principles of Africentricity or the tenets of Black nationalism. What they could identify with was the desire for empowerment through increased economic opportunity and freedom to live wherever and however they chose. They chose to remain close to other people of color, understanding the importance of supporting Black institutions and businesses and building a communal spirit and sense of purpose. Essential to these ambitions was the opportunity to send their children to a public school that met their needs—or to a private school, if it was more accommodating or desirable.

It was no coincidence that those of this philosophy were highly represented in the school choice movement: Polly Williams, Larry Harwell, and I, the Black nationalists; Zakiya Courtney and Virginia Stamper, the Pan-Africanists; and Brother Bob, the DuBoisist.

While it was rarely stated explicitly, parental school choice threatened the stranglehold of the missionaries because it pushed the agenda of the nationalists and Pan-Africanists to the fore. Democrats were fearful of what school choice might spark. First it's education, then it's economic development and Black subdivisions—and God knows what next. Aren't African Americans comfortable on the reservation?

At dinner in Washington we discussed how inspired we were by the opportunity to tell all of America our different stories, rationales, and hopes. We had come together on short notice and while there was obviously only limited thought given to who would participate, it was certain we had an excellent team that would not back down from controversy, that would capably represent Black America and its diversity. Thus, our first night in the nation's capital took on a warm and festive mood.

The next morning, before meeting with the president, we were escorted into a small conference room in a far-off corner in the lower level of the White House, where we were greeted with a light breakfast and heavy conversation with Lamar Alexander, secretary of education and the author, we were informed, of a federal school choice plan called the Educational GI Bill.

Joining us at the breakfast meeting were Governor Tommy Thompson and Mayor John Norquist, both of whom had left their political hats in Wisconsin and took on the demeanor of team members. Thompson and Norquist knew everyone in attendance well enough to refer to them by first name and were quick to put everyone at ease with jokes and encouragement. Thompson suggested that we be aggressive in our statements during our meeting with the president and equally assertive when the media approached us later.

Representing opposing political parties, both politicians came to the table with different political agendas. But like us, they were on a common mission and were like-minded in their determination to see school choice instituted nationally. We were key to that scenario and their presence, in some respects, symbolized the singular ability of school choice to bridge ideological breaches that no other initiative could or would.

Norquist and Thompson both expressed support for the Educational GI Bill at the onset of the breakfast meeting, which provided Alexander with an easy lead-in. His proposal called for a $500 million federal Parental School Choice Program. Under the plan, low-income parents could avail themselves of $1,000-per-child scholarships that would be passed along to whichever public, private, or religious school they chose to have their children attend. In some respects, the program was patterned after our choice legislation, and while it was sure to find support from low-income parents around the country, support among Democrats would be hard to come by.

"You folks could be our greatest advocates for this bill because you're living examples of what something like this can do," Alexander said. "Opponents will say we're trying to destroy the public education system, which is preposterous given the [budget] increases this administration continues to advocate for public schools. This is about options—choices that some people now avail themselves of, but which an entire segment of the population cannot."

America cannot afford to lose the talent and promise we do each year when thousands of minority and poor children drop out of school, he continued. In some communities, including Washington, D.C., the Black dropout rate is more than 50 percent. "That is an American tragedy that does not fit the image we have promoted of ourselves." School choice, or the Educational GI Bill, would offer alternatives and perhaps provide a second chance for thousands of poor youth in urban America who might otherwise end up in the criminal justice system.

Obviously, Black people were not the sole targets of school choice or the Educational GI Bill. Most of the urban poor are in fact White, just as most of those on welfare and public assistance are White. But we got Alexander's drift and it was obvious from the nods and acknowledgments around the table that we were of one accord.

Courtney asked the secretary about the tuition offered under his bill, to which he responded that it would conceivably increase. "But for now, we have to deal with a small amount to get our feet in the door. We recognize many private schools' tuition is three times higher, but that will be addressed later."

I asked why there was no financial support from the Republicans for our movement. He responded, "There is a great deal of support for what is happening in Wisconsin and for Williams's historic movement, but we don't want this to be a GOP movement. It's about what you are doing, what poor Black parents are demanding, not what we want."

Alexander stated the obvious: in order for the school choice movement to grow, it must be orchestrated by poor and Black parents. Assistance from the Republican Party could injure the campaign by giving the impression that it was a Republican initiative from the start. Several of us nodded our agreement with his assessment. It was imperative that we maintain our leadership of the initiative and our focus on empowering Black parents.

If it's hard to maintain a public appearance of being cool in the face of an unusual and even historic situation, each of us should have earned an Oscar. Even if we were heart-poundingly nervous, we didn't reveal our discomfort before the cameras and reporters who took up every inch of space in the conference room to which we were escorted after our meeting with Secretary Alexander.

We learned two things en route to the conference room adjacent to the Oval Office. The White House is a stunningly regal facility. Its majesty and elegance is mind-boggling, even if the decorum may be, by many Black folks' standards and taste, drab and conservative. The maze of offices, corridors, and hideaways boggles the mind. The second thing we noticed was that other than servants, there weren't many Black folks in the Bush administration, or in the entire White House.

President Bush was sandwiched by aides and Alexander and trailed by Michael Joyce, president of the Bradley Foundation, a man whose seemingly demure demeanor belied an enormous intellect and power. The president smiled at the assembled reporters, nodding in the direction of familiar faces as he made his way to his seat at the center of the table. His amiable expression implied that we should relax and savor the moment, for in many ways it was indeed historic.

Janette Williams looked around the room in astonishment before locking eyes with me. The instant communication spoke volumes about how fate and opportunity can detour a seemingly uneventful life. I glanced over at Zakiya Courtney, who always reminded me of an African queen and who now looked regal in her African gown. As usual, Courtney appeared to be in total control. I then peered over at Brother Bob, who looked comfortable as well. The thought hit me that Brother Bob answered to a higher power, and for him this was small potatoes. Milwaukee's Mayor Norquist scanned the room as if imagining himself one day orchestrating a meeting of heads of state. Though doubtless a political creature, Norquist, unlike many of his colleagues, was willing to take an unpopular position based upon principle. Indeed, his support for and leadership of the school choice battle put him at odds with close friends in the Wisconsin Democratic Party, but earned him in return new friendships among minorities and poor residents as well as political independence. It also carved a place for him in the vanguard of the new centralist Democratic Party.

President Bush offered the first greeting and handshake to Thompson. Thompson, like Norquist, was no great orator, but carried issues with force, conviction, and a simplicity that masked—probably intentionally—his political genius. Thompson and I first met at the *Milwaukee Community Journal* during his initial gubernatorial bid. He opened his presentation by noting that he didn't expect to secure more than 10 percent of the Black vote—if that—but offered something to Black voters that neither Democrat or Republican had previously put on the table: honesty.

I clearly remember Thompson saying that there would be issues over the years on which conservatives and African Americans could reach common ground, and it should be those issues, not partisan politics, that should define our relationship. "I'm for Black people controlling their community, agitating for their fair share, and being treated as I would like to be treated. I'm for Black people setting their own agenda. That's only right. It's your community and you know what's best," he said.

Thompson said he supported desegregation: "I think it's needed to bring us all together, but I don't think it offers the remedy for education that some Black leaders think it does. And in some respects, it suggests you have to have White people to educate you, or your children have to sit next to White kids to learn. If I were Black, that would be insulting to me."

Thompson was crucial to our victory. Some Black folks wouldn't even have entertained the thought of working with him simply because he's a Republican. That's not only myopic, it is politically naïve. After all, Richard Nixon signed an executive order calling for affirmative action to include minorities in government contracts. We wouldn't be defending affirmative action today had it not been for a Republican. Thompson supported the Black district plan, appointed all the county's Black judges, and put into place the state's strongest minority business enterprise program—as local Democrats have been dismantling theirs. Who is our friend and who our enemy? Can we even afford to think in such partisan terms?

True to his word, the governor had fought behind the scenes on several campaigns orchestrated by Black leaders, including Polly Williams, and had put money and opportunity in our hands on policy matters from welfare reform—he named Opportunities Industrialization Center (OIC) the lead agency—to school choice. How strange that the fates had worked to put Thompson and me together again to talk about one of those very issues—this time with arguably the most powerful man in the world.

Bush opened the meeting by declaring his support for school choice and offering us up as members of a vanguard of parents and social activists who were willing to challenge the status quo to provide opportunities for poor children. Parental rights and responsibilities should take precedence over bureaucracy and efforts to maintain failed systems, he said, offering choice as the epitome of a civil rights campaign that will ultimately shake the foundation of the education system.

The national debate, President Bush continued, should be one that looks at the needs of the children, particularly poor children in urban settings, not the needs of the bureaucracies or teachers unions. He then went around the room seeking our individual and collective impressions about school reform in general and school choice in particular.

Courtney detailed the struggle, applauding the parents—many illiterate and poor—who came together to advance an agenda they hoped would lead to quality education and thus better futures for their children. They would not be moved or intimidated, she said, adding that school choice is a mechanism to empower poor parents, many of whom have been erroneously typecast by the media and educrats as being apathetic or uncaring about their children's welfare. In addition to everything else, the campaign for school choice should dispel the stereotypes and prove to the world that Black parents prioritize the needs of their children and are resourceful and tenacious when it comes to their charges.

First the Fraziers and then Janette Williams brought to the table the stories of their children and the importance of providing the private school options for them. The Black schools provided something the public schools could not or would not, they said, and the family atmosphere provided a communal support network not offered by the impersonal and seemingly uncaring public school system.

President Bush then turned to Brother Bob, who emphasized the importance of including a value-centered high school as an alternative for poor parents, a possibility that was being challenged in Milwaukee by the denial of Messmer High School to be granted status as a choice school.

Brother Bob surmised that Messmer was denied that opportunity to participate not because it offered religious classes or began the school day with a prayer, but because it was perceived as a threat to the status quo. The same children who failed in the public schools prospered at Messmer, he said, raising questions the educracy didn't want to address.

My remarks attested to the truth of Brother Bob's words. Through my son Malik's educational experience I also served as a bridge between Messmer High School and Milwaukee's premiere Black independent elementary school, Harambee. I told the president that the school choice movement gratified me personally because it evoked one of the most impressive groundswells of support that I had witnessed in nearly two decades of Civil Rights movement involvement as an activist journalist. It was gratifying to see low-income parents taking the initiative to improve the quality of their lives and putting everything on the line to open the doors of opportunity for their children. School choice was refocusing the Civil Rights movement, shifting the battle from fundamental rights to equal opportunity. An empowering tool to level the playing field, school choice could tear down the plantation walls and provide the bricks for a stronger community.

To each of our comments, the president nodded in agreement or asked follow-up questions. The press took in every word and gesture—if they were looking for a weakness, they found none. Nor did they see stereotypical Black folks that have become the media norm, used to fuel prejudices and racial fears. Instead they saw articulate, caring Black parents, activists and educators, all committed to a cause and refusing to be labeled or derailed from their purpose.

As we laid out our agenda before the world and stood for a few moments on equal footing with the president of the United States, the media and the political status quo had to take note. This was an important moment for America's poor. A proud moment for Black America. And a turning point for the Civil Rights movement.

Maybe school choice would serve as the catalyst for a national movement, one that embraced the tenets of Black nationalism and would empower Black America. In just the short time since our movement made national headlines, activists were calling up and inquiring from all across America: Cleveland and Indianapolis, the Twin Cities and Washington. The problems we encountered with the Milwaukee public schools were apparently not unique, nor was the impotency of the political structure to solve the myriad socioeconomic ills confronting Black America.

Traditional Black leadership either didn't have a clue or was too intent on maintaining relationships to tackle the real issues. Many activists and poor parents quizzed us on our campaign with an eye toward initiating similar crusades in their own communities. There was also confusion about the NAACP's resistance, and fear about incurring the wrath of traditional allies who not only would turn their backs on us but also would undermine this effort and punish supporters—whether or not they were successful.

MEETING THE PRESS

After further presentations by Alexander and Bush, we were taken aside for an impromptu media session, where representatives from around the country bombarded us with questions about school choice and the direction of educational reform. As expected, some of the questions focused on the coalition with Republicans and on our rift with some Democrats and the NAACP over school choice. While most of us were polite, the tone of several of the questions prompted an occasional sharp retort.

At one point Courtney asked a reporter if he thought Black folks were not intelligent enough to set their own agenda and questioned the reporter's motivations and obvious prejudices. As a member of the press, I took personal offense at a question about how parental school choice was straining Black relations with the Democratic Party, offering that Black America is not in the hip pocket of any political party.

"There are many issues on which we differ with the Democrats," I bristled. "We're not pawns of anybody, and to be truthful, most Black folks are not members of any party, nor do they look at White people as being our saviors. It's insulting to suggest that we are obligated to follow a script or that we don't know what's best for our children and ourselves.

"As a matter of fact, I know more racist Democrats than I know Republican racists, if for no other reason than we deal with them more. It has long been my experience that the farther left you go, the closer you get to the right. And it goes the other way too. There are liberals who make racist statements and right-wingers who are very liberal.

"Black America has been used by one party and ignored by the other. We are not fools. We do what is necessary to survive, recognizing that to achieve our goals we must set our own agenda and forge alliances with whomever is willing to support that agenda, irrespective of party."

For the most part, the media slant was positive and the reporters' questions seemed to suggest that they were developing human-interest stories or at least unbiased accounts of the day's events. If nothing else, the reporters left the briefing knowing we were committed to our cause and determined to let the world know that it was no longer business as usual. The interests of the Black community would take precedence over political parties, alliances, tradition, or history. If integration is to come, we announced, let it come naturally, among equals.

We left the White House not as victims, but as victors, having redefined the commitment of Black parents and having shifted the Civil Rights movement away from accommodation/assimilation and toward Black empowerment.

AID TO THE CAUSE

Later that day we met with half a dozen supporters, including Michael Joyce and representatives from the Congress of Racial Equality and the National Center for Neighborhood Enterprise. Away from the lights, cameras, and notebooks, the mood was light, even festive, as we took turns analyzing the day's events.

This was the first time most of us had had a chance to engage in a fruitful dialogue with Michael Joyce, who was introduced to me months earlier by Polly Williams at a social function as "one of the most powerful men in America." Many of us held Joyce at arm's length, not only because of his position as president of the neoconservative Bradley Foundation but also because of our fears that any association with the Foundation or the Republican Party beyond the superficial would taint our campaign.

Nonetheless, Courtney, Brother Bob, and I were unified in our curiosity and desire to pick Joyce's brain, to separate fact from fiction. We didn't know the details of how or by whom this meeting with the president had been arranged, but it was our suspicion that Joyce had had something to do with it—a testament to his influence and support for our cause.

In many respects, Michael Joyce—who at one point referred to himself as a former liberal with children—perfectly fit the description of a neoconservative offered by Daryl Michael Scott in his masterful work *Contempt and Pity:*

> In the mid-1960s, a number of racial liberals became disillusioned with the direction of racial liberalism and its response to the social upheavals of the time. These "neoconservatives," as they became known, believed that most liberals were too apologetic for what they viewed as the riotous behavior of urban black citizens, and emphasized the need for law and order. More importantly, they also tended to have serious reservations about preferential programs such as affirmative action and efforts to promote integration such

as school busing. They reasserted the traditional racial liberal call for a color-blind state, which would protect only the civil rights of individuals. Alienated from the mainstream of the Democratic Party which embraced the use of the state to achieve the new goals of racial liberalism, the disaffected racial liberals began to support the Republican Party, which eventually rejected the use of the state to promote economic equality and assimilation. Increasingly, racial neoconservatives have called for a color-blind society as well.[3]

However, Joyce defies traditional categorization. Slight of build, wearing glasses, in his stylish double-breasted suit he could easily be mistaken for a college professor or a scientist. He carefully chooses his words and his extensive vocabulary is not forced or condescending, although he can quickly trip you up with a question about a 1960s R&B artist in a sentence that started with a statement about the post-cold war European economy or Thomas Jefferson's foray into Deism. His wife, Mary Jo, a former model, is a personable, articulate woman who teaches piano and prefers homemaking to sharing the limelight with her husband.

We bombarded Joyce with questions ranging from his personal and political history to racism in America, from his views on school choice to his perception of the notion that vouchers were being advanced with the intent of destroying the public education system.

Pleasant and unassuming, Joyce talked about his early work with and for traditional Democratic causes and leadership. His views slowly evolved over the years, he said, as he sensed that America was swaying away from the tenets of the Founding Fathers, away from a national sense of oneness and a culture rooted in Christian values and social responsibility essential to "Americanism."

Racism has no place in our culture, continued Joyce. It is contrary to every religious belief, a cancer that undermines the very tenets of the Constitution. African Americans must understand that they cannot erase racism until they see that this disease infects people on the Right, the Left, the Middle, and all shades in between. Racism is a manmade disease that does not discriminate.

Black Americans often find themselves being used as pawns in a complicated political game that keeps them powerless. For Black America, the safest strategy is to be pragmatic, realistic students of history. Keep your friends close and enemies closer, Joyce seemed to say. Build bridges wherever there are issues of mutual concern and benefit. Black America must see the importance of integrating—but not assimilating—with all aspects of society, opening the doors of opportunity, tearing down the walls from the inside as well as the outside. And the Black community must do that from a position of strength.

To our surprise, Joyce was vehement in pointing out the failings and naïveté of the GOP. Republicans had all but ignored Black America since the end of War World II and by doing so had made themselves an exclusionary political social club of limited vision. In truth, both political sides have faults; neither is particularly open-minded in its approach to solving the myriad of social and economic maladies plaguing urban America. And as such, both parties are directly or indirectly responsible for the declining values and mores of America. Political parties and political ideology should always take a back seat to the tenets that made America great: the vision of the Founding Fathers for a society where people are treated equally and fairly, and without regard to social or economic status. Those with the talents, discipline and perseverance to achieve financially or otherwise should be allowed the luxuries that come with affluence.

Joyce theorized that Dr. Martin Luther King Jr.'s vision more closely represented the country's interest than any other American's before or since. Politics can define that goal, but none has yet articulated how to get to King's promised land, where all people are judged by the content of their characters rather than the color of their skin. That is a moral problem that must be solved through cultural transformation.

School choice was the most important battleground in America, asserted Joyce, because it spoke of the importance of Black empowerment as a mechanism to break the monopoly and open America's eyes to the dual public school system, the two Americas that must be merged if the country is to reach its proper place on the world stage. The plantation gatekeepers don't just wear GOP suits—they also wear sports coats manufactured in Democratic Party factories, he said. Black Americans hold the key to America and indeed America's Black poor, if given the chance, can bridge the gap between the two Americas that define and divide our country. Without knowing it, Joyce recited the African cultural adage "I am because we are," which means that America can go no further than its least privileged citizen.

It became clear to us that Michael Joyce was not a conservative in the traditional sense. His vision and ideology transcend artificial political boundaries. He was an idealist who took seriously the Constitutional creed that all men are created equal, and we should be allowed to grow and prosper, to reach our God-given potential, unencumbered by color or creed. To many of us, parental school choice was an empowerment issue, a civil rights imperative, or simply a matter of opportunities and options. But to Joyce it was a grander struggle that could serve as a catalyst for social, political, and cultural change.

Michael Joyce's tacit support was critical to the choice movement, as was the Bradley Foundation, an organization we at times lambasted and publicly and politically retreated from because of its link to Charles Murray, author of *The Bell Curve*, which asserted a racist theory of White and Asian intellectual superiority. Joyce and company explained that although the Foundation had funded a fellowship for Murray, they rejected his theories, which they considered appalling. In fact, the Foundation cut off funding after the book's conclusions came to light. However, Joyce and the Foundation were permanently stereotyped and ostracized. That ostracism put us in an awkward position, one that not only invited negative media scrutiny but also fueled chiding from the opposition—and some Black supporters as well. The Foundation's conservative bent didn't spook us. As the 1996 Joint Center for Political and Economic Studies National Opinion Poll illuminated, there are many items on the conservative platform that Black Americans—and nationalists in particular—identify with, although our worldviews are vastly different. The allegations of racism via the Murray connection were another matter, however.

Despite what was often a fair-weather friendship, we privately acknowledged that without the Bradley Foundation the uphill climb would have been much steeper and our casualties far greater. The Foundation was never involved in the planning, coordination, or leadership of the movement; its assistance was neither sought nor required. In fact, it was our imperative to keep this movement in Black hands from beginning to end. Nonetheless, the Foundation did indirectly help fuel our train as it traveled the latest Underground Railroad: when opponents derailed the train by maiming the school choice initiative, it was the Foundation that came up with several million dollars to provide scholarships through PAVE to the Black children who would otherwise have been left by the wayside. The Foundation also reportedly funded the institution of which Clint Bolick was the director.

Joyce was also involved with putting pressure on key Republicans to support our cause and was reportedly instrumental in forging a truce between the governor and Mayor John Norquist to advance our crusade. The Bradley Foundation, at the urging of choice proponents, also underwrote a promotional campaign the first two years of the program to advertise participating schools when Grover refused to follow the legislative mandate to do so.

After the publication and resulting outcry over *The Bell Curve*, several White missionaries led by junior college instructor Charlie Dee facetiously called on the Bradley Foundation to atone for funding Murray by allocating funds to help the underprivileged. The critics conveniently failed to mention the Foundation's prior and current contributions, nor did they acknowledge the dozen grants earmarked at that moment for Black organizations whose programs ranged from business incubators and job-training programs to a Black police organization and a nationally renowned but financially strapped African dance company, Ko-Thi. All of these recipients made the decision to apply for Bradley Foundation grants fully cognizant of the ribbing they would take, but also aware that none of those who lambasted them would put their money where their mouths were. The Bradley Foundation, despite its conservative leanings and links to neophytes like Murray, made a point of offering grants with no strings attached and no preset conditions other than financial need.

As Malcolm X said, freedom *by any means necessary.* "Let the White folks with the money wage that war of words and rhetoric; for us it's about principle and empowerment," said an activist at one of our weekly meetings. While we had right on our side, right by itself isn't enough when you're going against the large war chests and political might of the teachers union, the NAACP, the ACLU, and a political newcomer to Milwaukee, People for the American Way (which we took to mean the old way of two societies, social injustice, and institutional racism). When we needed bullets and the Bradley Foundation extended its hand, we accepted them without judgment. Michael Joyce continued to be a very powerful ally.

After meeting with the president and the press, our school choice delegates flew back to Milwaukee separately. As I looked down upon the nation's capital from ten thousand feet, I couldn't help but think about the dichotomy that Washington, D.C., poses for America. A half-mile away from the grandeur of the White House and the Capitol—the seats of world power—are slums that breed poverty and despair. Washington, D.C., has one of the worst public school systems in the country, but lawmakers, most of whom send their children to private schools, refuse to authorize parental school choice for the D.C. poor. Even Rev. Jesse Jackson, who vigorously opposes school choice, sends his children to the best and most expensive private school in the D.C. area.

What hypocrisy! But what else is new in Washington?

In the days following our return to Milwaukee, there was much talk of our historic meeting with the president of the United States and our opportunity to present our side of the story before the national media. We also discussed new opportunities to move our struggle for equality and justice beyond education and alliances that could be forged toward that end. We envisioned expanding our crusade to a national level, linking grassroots campaigns around the country. The school choice movement had provided a clear design for a bottom-up movement that was just the beginning.

Exhausted but fulfilled, we concluded our sojourn to the nation's capital having planted a seed that, someday, would hopefully grow into a mighty African baobab tree from whose powerful limbs would blossom a sweet and fulfilling fruit.

THE SECOND
EMANCIPATION PROCLAMATION

The function of freedom is to free somebody else.

—TONI MORRISON

TEARING DOWN THE PLANTATION WALLS

The Civil War is over. The North(side) won. Slavery has again been abolished; the sons and daughters of Africa set free. The educational chains have been cast aside; the plantation walls torn down.

June 10, 1998, will go down in our "His-story" books as the day the Wisconsin Supreme Court issued our second Emancipation Proclamation. With its decision affirming the constitutionality of the expansion of Wisconsin's Parental School Choice Program to sectarian schools, the Supreme Court, led by Patrick "John Brown" Crooks, replicated President Abe Lincoln's most enduring executive act some 125 years earlier. As a result, this year's celebration of Juneteenth Day will have more current relevance, as up to fifteen thousand low-income, mostly minority families will be able to send their children to the same schools the modern analogues of slave holders, overseers and missionaries send their offspring to.

Equally important, with the "South" now in flames and the victorious troops marching through "Vliet Street" (where not by coincidence MPS

Reprinted with permission from *Milwaukee Community Journal*, June 1998.

and MTEA headquarters are located), the handwriting is on the wall for the education system that kept Black and poor families trapped in mediocrity and servitude. The court decision means the system will be forced to self-assess, to empower parents, and more important, finally to educate all its charges. Reconstruction is around the corner, brothers and sisters. Black and poor families will again reap the benefits of a newfound freedom. If some think it is better to remain on the plantation as sharecroppers or to trust the new "morality" and sense of responsibility of the former slave holders, so be it. That is the choice of a free people. Yet, condemn not those who pack their meager belongings and leave the plantation, guaranteed for the first time an opportunity to avail themselves of the liberties that are offered free men and women.

Some may think me flippant in making this analogy. No apologies are forthcoming. For there is significant parallel here that transcends coincidence: indeed a war has been fought—a Civil Rights war—that pitted slave holders against "captives," people of color who like their shackled ancestors, were denied first-rate educational opportunities and thereby the amenities of citizenship. These descendants of African kings and queens were not allowed to live the American dream, for in reality they were destined by lack of educational opportunity—or the resources to secure them—to second-class citizenship.

There are many who believe this affront was initiated out of fear: an educated "captive'" will learn to pick his or her lock. A brainwashed, miseducated or ignorant slave will serve his master faithfully. Throw in a few Uncle Toms and House Negroes to spy, defuse, and sabotage and the methodology of apartheid can easily sustain itself in Milwaukee with MPS assuming the role of the overseer.

But they underestimated our resolve, our passion, our determination. They didn't include "Justice" in the equation, and apparently didn't understand that when Right is on your side, you always have an advantage.

For the record, this educational civil war has been waged my entire life. It has been a war fought not only over the basic rights of U.S.-born citizens of color to receive a constitutionally guaranteed education but also over what and how these children would be taught. It is a war with clearly defined adversaries, although many have jumped sides on occasion, and the uniforms of others may have prompted confusion at various times. It is a war that has seen a shift in military tactics ranging from efforts to desegregate to a strategy of annexing ourselves, creating a separate Black-controlled school district. It has pitted brother against brother, White against Black, White against White, Negro against African, and Black against Black. It is a war that has forced a reassessment of friendships, allies, and tactics and left Black Americans with a firm understanding of the adage, "we have no permanent friends, nor permanent enemies, only permanent issues."

It is a war that has been fought with street soldiers, mercenaries, women, and children. And, while there has been bloodletting, primarily it has been a war fought on a metaphysical plane; in the courts, in the legislature, at hundreds of community meetings and prayer vigils. There has been much physical conflict as well, as parents chained themselves to buses, staged endless demonstrations, marched thousands of miles. They also wrote volumes of letters, appeared at endless hearings, and lobbied hundreds of politicians and civic leaders. Often it seemed like they were merely spittin' into the wind, but in retrospect each effort chipped away at another brick in the plantation wall.

It is a war that has waged on and on and on and will resume on another battlefield once the smoke clears. It is a war that did not begin as some believe with the School Choice movement (which, incidentally did not start with Governor Thompson's bill in 1988, or Polly Williams's legislation of 1989; in truth, the first campaign for School Choice was initiated by a Black group in 1970, which was funded and supported by the Social Development Commission). It is a war that saw Black professionals pushing for a Civil Rights statute a decade before I was born and their children chaining themselves to a school yard fence a generation later.

It is a war rooted in the intrinsic battle over the minds of our children, an educational war that directly impacts our cultural stability, our economic potential and even our religious foundation. It is a war that is both about civil rights and silver rights. History, and His-story. Justice or J.U.S.T.U.S.

It is a war that has been fought on many venues, but has seen but two sides: Black America against people who have tried to deny, limit, or miseducate our children. The enemy at various times has been Republican, Democrat, Jewish, and Christian. They have been rich, middle class, and poor. They have been White and Brown and Yellow, and often came in Black face. Sometimes they were motivated by misguided beliefs. Other times they were trying to uphold the tenets of White supremacy: to maintain the system of apartheid that has distinguished Milwaukee, but is no less evidenced elsewhere throughout America. It can be seen in urban and rural areas where the parents of Black children, the sons and daughters of slavery and oppression, strive for equal opportunity, the benefits of American citizenship, and the tenets inherent in the Constitution of the United States.

Some of those who blocked the doors or detoured dreams were hate-filled; others were trying to guarantee their job security. Let "His-story" judge them; because in the final analysis, it was oppressor against the oppressed, there was no middle ground, no gray area.

The history books—at least ours—will show that this war has been about empowerment and has been fought at many different levels, using many different strategies. Often we've fired salvos at the wrong enemy or used inappropriate weapons. We wasted years riding a freedom train called "court-ordered desegregation" without understanding the track didn't lead to the Promised Land.

We've lost a few good fights along the way, including the proposal to carve out our own district—the North Division School District.

We did show what could be done at Malcolm X Middle School, when parents and truly concerned and dedicated teachers are in charge. But North Division is another battle, one as yet undecided.

Another lesson learned the hard way centered on our inability to see the spies and double agents in our midst. The Leon Todds, a.k.a. Benedict Arnolds, who work for the other side, wreaking havoc and terrorism under the flag of Negritude. We allowed him and his cronies to get into a position of power on the school board, and then cussed ourselves as he stabbed one of our generals—Howard Fuller—in the back, and then went about the task of systematically undermining or sabotaging reforms and criticizing African-centered education and Black parental involvement.

Those battlefield lessons were learned the hard way, as we also learned that yesterday's allies may become today's enemies, or when all is said and done, this is a battle that only we can win or lose, for others have their own agenda. In that respect, each battle must be fought separately. Today one group will join us in battle and tomorrow another may offer us munitions.

Therein lies the strategy of success. Ten thousand ants can eat the mighty elephant, our ancestors once said, and our 60-year battle for quality education has proven that.

This battle over empowerment includes the ability to make sure our children are educated but also to control what they are taught, and by whom. As the war evolved, we learned that empowerment can be achieved through various avenues—through charters, site-based management and Black independent schools. It most certainly can be achieved through

School Choice, which is not about the separation of church and state, but about channeling "our" money to institutions of our choice, where we, the parents, feel our children will get the best education. If that is at Harambee, with its African-centered curriculum and proven administration, so be it. Whether that means Messmer, the only high school in the city where the Black and White GPA is identical, more power to you. If that is in a planned Black Baptist or COGIC school, the Chapter 220 Intradistrict suburban "integration" program, a public/private partnership school, or in a tree house . . . then as the African affirmation goes, "Oshai" (and so it is).

We are not a monolithic people. One shoe does not fit all. Thus, parents should be the decision makers as to where their children go to school and should have the option of transferring if the school isn't serving their needs. They should also be allowed to be a part of the educational process, both as a policy maker and as overseer.

Many of those on the other side of the battle line don't think so. They want all Black children to remain enslaved, confined to the plantation, forced to accept second-class citizenship, trained to be good servants, or worse—miseducated, with low self-esteem, bred for the prison camps. In truth, effort upon effort to empower parents, through site-based management to having a greater say in the allocations of resources, or even in questioning teaching techniques or challenging unqualified teachers, have been met with resistance, not just from the teachers union, but from board members as well. Is it any wonder that accountability has been a myth and parental involvement a joke? Is it any wonder why the war wages on, and on and on?

School choice, we recognize, is but a battle in a war waged to break the chains that bind African Americans; limiting their access to the benefits of a democratic society, restricting them to second-class citizenship.

What we're about, the reasons for this war are often confused because the propaganda machine is controlled by the plantation owners, as are many politicians, teachers and even civil rights leaders. You can tell them even when they're not in uniform because they're the ones defending the plot against the Massa' or turning us in when we plan our escape via the Underground Railroad.

You'll hear them questioning the court's decision on expanded School Choice, suggesting we are better off back on the plantation or that it will lead to segregation (as if the schools aren't already segregated). They'll probably question who paid for our bullets and erroneously infer choice participants are stealing from the plantation's treasury (as if we should care). The reality is we're never better off on the plantation, sitting at the Massa's table (desegregation) doesn't ensure quality education or that you will be accepted, and the so-called plantation money is from our own sweat and blood. It's our damn money! Call it payback, reparations, whatever you want. But it should follow our children, not the overseer.

Yeah, we'll celebrate our latest battle, this historic victory against overwhelming odds, but we also recognize there will be many more battles to come. There are thousands of other "prisoners of war" we must free. The war isn't over until all our children get the opportunity to reach their potential, when they can hold their heads up high with a sense of being and purpose. When they all have a foundation to stand on and a future they can visualize.

This is a war for our children, and their children. And we will win it, or die trying.

Hotep.

—Mikel Kwaku-Osei Holt

OPENING THE DOORS TO RELIGIOUS SCHOOL CHOICE

The above editorial was my initial reaction following the Wisconsin Supreme Court's ruling on the expansion of school choice to sectarian schools, a decision that rocked the state and shook the educational world. Our battle to secure opportunities for 1,500 low-income families, and in effect alter the educational debate, had reached a new plateau on June 10, 1998.

The bar, of course, was to rise even higher. Five months later the U.S. Supreme Court refused to review a related challenge of the Parental School Choice Program, thus reaffirming it. We hoped that this phase of the war was over. History, however, suggested it was not.

Who could have guessed where the decisions made in Urban Day Community School nine years earlier would lead us? At the time, it was just a matter of righting an injustice, spitting in the face of the Establishment, forcing the educracy to explain its ineptitude, and pressuring it to finally respond to our cries. Our ultimate aim was to shift the power paradigm. Our ambition was to induce the system to undergo a metamorphosis, resulting in an institution that truly served the needs of *all* children, regardless of race or economic status. The short-term goal was to provide low-income children with access to an educational environment with a proven history of academic achievement.

The efforts of that small group in 1989 would have a snowball effect that would drastically alter the status quo, moving Milwaukee—known nationally as one of the least livable cities for African Americans—to the vanguard of educational innovations. The limited Parental School Choice Program for which we had fought so hard nine years earlier had evolved into a more comprehensive voucher program. Charter schools would follow, offering even greater options to a community tired of excuses and false promises.

The state supreme court's original ruling on March 4, 1992, affirming the constitutionality of school choice in Wisconsin shifted the debate for low-income parents from giving their children the option to attend an independent school to ensuring that there would be space available in that school. The bottom line is that there would not be enough seats for the number of families wishing to participate in the Parental School Choice Program. At maximum, there were only six hundred seats in the various nonsectarian schools.

Also, the school choice legislation allowed for only 49 percent participation, which in many respects was acceptable, but was certainly limiting. If you only had 250 seats at a school, you could use only half for choice. At Harambee, for example, the board's goal was to maintain an even mix of paying and choice students, recognizing that many choice parents were unfamiliar with the demands and obligations that went along with private schools, and because the mix worked out well in maintaining our communal networking system. The concept of "each one teach one" was altered at Harambee to "each one embrace one," helping him or her along. Another consideration was the necessity of redirecting resources to bring a majority of the new choice students up to par academically.

Interestingly, opponents of school choice always used Witte's biased and flawed 1991 study to assert that the program wasn't making substantial academic impact after its first year. Aside from the fact that six subsequent studies, including two from liberal antivoucher groups, documented impressive results, choice adversaries never mentioned—whether intentionally or not—that most of the choice students were on average *two years behind* when they were enrolled!

A study by Sammis White and Howard Fuller dispelled the lie that school choice was skimming off the brightest and best students. There was truth to that assertion, but not in the sense that opponents intended. Academically, most choice students were on the bottom of the ladder; a majority came from single-parent households with incomes far below the poverty level. Most of these students had immense potential, but it had remained untapped under the MPS umbrella. These potentially bright candles were never lit—but private schools have historically been able to pull that genius to the surface.

As the world has since witnessed, the Wisconsin Supreme Court's 1992 ruling on our original school choice initiative was but the beginning. By the next year, the number of choice schools doubled, as did the number of participants. There was soon a waiting list of more than four hundred children, signifying widespread support of the program and highlighting the program's inability to accommodate all those interested. It soon became obvious that the desire to escape the plantation was far greater than the seats on the Underground Railroad train. But even with another $1.6 million contribution to PAVE, the effort to serve everyone in need came up short, particularly with poor parents required to pay approximately half the tuition.

Hoping to open the doors to religious school choice by sneaking through a side window, parents once again contacted Clint Bolick and the Landmark Legal Foundation Center for Civil Rights, seeking a legal remedy. Bolick responded on August 31, 1994, with a suit filed in U.S. District Court challenging the constitutionality of the state's ban on religious schools participating in the choice program. His brief theorized that the exclusion of Messmer High School, a value-based school, and Central City Catholic schools violated low-income families' first amendment right to free exercise of religion. It was a brilliant, if controversial, tactic—but it soon became clear that the suit could be tied up in the courts for a decade. Our problem was more immediate, and there seemed to be only two options available to us.

The first was a substantial expansion of participating schools, a prospect that could be difficult to achieve given the unexpected closing of choice school Juanita Virgil Academy in 1991 and the ammunition that gave opponents who asserted that school choice was unstable. As Williams noted in several interviews, the school's closing was an unfortunate scenario, but one that generally happens in the real world of accountability. Virgil Academy was a business that failed. Parents took a chance and some were hurt in the process. But they were strengthened by it, and the task before us then was to ensure that mechanisms were put in place to guarantee it wouldn't happen again. New schools were part of Williams's plan, and would be eventually crucial to the continuation of the program, but it was obvious that they must be nurtured. In addition, safeguards must be put in place to weed out the fly-by-nights who would be attracted by the smell of crisp dollars, which weren't as plentiful as it may have seemed. Williams also noted that dozens of MPS schools undergo the same problems as Virgil Academy, but instead of being closed are left open—even as the students continually fail. That's what accountability is about. Under school choice, if parents don't like an institution, they can remove their children, and the schools will close. In MPS, they are forced to suffer unless they have the financial resources to leave the system.

The limited number of choice seats, coupled with growing public interest in the program and the continued failures of MPS, soon sparked a new parents' movement to expand the Parental School Choice Program. Williams found herself besieged with requests to introduce new legislation, not just from parents involved in the original movement who were still reeling from the refusal of the state to include Messmer and St. Joan Antida high schools in the program, but also from parents from several Central City Catholic schools that were under threat of being closed because of dwindling financial support from the Catholic Archdiocese.

The Archdiocese had undertaken a study during the early 1990s on the declining number of Catholics in the Central City and was close to merging several of the parishes, which would have meant the closing of several Catholic schools. While enrollment in the schools was steady, few Black parents were actually Catholic, putting the Archdiocese in a difficult position. When word reached Williams in January 1994 that St. Leo's, one of the most revered Central City Catholic schools, was being targeted for closure, she acted quickly.

On a cold February morning, Williams stood on the steps of the school with Mayor John Norquist, St. Leo's staff, and a dozen community residents to announce a bill to expand the state's Parental Choice Program to include sectarian schools. Williams hoped the bill would be included as part of the budget and debated within a few weeks in the Joint Finance Committee. She acknowledged to reporters that she had planned to introduce legislation to expand school choice to religious schools at some point in the future, but the immediacy of St. Leo's plight had forced her to adjust her plans. Her proposal would come in the form of an amendment to the current school choice legislation rather than a separate bill.

Mayor Norquist, a staunch supporter of choice and vouchers, declared that the plight of St. Leo's parents further exemplified the need to expand choice. The mayor said that his daily discussions with civic and business leaders convinced him that MPS is a major impediment to efforts to expand Milwaukee's business base. The quality of education is a major concern of businesses, and the abysmal failures of MPS hindered the city's efforts to retain and attract new businesses. Expanding school choice would serve the dual purpose of forcing the public schools toward change and greater accountability and ensuring a larger pool of academically sound workers through the private-school networks.

Although Williams's amendment never saw the light of day—it was unceremoniously tabled in committee—that defeat didn't signal the end of crusade. Instead, it sparked a new grassroots movement. Taking the lead in that endeavor were Zakiya Courtney, Messmer High School principal Brother Bob Smith, and Hispanic choice parent Pilar Gonzales, who helped create Parents for School

Choice (PFSC), a new organization that pushed not only school choice but eventually public school charters as well. Under Courtney's guidance, the group forged alliances with prominent business and civic leadership to advance its agenda.

Early in the process PFSC worked with Williams, but it soon became obvious that an ideological clash would keep the parties on different trains. Williams had suspicions about the business community's involvement, although initially she attended several meetings with the Metropolitan Association of Commerce Executives, led by Tim Sheehy, who had brought in George and Susan Mitchell as consultants to work behind political lines to press for an expansion of school choice.

Williams agreed in principle with the goals of PFSC, but preferred to continue with her own networking base, which she hoped to expand through a new organization she created called Milwaukee Parental Assistance Center (MPAC), a resource and advocacy organization that focused on educational issues. Williams's base of support was the grassroots network that she had groomed to take on other challenges, including electoral politics and economic development issues. She secured a grant from the Bradley Foundation to start the organization, which at one point was headed by her aide Larry Harwell, whose statistical skills and analytical abilities had proven to be crucial to the advancement of not only the school choice campaign but also county and state redistricting battles.

While Williams laid the groundwork for expansion of school choice, working behind the scenes and ultimately emerging with several key amendments, PFSC planned the first step in the historic journey under the guise of a major public celebration to highlight the contributions of schools and individuals to the school choice movement. Among the invited guests was Governor Tommy Thompson, who several months earlier had responded negatively when a news reporter asked him about expanding school choice to other Wisconsin communities or to religious schools in Milwaukee. Emphasizing his support for choice, Thompson nonetheless said he wasn't interested in expanding the program yet; he was awaiting more conclusive studies to show the program's success and an expected shift in the political leadership of the state assembly to the Republicans. He noted that major studies conducted by Cecilia Rouse of Princeton University and Jay Greene and Paul Peterson of Harvard University concluded that students participating in the program were showing significant academic achievement, while University of Wisconsin professor John Witte's annual research consistently showed that parental satisfaction with the schools was high. But politically, it wasn't yet time to take on the battles that new legislation would bring.

The growing army of choice supporters, however, had a different idea. As Thompson was to learn during the PFSC school choice celebration at the

Milwaukee Area Technical College on October 29, 1994, the politically correct time is when demand is matched with opportunity and political expediency. Such was the case on this day, when after sitting through several skits by Black, White, and Hispanic children and presentations from Brother Bob and Zakiya Courtney, Governor Thompson was asked before the glare of television cameras, several hundred celebrants, and a half-dozen politicians to entertain the possibility of championing legislation to expand school choice to religious schools.

Obviously caught off guard by the staged event, which had been sold as an awards ceremony, Thompson seemed to be lost in thought for several moments before, smiling broadly, he announced that he would give the matter serious consideration. The outburst of applause signaled not only a recognition of his commitment but also an acknowledgment that once again the Freedom Train would be leaving the station.

SUCCESS IN THE SUPREME COURT

Three months later Governor Tommy Thompson announced he would introduce legislation to expand school choice to religious schools. His announcement was met with applause from the low-income community, although there was an undercurrent of concern that this battle would be much harder than the previous campaign, not just because of the constitutional questions that could easily derail the Freedom Train but also because the first time around we had caught the opposition unprepared. They had not only underestimated the depth of community support but also were astonished by our ability to establish a bipartisan and multi-ideological coalition. This time they would be prepared and were obviously willing to expend all munitions to win the war. And that included a propaganda war in which they would rally the White media against us and an all-out effort to break up the political coalition that benefited us the first time around.

Though the strategy for advancing the new choice program was similar to the original campaign, this time the road was much rockier; the teachers union and the American Civil Liberties Union were clamorous in their opposition to the new proposed legislation, and several key Democrats who were sponsors of the first bill, such as State Representative Spencer Coggs, were steadfastly opposed the second time around. Coggs said that he had reservations about the bill because he "feared it was unconstitutional." Coggs's rationale sparked a heated reaction from parents particularly after he said during a spring 1995 hearing that he had conferred with several prominent community elders who endorsed the measure, but that he still felt uncomfortable embracing it.

Gwen Moore, who had since been elected to the state senate, was much more vehement in her opposition to the new proposal and found herself under attack from PFSC. Like Coggs, she expressed reservations about the constitutionality of the measure as well as fears that the measure would have a negative impact on MPS. Moore also let it be known that she was a strong supporter of the MTEA, a fact that incensed many in the Black community who viewed the union as the greatest impediment to school reform.

Most of the negative and sometimes incendiary comments about Coggs and Moore were intentionally kept out of the Black media. As in the case of the initial choice movement, the *Milwaukee Community Journal* served as the primary source of community reporting on the campaign, and it was our decision not to publicly fuel unnecessary divisions. We made note of Coggs's and Moore's opposition and provided them with a forum when they asked for one, but generally saw no benefit in providing school choice opponents with more ammunition. Moreover, both Black lawmakers were valued soldiers in an ongoing war for Black empowerment and justice, and their contributions and leadership would be critical in other campaigns. To attack them over this issue could be self-defeating.

State Representative Antonio Riley, elected the year before, emerged as a more-than-adequate replacement for Spencer Coggs and Gwen Moore. Also an African American, Riley was eager to expend political capital advocating on behalf of the parents and community leadership who championed the expanded program, even to the point of antagonizing Democratic Party leadership. In fact, Riley's support cost him key committee appointments, prompting him to join Williams in blasting the Democratic Party leadership for "selling out to the teachers unions" over loyal Black supporters.

As it turned out, Williams's and Riley's support was helpful, but not necessary: as the governor had hoped, the Republicans took control of the assembly, and passage of the expanded school choice legislation was a foregone conclusion. Personally guided by Assembly Leader Scott Jensen, a former chief of staff to the governor who had made an unprecedented and rapid climb to his present position, a hearing on the measure on March 29, 1995, drew hundreds of low-income parents to Madison. As had been the case five years before, White out-state lawmakers were left with little doubt that school choice was not only viable, but a top priority of the urban poor, who saw it as a weapon to break the chains of mediocre education. Black parents showed up in large numbers for the hearing, and their presence was not ignored by the politicians, who always seem to be looking over their shoulders.

Six weeks later Williams introduced amendments to the legislation, including provisions to increase the number of participants from 3 to 7 percent of the MPS total and to allow low-income families with children already in private schools to participate (the provision which had been taken out of the original bill during the senate negotiations). She also amended the legislation to keep the funding tied to the state aids formula instead of shifting it to Chapter 220, a shrewd maneuver that increased the financial allocation to nearly $4,000.

Soon the governor expressed his support for her amendments, and one week later, on May 17, the Joint Finance Committee approved the measure by an 11-5 vote and included the proposal in the 1995 budget bill, where it was immediately passed. The ink didn't have time to dry before Thompson added his signature to the bill, making Wisconsin the first state in the country to enact a Religious School Choice Program.

Within two weeks, one hundred private schools had indicated their interest in participating in the program, and a central clearinghouse was receiving an average of one hundred calls a day from Milwaukee low-income families seeking registration information. If there was ever any doubt about the community's interest in the program, it was easily dismissed by the flood of calls.

Yet history was set to repeat itself in more ways than one.

Again the *Milwaukee Journal* and *Sentinel*, joined by the neoracist *Shepherd Express Weekly*, editorialized that school choice was a right-wing conspiracy to destroy or privatize public education and segregate the (already segregated) public schools, and would generally mean the end of the world—at the same time they admitted that the public school system was ineffective, the school board was rudderless and inept, and the MTEA presented a major obstacle in the advancement of education reforms. In essence, the White press was telling frustrated Black parents that the system was rigged against them, but to escape the plantation was not an option. Apparently, the message was "stay and suffer."

Department of Public Instruction head Herb Grover had since left office and was replaced by John Benson who, like his predecessor, made no secret of his support of and allegiance to the state teachers union. Following in Grover's footsteps, Benson responded to the passage of the religious school choice legislation with a tirade of insults and unsubstantiated prophecies of doom, including the prediction that racist groups and terrorists would start schools under the program. Although he, too, acknowledged the abysmal state of public education in Milwaukee, Benson made known his intent to undermine the program if possible. At one point he announced that he was hiring a special consultant to develop a reform plan for MPS. There was momentary hope from Milwaukee parents until it was discovered that the $20,000 "research and development grant" would be awarded to Maury Andrews, the former president of the state teachers union! Months later Andrews's recommendations were soundly rejected by all parties in the school reform debate, including the teachers union, although they would resurface three years later when the MTEA-controlled school board and the national missionary organization People for the American Way (PFAW) needed a diversion to offset the growing support for a breakup of MPS.

The response from the teachers union was also predictable: officials announced a lawsuit in conjunction with the ACLU to halt the program before it could get off the ground. This time, they were successful in getting an injunction—but not before several hundred parents had signed up for the program.

The injunction, filed in Madison Circuit Court, centered on the constitutionality of the new legislation. It bypassed the circuit courts and made a beeline for the Wisconsin Supreme Court, where it was stonewalled by a split court, 3-3, after Justice Ann Walsh Bradley withdrew. The split meant the case was sent to a lower court for consideration, where Religious School Choice was declared unconstitutional, although the judge maintained provisions expanding the program to fifteen thousand students.

Proponents, led by Clint Bolick and Governor Thompson, immediately appealed. And finally, on June 10, 1998, after weaving its way through the appeals process, the case was again heard by the Wisconsin Supreme Court, this time with a new member, Justice Patrick Crooks, who had replaced one of the antichoice justices. It seemed that the entire state took a deep breath as the court decided the case, analyzing testimony from representatives of the teachers union, the ACLU, and the choice army. Pundits had theorized that the court would rule in our favor because Crooks was considered a supporter of choice and, assuming that Bradley would again withdraw, the balance of power was in our favor. As it turned out, our prayers were answered, and on a bright sunny day in June the streets of Milwaukee's Central City looked a little brighter. The hopes of thousands of Black parents appeared closer to reality as another brick in the plantation wall crumbled.

The state supreme court's decision was met with cheers and tears during an impromptu celebration held at Messmer High School two days after the decision. It was an unusual gathering, drawing scores of low-income parents and their children along with activists including Howard Fuller and Zakiya Courtney and behind-the-scenes proponents such as Michael Joyce and even MPS Board Director John Gardner, one of three board members who publicly supported school choice.

WTMJ television and radio talk show host Charles Sykes received applause for raising funds for PAVE scholarships for low-income families and for his unwavering support for school choice and Black self-determination. Choice advocate Pilar Gonzales was honored for her tenacity and dedication to the cause. Praise was heaped on Fuller, George and Susan Mitchell, Williams, and the mayor. And, of course, we couldn't forget the thousands of parents who worked toward a goal that never should have been necessary in the first place in a country that touts itself as the land of equal opportunity and the greatest democracy on the planet. Under Brother Bob's ministerial lead, the community offered thanks to our God for leading us to a new Promised Land.

We recognized that the battle was far from over. Even as the national media converged upon Milwaukee to publicize the historic decision, they were quick to note that opponents had pledged to take the case to an even higher authority: the U.S. Supreme Court. But for now, there was victory and hope, and there were new choices for low-income parents. And, as Board Director Gardner noted, there would be movement on the part of the status quo to implement reforms in order to compete against the private schools they previously could ignore. What few reforms had been implemented in recent years were the response of an MPS board threatened by the Underground Railroad called school choice, Gardner noted during his comments. "There will be more movement now, and everyone will benefit as a result," he theorized.

A VOICE OF REASON

We had escaped the plantation, and not unlike our ancestors of 150 years ago, we find it necessary to keep looking over our shoulders, to make sure the slave catchers are not on our heels. There are some among us who believe the school choice victory will be taken away from us, even though the state supreme court has affirmed it. History has taught Black America not to assume we have achieved; the enemies of freedom are always waiting for an opportunity to steal our thunder, to reshackle us.

Indeed, that was the case in Milwaukee, where hope upon hope had been dashed, and victories, like North Division High School, were quietly taken away from us in the dim of night. It's hard to be optimistic in a society where Black victories are few and the rules of the game keep changing.

One grandmother who attended dozens of organizational meetings and rallies, but never really felt we would win the battle, made a deep impression upon me. She has been through the wars—both local and national—and while she is a "good Christian" filled with hope, history's hard lessons taught her to be pessimistic. This woman has lived through more struggles than any of us can imagine and has seen victories unfulfilled and promises unkept.

She once asked about the values of "people who would fight to keep another group of people from accessing a program that would improve their lives." She questioned the rationale of NAACP members who "are themselves the victims of race hatred and bigotry, but can stand like George Wallace blocking the door of educational opportunity for poor children." And she expressed curiosity about the future of a country in which, 150 years after the Emancipation Proclamation, Black people have to fight so hard just to "*think* about freedom. And then worry if what they give us will be taken away later. I seen it happen too many times. Don't they know that this country will never be good in God's eyes until those on the bottom have at least the same opportunities as those at the top. Let our God-given abilities not be hindered by bigotry or class or religion. But Lord, sometimes I don't think this country will make it."

I never knew the woman's name, and I haven't seen her in several years. She wasn't at the victory celebration and hasn't been to public hearings about charters that have followed our crusade. I hope the sister is doing well and that she's wrong about this victory and America. School choice has the potential of opening previously closed doors, of equalizing the equation, of spearheading a national movement that will end with America becoming the America that this grandmother and Dr. Martin Luther King Jr. and W. E. B. DuBois and Malcolm X envisioned. Maybe not a truly integrated society, but at least an interracial democracy. If not a melting pot, at least a Caesar salad in which all ingredients are equally important.

As for the School Choice Program, Howard Fuller said it best when he declared at a December 1998 educational reform rally, "We are not going back [to the way things were]. We're not giving up these gains, and we will not retreat. Hopefully, some day, the opponents of school choice [and] parental empowerment will be willing to sit at a table and honestly talk about what's good for all children. Maybe some day we won't need school choice. But until then, we're clenching this victory to our bosom and not letting go. We're not going backward ever again."[2]

Civil Rights and Wrongs

Who but parents would care more for their children's educational future? Who but villains would deny them this right? Who but hypocrites would exercise that right, yet deny it to others?

—Kevin J. Walker

The battle over the direction of the Civil Rights movement continues in a new theater, dominated by three contrasting ideologies offering Black America divergent paths to the Promised Land of freedom and equality. These ideologies are represented by the assimilationists, neoconservatives, and nationalists—opposing platforms advanced via political positions that I cautiously call the Black Left, Right, and Middle, respectively.

This analogy is not meant to be confused with the politically limiting categorization of liberal, conservative, and moderate, although there is parallelism. It should be understood that these often confusing and intentionally misleading labels carry different connotations in the Black community than they do in White society. A 1996 Joint Center for Political and Economic Studies National Opinion Poll on social attitudes revealed that most Black Americans are socially conservative while politically liberal.1 If you gave an average Black American a political quiz, chances are that he or she would respond like a conservative but deny membership in that group. Chances are he or she votes for a liberal Democrat, and admires and supports an Independent (yet assumes a vote for the Independent is a waste because the two-party system is too strong), but will probably never join any political party.

That contradiction is not as confusing as it would appear. On issues like crime—where we are more often the victims—as well as nuclear family structures, abortion, and vouchers for religious schools, Black people take what could be considered conservative positions, even though we don't call them such.

Politically, African Americans primarily vote Democratic because that party has upheld our rights, protected us through the use of federal troops when necessary, and opened doors of opportunity through the courts over the last four decades. The Republicans have essentially stood by during—or under the administration of Ronald Reagan have openly fought—civil rights initiatives, sanctions against the racist apartheid South African government, and even a national holiday for Dr. Martin Luther King Jr., an action that many viewed as being symbolic of the GOP's callousness toward racial harmony.

But remove the labels and you find that most African Americans advocate nonpolitical solutions to the socioeconomic ills that hold back Black America. Supporters of school choice have been accused of being pawns of conservatives, when in fact they view school choice as a progressive initiative that empowers poor parents. It is also well known that the basic tenets of Black nationalism—strong cultural values, advocacy of the traditional nuclear family, and self-determination—can be construed as conservative tenets. Indeed, one is hard-pressed not to typecast Black historical figures from Marcus Garvey to Minister Farrakhan as conservative, despite their distrust and rejection of America's two dominant political parties. Malcolm X, for example, espoused limited government intrusion into the affairs of the Black community (save for removing racist barriers), family values, and disdain for immorality, including fornication and out-of-wedlock births. Where would you place him on the "political" scale? Would his rhetoric have been less truthful, or his support base less entrenched had he someday declared himself a Republican, or a conservative? Actually, because of the confusion over the meaning of those terms, and Black America's inability or unwillingness to look beyond the labels ourselves, we are as much a victim of political typecasting as the rest of society.

A case in point: several years ago the League of Martin, a fraternal and activist group of Black police officers in Milwaukee headed by Black nationalist Leonard Wells, invited PBS broadcaster and economic empowerment advocate Tony Brown to be the keynote speaker at the organization's annual dinner. Brown, highly regarded in the African American community, particularly among the Black middle class, received three standing ovations for his comments, most of which outlined his philosophy as detailed in his book *Black Lies, White Lies*. After his presentation, a Black officer with whom I was seated called Brown "one of the most revolutionary visionaries" he had ever heard. I agreed, adding that it was too bad some folks couldn't see beyond his membership in the Republican Party. As soon as I made that pronouncement, the brother's demeanor changed 180 degrees, and he fell just short of calling Brown an Uncle Tom by association.

Such is the dichotomy of Black America—a dichotomy that underscores the power of the propaganda machine and the efforts of Democrats and mass media to politically paralyze the Black community by establishing false and misleading categorizations.

LIBERALS, MODERATES, CONSERVATIVES

Clearly, conventional political/ideological labels don't describe Black America very well, but it may be useful to note briefly how these terms are perceived and interpreted within the Black community.

The term liberal is often associated with left-of-center Whites and Jews—not to be confused with progressives—who advocate on behalf of and often in spite of Black people, but are generally in tune with the downtrodden on many issues. Also under the category of liberal are those Whites who often have a patronizing attitude toward Black people. Among this group are apologists whose oft-condescending remarks are rooted in unacknowledged racial prejudice.

To their immediate political left are the socialists and communists, both of whom have histories of supporting traditional civil rights issues such as police brutality and institutional racism. Although they too often enter the debate with a self-righteous indignation and paternalistic attitudes, they generally have a better feel for the fundamental Black liberal issues of justice and equality.

The term missionary refers to White liberals who try to impose their culture or values on Black America. They are the liberal moralists and often the poverty pimps—those who profit from social welfare programs. Even though missionaries are supposedly people of good will, the word missionary has acquired a negative connotation. There is a West African proverb that frames many cultural nationalists' perceptions about missionaries:

And first they sent in the missionaries, who told us we were savages and were worshipping the wrong God.

And so they gave us their God, and then they taught us how to pray. And then they told us to pray with our eyes closed and our hands clasped together.

And we listened and did as told and opened our eyes to discover the chains around our wrists and our country stolen from under us.

Though seldom referenced in Black political or social circles, moderate describes anyone who is not liberal or conservative, whose political philosophy is more centrist, embracing elements of the left and the right. But the term encompasses more than that.

Just as black is the accumulation of all colors, moderate is in many respects the accumulation of various philosophies of the left and right that fall under the umbrella of Black empowerment and self-determination. Black/cultural nationalists are, in my analogy, essentially moderates. While most embrace so-called conservative causes as being pro–nuclear family, they may also be pro-choice when it comes to abortion. A moderate may be tough on crime (as most African Americans are) but opposed to the death penalty and may advocate programs dealing with the socioeconomic factors fueling crime. Black moderates promote a color-blind society while embracing affirmative action, realizing that America is a long way from a nonracial utopia (Dr. Martin Luther King Jr.'s dream). Moderates are generally politically independent, pragmatic, sensitive, and open-minded.

One can assume that most White Americans fall within this category. Like most Americans, they harbor some prejudice, and are usually nationalistic in their worldview. They will be quick to say they are not narrow-minded or intolerant, although they will generally put White America before America in general—and surely before Black America. They are primarily Christian and would most likely feel more comfortable in a White segregated church than in an integrated one, although that is not an issue of racism but one of custom and culture.

The label of conservative has taken on a distinct albeit misleading connotation in the Black community. A Black conservative, for example, is automatically assumed to be a Republican, while a White conservative is thought to be a racist. A White Democratic conservative, as many of the Southern bigots labeled themselves, is apparently an excusable enigma. Little thought is given to these Southern Democrats, who were at the forefront of the anti-Black Civil Rights movement campaigns of the '60s and '70s. That philosophy and mindset, which continues today, has apparently been forgotten by black assimilationists, who view the Democratic Party as the only acceptable political avenue for Black America.

Republicans are generally thought to be mean-spirited middle- and upper-class professionals, their policies anti-Black and antipoor. Many in the Black community erroneously assume that Black conservatives are by association "House Negroes," or sellouts. Indeed, remove the political label and you'll find many of Black America's greatest leaders would be considered conservative today. Malcolm X and Booker T. Washington are the most obvious. Minister Louis Farrakhan, arguably the most powerful and influential Black leader of the last decade, fits the profile, although he publicly offers nothing but disdain for both Democrats and Republicans.

Too many Black Americans have allowed the media and Black gatekeepers to pigeonhole conservative ideology to political categories, when our culture embraces tenets of each major ideology. According to the 1996 Joint Center for Political and Economic Studies national opinion poll,

> Although Blacks overwhelmingly consider themselves Democrats, they divide themselves fairly evenly into thirds under the labels of liberal, moderate, and conservative.
>
> Young people in both the Black and the general population are more apt than their elders to identify themselves as Republicans; this does not constitute evidence of a trend among Blacks toward joining the GOP, however.[2]

The study showed that, for the most part, Black Americans agree with the general population on economic matters, crime, and social welfare, but they favor smaller tax cuts than do Whites. Self-categorization aside, it is safe to say that most African Americans would fall within the category of "moderate."

Putting generic political labels on African Americans does us a disservice because our worldview, experiences, and history in this country have forced upon us a unique perspective that defies common civic definition. Clearly, traditional categorization doesn't adequately capture the political views of the African-American community. However, the lines are drawn more definitively regarding the three dominant Black ideologies: assimilationism, neoconservatism, and nationalism.

ASSIMILATIONISTS: THE BLACK LEFT

The most publicized position is offered by familiar—albeit increasingly suspect—faces who essentially offer tired tactics that begin and end with cultural and political assimilation. Their greatest advantage is not in leadership, and surely not in their recent track record, but in their partnership with status quo political machinery, the liberal White media, and, ironically, various labor factions with a vested interest in maintaining a veiled apartheid-state status quo.

For my reference, the Black Left (at the gate) consists of the assimilationists/integrationists, liberal Democrats, reformists, and socialists/communists. The Left includes Rev. Jesse Jackson, Manning Marable, and Rep. Maxine Waters.

NEOCONSERVATIVES: THE BLACK RIGHT

Neoconservatives represent the moral vanguard. They deem it best to take a higher ground in the struggle for justice and equal opportunity, bearing a flag oft smeared with political ink. Complementing the Black Right's moral imperatives are calls for market-based solutions through entrepreneurship and reinvestment in the Black community: Black America can only secure its position of equity through hard work, sacrifice, an enlightened entrepreneurial spirit, and adherence to the tenets of capitalism. Add a strong spiritual component and you have the cornerstone of neoconservative ideology.

The Black Right(eous) includes neoconservatives, conservatives, and religious moralists who see the path to complete integration blocked by African Americans' own ethical weaknesses, cultural deficiencies, and lack of a work ethic. The Black Right includes Walter Williams, Shelby Steele, and Tony Brown.

NATIONALISTS: THE BLACK MIDDLE

Today, in ever-growing communities around the country, the voices of the assimilationists and neoconservatives are being drowned out by nationalistic cries. Nationalists look inward for strength, moral imperatives, and leadership, working to strengthen what is commonly perceived as a nation within a nation. Nationalists aim for control of institutions in their community, the empowerment of their children through culturally and technologically grounded education, and a program of cooperative economics that will result in job creation and community revitalization. They also advocate that the movement to solve socioeconomic problems within the Black community must be led, orchestrated, and implemented by Black people for Black people.

This Black Middle (passage) includes Black nationalists, Pan-Africanists, and independent political pragmatists who embrace what is commonly referred to as the Black Power movement agenda. The Black Middle includes Conrad Worrill, Mulana Karenga, and Minister Louis Farrakhan and was born of a school of visionaries that included Malcolm X, Marcus Garvey, Stokely Carmichael (Kwame Ture), and Booker T. Washington.

Nationalism covers a wide spectrum of philosophy, action, methodology, and strategy, even incorporating some elements of assimilation and conservatism. In often conflicting works, writers and social scientists ranging from Robert Smith and Harold Cruise to Wilson Jeremiah Moses have examined nationalism's parameters, assessing that it ranges from tacit involvement in community campaigns such as the integration crusades of Frederick Douglass and Dr. Martin Luther King Jr., to the advocacy for a separate state as espoused by Nation of Islam founder Elijah Muhammad to Marcus Garvey's Back to Africa Movement. Historians and sociopolitical scientists agree that a central theme runs through the various degrees of nationalism: self-determination and a conviction that Black solidarity is key to progressive change in America. By that measurement, one of the country's first nationalistic movements was led by Richard Allen in the late eighteenth century. Allen refused to abide by a Methodist Church requirement that Black and Whites pray separately, and led his fellow Black parishioners out of the Philadelphia Church to start the country's first African Methodist Episcopal Church.

True nationalists differ from the Kings, A. Philip Randolphs, Jesse Jacksons, and Julian Bonds in that we believe that the systemic racism that undergirds American culture has kept the playing field drastically uneven, and we are convinced by lesson of history that Black Americans must lead and control the movement to reach equality. That does not mean that we dwell on racism or use it as an excuse or that we occupy ourselves with some grand moral imperative to Christianize the Christians. Like Allen, we continue to leave our church and mosque doors open to all, but we don't have a problem with praying among our own—or with following the tenets of a Black Jesus.

Some Whites (and Blacks) are afraid of nationalism, mistakenly subscribing to the idea that it is anti-American and anti-White and advocates the overthrow of the government. Although some nationalists have given up hope of a nonracial, multicultural society, this fear is essentially baseless. Some nationalists believe that White America will never allow African Americans to truly integrate, and thus an African American's life must be one of either survival or separatism. Simply put, who wants to live next to, associate with, or waste energy chasing a dream deferred? Better to make the break.

But that doesn't mean that what's good for Black America isn't also good for America. For all intents and purposes, Black Americans hold dual citizenship. This is a signal that the solutions to the problems facing our community can and must be solved by us through self-empowerment, community revitalization, and cooperative economics. If successful, those efforts will result in strong communities and strong families, and will serve to break the cycle of poverty and despair in the Black community. Black nationalists are willing to address the sociocultural issues facing Black America including immorality, the dissolution of nuclear family, the deterioration of values and mores, and the proliferation of drugs and violence. Our solutions are rooted in African-centered mechanisms and a pragmatic ideology that if embraced widely will reverse the genocidal path we're following by removing the cloud of slavery that hovers over us. Integrationism has been compromised and for a variety of reasons has not addressed the key issues facing Black Americans. Black conservatives have not found a foothold in the community, and have limited appeal because of their association with political accommodation. That clearly leaves but one widely accepted—albeit often misidentified—philosophy.

Nationalists seek the right to control their own destinies. We reject the victim-ization politics of the Left and the NAACP as well as the assimilationist politics of the Left and Right, choosing instead to focus our energies and efforts on campaigns of empowerment, cultural grounding, and spiritual connection. Nationalists—like Jewish people, most Third World immigrants, and Asian Americans—believe in community building: if all things are equal, vote Black, buy Black, and glorify Black. We don't apologize for that—no more than Jews apologize for supporting their own, Iranian or Indian immigrants make excuses for forming co-ops to run Central City businesses, or Asian or Hispanic Americans ask pardon for their fight to maintain their languages and cultures. In fact, we should be able and eager to send our chil-dren to African schools, to keep alive our culture and connection to the Motherland.

Nationalists do not seek special favors or rewards. We will be the first to fight for America and democracy, but also the first to criticize bigotry and persecution of people of color. We strongly subscribe to the credo of the Black press, now the motto of the National Newspaper Publishers Association: "The Black Press believes that America can best lead the world away from racial and national antagonism when it accords to every person, regardless of race, color or creed, full human and legal rights. Hating no person, fearing no person, the Black Press strives to help every person in the firm believe that all are hurt as long as anyone is held back."

Unlike assimilationists and integrationists, nationalists are not afraid of alien-ating White sponsors by rejecting their advice and direction. Indeed, nationalists recognize that government and the White Establishment are part of the problem. As Frederick Douglass noted, power begets nothing without demand.

As Sterling Stuckey puts it, nationalism emphasizes "the need for Black people to rely primarily on themselves in vital areas of life—economic, political, religious and intellectual—in order to affect their liberation."[3]

In his eye-opening presentation at the Martin Luther King Jr. Commemorative Program at Michigan State University in January 1999, social activist Robert Smith hypothesized that there are six basic principles of nationalism: group solidarity and self-reliance ("only Blacks in the end can secure their freedom, no matter how great the support from their allies"); truth-telling (about White supremacy and racial dom-ination as well as Black failings); the importance of Black culture; race first; rejection of the pitfalls of a social movement, including chauvinism, cultural extremism, and religious extremism; and preserving and nurturing zones of institutional autonomy in the areas of education, media, religion, culture, and economics.

Those philosophically linked to integrationist and assimilationist agendas may in fact embrace several of these principles, even while disavowing nationalism as being too radical.

TEARING DOWN THE BARRIERS: DESEGREGATION

Each of the aforementioned ideologies offers a fundamentally different approach to the problems plaguing the Black population. The most revealing contrasts can be seen in the opposing views of the Black civil rights groups and the Black Left and Right over school desegregation.

As the 1992 U.S. Commission on Civil Rights study on Milwaukee's school desegregation program revealed, there was no pot of academic gold at the end of the rainbow. Desegregation has not resulted in integration or in better education. Throughout America, desegregation undermined neighborhood schools, which, although inequitably financed, held neighborhoods together and empowered more Black students than they are able to today. Equally important, the neighborhood schools provided for parental involvement in the educational process. Busing for desegregation meant a slow deterioration of the communal structure.

Despite evidence to the contrary, the Black Left views desegregation—which it erroneously continues to call integration—as a cure-all, the single most important wedge to hold open the door to equal opportunity and brotherhood. The Black Middle and Right see school desegregation for what it is. They know that neighborhood schools are essential public institutions that directly empower parents and define the community.

In *Black Lies, White Lies* Tony Brown suggests desegregation and neighborhood schools are not mutually exclusive. Desegregation, he surmises, means equality and choice. Its fundamental premise is tearing down the barriers—primarily those of salary, experience, and tenure. That does not mean the movement of bodies, which, unless it goes both ways, is another form of racism. If the most tenured teachers are not evenly dispersed, if White busing does not equal Black busing, if school facilities are not evenly distributed, then you still have segregation. Integration in such a context is a lie.

Locally, this scenario has played out with Black leaders such as Polly Williams and Howard Fuller in league with what some consider the Right and Walter Farrell and Black Democratic politicians such as State Senator Gwen Moore on the Left. With parental school choice as the fulcrum, the contrast could not be more startling. We can either continue down the path of educational mediocrity, placing our hopes and dreams for the future at the feet of the status quo (which has responded to our cries only with placebos and false promises) or chart our own course and shift the power paradigm—first through school choice, then through other efforts to control dollars and cultural sense.

POSITIONS ON SCHOOL CHOICE

School choice also provides a perfect point of departure to assess ideologies. Civil libertarians, Democrats, and those who belong to left-of-center political parties hypocritically oppose school choice on one of three grounds: (1) it will lead to further segregation, (2) it will hurt the public school system, that is, weaken the stranglehold of the teachers union or jeopardize the job security of teachers, educrats, and poverty pimps, or (3) it runs contrary to the constitutional provision of separation of church and state.

While condemning parental school choice, often calling it part of a vast right-wing conspiracy, the Left offers no solutions for the abysmal failure of the public school system and the harm it has reaped on literally millions of minority and poor children. They often ignore or brush aside the growing chorus of activists and educators such as Asa Hilliard who offer their own, more credible conspiracy theory: the failure of the public school has been plotted by entities who want to maintain the American apartheid system. Teachers unwittingly participate in this grand scheme, as do educrats who can't see the truth because it is blanketed in pension programs and administrative perks. Assimilationists are accessories before and after the fact through their silence and coalition with the conspirators.

The Black Middle (nationalists and Pan-Africanists) endorses school choice not only as the ultimate civil rights issue of the 1990s but also as an empowering mechanism for the urban poor in particular and African Americans in general. School choice allows a larger percentage of Black children to enroll in independent African-centered educational institutions or value-based religious, Montessori, or college preparatory schools. To the Black nationalist/Pan-Africanist, school choice can be an important tool in the campaign to break the shackles of educational apartheid, allowing us the opportunity to educate our own, thus opening the doors of opportunity for a new generation. Obviously, public schools will always serve as the primary educational tool for Black Americans; there are a finite number of school choice seats, even after the program's expansion to include religious schools. But here, too, school choice serves a dual purpose: sparking competition and accountability while educating the have-nots on the importance of community control of institutions.

Because the systems are themselves corrupted by entrenched bureaucracy and caste system politics, site-based management proves the best decentralization method—an important step in nation building, which is the central goal of Black nationalism. Because it shifts power and control from the educrats and poverty pimps to the people, site-based management is an obvious threat to the status quo.

The Black Right supports school choice because it breaks the stranglehold of an educational monopoly that has too long ignored the cries for educational reform and taxpayer-marketplace accountability. School choice is also a moral issue; it questions how society can limit or deny opportunities to a class of people because of their economic status. In a paradoxical sense, school choice is the ultimate example of affirmative action, opening the doors of opportunity to those victimized by apartheid. Additionally, the Black Right believes that school choice can provide at-risk children with opportunities that will deter them from antisocial behavior. It can break the shackles of poverty and its manifestations—crime, violence, and even out-of-wedlock births—by providing children with a solid education foundation, social mores, and (in the case of African-centered schools) a cultural imperative.

In the view of the Black Right, school choice can serve as the catalyst for systematic reforms that can reverse decades of sociocultural deterioration. It will provide thousands who otherwise would be denied quality education with what Malcolm X called a passport out of deprivation and despair. School choice will empower not only the students but also their parents and communities, giving them a place at the table of economic and cultural parity.

POWER STRUGGLES: BLACK LEFT VS. BLACK MIDDLE

The Black Right has yet to establish a significant base in the African-American community, although Republican support and access to the media (particularly talk radio) has in many ways provided it with a forum much greater than that of the Black nationalists. Some White Christian fundamentalists who plead common cause over issues such as morality, abortion, and family values have sought inroads into the Black Right, but have not been successful to any noticeable degree in the African-American religious community. However, the fundamentalist Baptist Church continues to have a large following in the Black community, and spokespersons such as Reggie White of the Green Bay Packers are warmly embraced.

It is commonly assumed that the Black Left and Middle hold the greatest credibility in Black America, and it is from these two conflicting philosophies that most Black leadership and support emerges. Black nationalism (the Middle) is emerging as the standard-bearer, backed by an ever-increasing majority of Black grassroots activists and poor urban residents.

One of the most illuminating contrasts between the Black Left and Middle is provided by two former Black congressmen Kweisi Mfume and Rev. Floyd Flake, who as liberal and loyal Democrats followed the party platform while in the United

States Congress. They endorsed an agenda that essentially echoed the platform espoused by the Black Congressional Caucus. Upon leaving Congress, however, Mfume and Rev. Flake took opposite paths: Mfume took over the helm of the floundering NAACP, vowing not only to continue its mission of advocacy of traditional civil rights issues and assimilationist agenda but also to reenergize the organization, reversing a spiraling national influence and credibility in the Black community. Rev. Flake, however, followed a more pragmatic path, one grounded in Black nationalism and the realization that little would change for the masses of African Americans as long as they were aligned with either major political party. Instead, Black America must look inward for wisdom, strength, and solutions to social ills. Thus, while Mfume clothed himself in a traditional assimilationist checkerboard flag, Rev. Flake adorned a Kente cloth robe and waved the Black liberation flag of self-determination and Black Power.

Mfume and Rev. Flake's positions on school choice epitomized the variance in their philosophies: Rev. Flake viewed the initiative as a boon to the community, while Mfume and the NAACP sided with groups such as People for the American Way that seek to sacrifice black children to the failing status quo as long as there remains even a glimmer of hope of achieving the goal of a raceless society.

NATIONALIST SUPPORT: REVEREND FLOYD FLAKE

Rev. Flake left Congress inspired to empower Black America through economic development and educational initiatives, much like Robert Woodson of the National Center for Neighborhood Enterprise and others who were dismayed by the economic backslide of African Americans over the last forty years. His years in Congress brought him to a frustrating realization: national policies, whether Democratic or Republican, brought few immediate benefits to the millions who struggled for day-to-day existence. Perhaps the church could do at a local level what lawmakers and traditional Black leadership—however well intentioned—could not or would not do.

Stressing a formula of self-actualization, Rev. Flake's church, Allen African Methodist Episcopal, has undertaken a major economic and educational development program that has transformed its Queens, New York, neighborhood. Rev. Flake's philosophy, in many respects reminiscent of Booker T. Washington's—with undercurrents of Garveyism—centers on improving social and economic conditions through reinforcement of moral and cultural values and reinvestment of Black capital in the Black community, including job creation. Self-determination and self-help will instill pride, self-worth, and a sense of community and purpose.

His is a simple premise: A Black dollar must touch four Black hands before departing the community, and this community will consist of a people who pray with each other, don't prey on each other, and see themselves as descendants of greatness. A Black church that hires a Black construction firm can ensure that goal. The dollars touch the hand of the congregation leader, the construction owner, the Black supplier, and the Black worker. A Black bank and Black insurance company complete the cycle.

During a summer 1998 speech in Milwaukee, Rev. Flake implored Black clerics to "cast down their buckets where they are" in the tradition of Booker T. Washington—to rebuild their communities, set moral imperatives, and "educate our own to become productive citizens." Waiting for others—including White philanthropists, traditional civil rights groups, or the government—to solve Black problems is a fruitless venture that has left the Black community's agenda devoid of economic stability and its people caught in an abyss of low self-esteem and moral turpitude, continued Rev. Flake.

He asserted that by aligning themselves with traditional coalitions, the civil rights leadership has abdicated its responsibility to Black America and instead allowed others, some of whom have conflicting agendas, to set our course. As a result, Black America continues to wallow in despair, while others have benefited from programs earmarked for Black Americans. Affirmative action, although a noble and just concept and potentially effective mechanism, is not a cure-all for what ails Black America. It benefits White women more than any other group and aids very few Black Americans. Likewise, the liberal philosophy agenda is not necessarily Black America's agenda, and by focusing our efforts solely on Democratic Party initiatives instead of those that empower the Black community directly, Black leaders have subjugated our campaign for equality.

Rev. Flake took some flack for the latter hypothesis when he encouraged Black New Yorkers to split their vote among Democrats and Republicans during the 1998 congressional elections. His premise was simple: we are taken for granted by the Democrats and ignored by the Republicans. A 20 percent Black Republican vote would result in a net loss to the Democrats, forcing a new respect and accountability. Conversely, any entrance into the GOP will open new political doors and provide access to the power brokers.

Similarly, Rev. Flake surmises that school choice speaks to the new Black agenda of self-empowerment. Like most African Americans, the former congressman soundly rejects the oft-heard public-school premise that Black children are somehow educationally deficient, that poverty has affected Black children so adversely that they cannot compete—unless, perhaps, they sit next to White children and something happens to rub off.

Bull! Poor Black children do not learn because no one teaches them, or because teachers have low expectations for them, or because bureaucracies and burdensome regulations block the efforts of good teachers. That system continues because people are afraid to challenge the entrenched status quo.

Said Rev. Flake in an article in *Policy Review* entitled "No Excuses for Failing Our Children,"

> The current political order is unwilling to rock the boat. Co-conspiring politicians remain wedded to a system of waste and mediocrity because of the fund-raising prowess of teachers unions and other interest groups. Inner-city politicians, whose children more often than not attend private schools or the best public schools, are protecting a system that discourages reforms, chokes choice, and ultimately condemns children to a life of social and economic dysfunction.
>
> I am not against public schools. I am against unresponsive and irresponsible public schools where educational mediocrity goes unchallenged. I am against public schools that only expect the least from our children. I am against public schools where improvement is stifled by strict union rules and regulations. I am against public schools that imitate the despair of their surrounding neighborhoods and fail to conquer that despair with the tools of learning and the virtue of hope.
>
> There is no excuse for this. Poor children can learn. Set the standards high, and children will meet those standards.[4]

Vouchers can be instrumental in reversing a social and political condition that has left the Black community economically and culturally paralyzed. Rev. Flake understands the difference between education and learning, as well as the importance of controlling both processes. We are one of the only ethnic groups in this country that allows others to teach its children, and it is not coincidental that African Americans and Hispanics are seemingly the only ethnic groups suffering from educational morass.

Controlling the education process ensures that children will have not only a sound educational foundation but also a moral compass to guide them throughout life. Rev. Flake, at the vanguard of a more progressive and pragmatic Black leadership, challenged those in positions of power to reassess their positions, to analyze where the so-called Freedom Train has taken us and where the traditional coalitions with White missionary organizations have gotten us—and then to make appropriate changes.

Rev. Flake said that if you're happy with the state of America and believe allocating more funds to welfare is going to empower Black women, then so be it. If you believe tolerating or turning your back on out-of-wedlock births and single-parent households is the key to self-empowerment and equal rights, then follow that path. If instead you would like to make serious gains in jobs creation, Black business growth, cultural pride, and family stability, then another path must be followed. It must be one led by us and exclusively for us. Only through a position of strength may one stand eye-to-eye with both allies and enemies. That cannot occur when one side or the other is on its knees.

Religious school choice targets taxpayer funds—our so-called public money—to institutions that we control. School choice puts poor Black children from broken families in loving, nurturing environments. That less-fortunate Americans should be denied an opportunity to avail themselves of educational opportunities accessible to the wealthy is immoral. For those who block the schoolhouse door to then claim that they are our friends, that they care for our well-being, is immoral.

School choice should be advanced in spite of this hypocrisy, avows Rev. Flake. Black America must take a leadership role in advancing programs that benefit Black children. Far too long we have allowed others to miseducate our children. And where has it gotten us?

ASSIMILATIONIST OPPOSITION: KWEISI MFUME AND THE NAACP

Beset by financial instability and declining membership, the nation's most renowned civil rights group found itself taking a back seat during the early 1990s to the bolder and more progressive nationalist groups, including the Nation of Islam, the National Black United Front, and the African American Leadership Summit. Compounding the NAACP's problem was the perception among many younger, less-patient, and less-obliging African Americans that the organization's mission had run its course.

Many felt that the days of marching to achieve integration, lobbying for civil rights legislation, or combating gerrymandering practices were all but over, while direct action through community building—economic development, cultural consciousness, and a new war against inadequate urban public schools—was the tactic of the day. School desegregation had not achieved its goals of enhanced and equitable educational opportunity. The social welfare programs of the '60s and '70s had not catapulted Black Americans into the economic mainstream.

Indeed, those battlefield strategies, while worthwhile in many respects, served only to take Black America to the starting line—winning the race would require a wholly different philosophy, one that many felt had more to do with training the athlete than focusing on the conditions of the track or the (political) climate. Some suggest that we have not admitted to losing this race, even though the evidence—entrenched poverty, dysfunctional families, an ever-widening gap between Black and White middle class, teen pregnancy, academic impotency—stare us in the face.

Some nationalists went so far as to suggest that the Left's strategy was to teach Black Americans to run like Whites, become bosom buddies with the referees. If the African-centered and historical culture of Black heritage had to be tossed aside, then so be it; they were willing to doff their red, black, and green track uniforms and cut their dreads or naturals (and use skin lightener if available). Second-generation Black Americans consider such ideas a sellout, a "White-ice-gets-colder" denial of culture and heritage.

One of the best analyses of the NAACP/assimilation philosophy is offered by Amos N. Wilson in his groundbreaking work, *Blueprint for Black Power*:

Besides seeking to attain full and equal civil rights, the groups which make up the assimilationist leadership establishment see the integration or assimilation of Blacks into virtually all social areas with Whites as their ultimate social and political goal. Their penultimate goal appears to be that of total psycho-social, politico-economic merging of Blacks with Whites to the point where the Black community will lose its ethnic identity, residential and cultural distinctiveness, self-reference and visibility as an African people or as a community of persons of African descent. They seek to not be seen as possessing "color" but to be characterized in deracialized abstract terms.

The moralistic coloring of this leadership establishment follows from its belief that separation by race is morally reprehensible, that ethnic exclusivity is morally unconscionable. More pertinent, however, is its belief that racism, especially in the form of White supremacy and all that it implies, represents a fundamentally moral problem—a problem founded on racial prejudice, stereotypes, deviations from Christian ethics, and lack of racial or humanistic enlightenment and moral will. The assimilationist/moralistic establishment essentially overlooks the economic rationale for one race dominating another. Consequently, while pursuing legal and legislative remedies for racial discrimination, while vigorously protesting racial injustice, this group advocates what Cornel West calls the "the politics of conversion," or a "love ethic." [5]

Wilson goes on to charge that the failure and/or refusal of the NAACP to realize ethnically based, sociocultural, politico-economic plans for African-American people—"things essential to their survival and advancement"—has hindered and supplanted the effectiveness or relevancy of the groups:

> In fact, these organizations have a history of opposing and seeing the drafting and execution of such plans as racist, nationalistic, separatist and self-segregating. While this opposition may point to a lack of confidence in the idea that such developmental plans are intellectually and organizationally achievable or desirable for Africans, it appears to be motivated more by the unfounded belief that the inevitable assimilation of Blacks and Whites will make such efforts on the part of Blacks unnecessary. By becoming indistinguishable from Whites, Blacks would thereby automatically inherit the power, prestige, privilege and material advantages Whites already enjoy. Thus, the pursuit of power by Blacks, which would require the full active development of ethnically based organizations and institutions, is perceived as counterproductive, as a hindrance to racial merger—the supreme goal of Black assimiliationists.
>
> Consequently, the assimilationist leadership is terrified by the Black Power movement. It readily allies itself with dominant Whites to mortally combat such. Evidently, a racial balance of power that can protect the human rights and ensure the exercise of freedom and justice of Blacks presents an undesirable alternative to what is a patently false race-merging fantasy, a delusion having absolutely no substantiating foundation in human history.[6]

Wilson's assessment is perceptive and accurate and complements famed social critic John Killens's "Declaration on Integration" in his book *Beyond the Angry Black:*

> Integration comes after liberation. A slave cannot integrate with his master. In the whole history of revolts and revolutions, integration has never been the main slogan of the revolution. The oppressed fights to free himself from his oppressor, not to integrate with him. Integration is the step after freedom when the freedman makes up his mind as to whether he wishes to integrate with his former master.[7]

Nationalists have made such inroads because most post-Civil Rights movement Black Americans recognize the folly of trying to ignore their ancestral heritage.

They have graduated from colleges with Kente cloth mortarboards, given their children African names, and attended churches where the choir sings draped in African robes—often with an African-featured Jesus, Joseph, and Mary beautifully smiling down upon the congregation. The NAACP's inattention to the demands of this new generation has cost them dearly.

Under Mfume's predecessor, Ben Chavis, the NAACP took bold steps to address the generation gap regarding Black youth. Chavis, engineer of this giant step to the Right, had angered the traditional civil rights community by partnering with Nation of Islam leader Minister Louis Farrakhan and National Black United Front (NBUF) president Conrad Worrill on several empowerment campaigns. Eventually Chavis abandoned the NAACP assimilationist agenda, espousing a more pragmatic and empowering philosophy of Black nationalism. In 1995, he publicly allied with Minister Farrakhan, first as a coordinator of the Million Man March and later in an attempt to create an independent political party under the flag of the African American Leadership Summit. The latter effort was considered a major threat to the civil rights hierarchy and its core support base, the Democratic Party, labor unions, White missionary liberals.

Chavis's transition from an integrationist who followed the traditional NAACP/liberal left agenda of gradual assimilation to a Black Power nationalist advocating self-determination and self-reliance sent shock waves through the NAACP and its base support, although to many it was a refreshing metamorphosis signaling a new direction for the traditional Civil Rights movement. To the millions who viewed the NAACP agenda as outdated, myopic, and out of touch and its policies patronizing and complacent, Chavis's push for self-empowerment through actualization of a Black agenda (versus continuing under White liberal leadership) was a breath of fresh air. But to the NAACP leadership—and to funding sources and support mechanisms—it was a devastating blow and a threat to the status quo.

Chavis's days were numbered, and even as he found himself submerged in a sexual harassment controversy, it was obvious that his all-too-brief marriage to the nation's oldest civil rights organization would end in a quick annulment, if not a divorce. The NAACP hierarchy, however, did see the value in Chavis's militant tone and rapport with Black youth. His call for Black empowerment struck a chord with both the hip-hop generation and with many of their parents who embraced Malcolm X as their hero and who saw the failed integration and victimization politics as barriers to true intrusion in America's melting pot.

Thus the NAACP sought out and induced a successor to Chavis who could relate, who could talk the talk of the streets, yet sing from the NAACP hymnbook.

Mfume, a former street hustler and high school dropout turned college student activist, radio disc jockey, and politician, fit the bill.

Mfume brought dynamism and a new slant to an old agenda. The mere fact that the former New Yorker had an African name and traveled a long way from "the mean streets to the mainstream" (as the subtitle of his book *No Free Ride* implies) signaled a more culturally attuned awareness. Mfume added a perception of grassroots concerns that had long been missing from an organization essentially directed and financed by liberal Whites. Hopefully, the stylish, hip-talking Mfume understood where young Black America was coming from and would translate that culture into collective action.

However, while Mfume's rhetoric was certainly fiery, the NAACP's core platform and methodology remained the same. Mfume quickly retreated from Chavis's nationalistic platform. Not surprisingly, within weeks of assuming the presidency in February 1995, he issued a scathing attack on vouchers, which he called an affront to public education and a conspiratorial plot by right-wing conservatives to destroy America's public education system (the country's only true vestige of socialism) and replace it with some unknown but surely ominous private enterprise.

Mfume's tirades against empowering low-income parents with educational choice have continued. The NAACP president stated in a People for the American Way newsletter drafted and circulated in Milwaukee in 1998:

> Publicly funded vouchers will skim off the best students—those whom private schools find desirable for their own reasons. Since families will have to make up additional costs, those in the upper- and middle-income brackets will be helped the most. . . .
>
> Skin color, religion, economic class, language group, need for remedial work—all these things would be barriers to acceptance and success in a system designed around the choices of the private schools, not the choices of parents and students.
>
> Education must be a fundamental guarantee for each child, and for our nation's precious democracy. Once again, we are called upon to stand up on behalf of our children and to fight back.[8]

What is most startling about Mfume's statements is his obvious willingness to perpetuate several blatant lies. Milwaukee's school choice program, as he well knows, does not skim off the best students, because the system is set up for random selections of low-income families, and it is not the schools that pick the students, but the parents who choose the schools. There are no additional costs, because participating schools must accept the state aid as the sole tuition supplement, whether it fully covers the costs or not. And, unlike public schools, which the NAACP readily admits are failing the overwhelming majority of Black and poor children, under school choice parents always have the option of leaving a private school at a second's notice if the school is not meeting their educational needs. Finally, most participating students are the products of single-parent households and were failing in the public schools—a primary factor motivating their transfer. Most met the profile of at-risk students who eventually drop out of the system.

But Mfume knows all of that, which makes his statements all the more curious. Were they really his? Many found it strange that his comments were almost identical to public pronouncements made by the head of PFAW during a December 1998 antichoice rally held in Milwaukee. Many believe Mfume's comments were actually authored by others, suggesting he is but a willing pawn.

It also conveniently escaped Mfume's public statements that the NAACP had all but ignored the national plight and ramifications of three generations of urban poor children who were being failed by public schools as it pushed its integration imperative.

They didn't hear the cries from Black parents in Chicago, thirty years after Dr. Martin Luther King Jr.'s final visit, who saw their children attending schools that relegated them to second-class citizenship. They didn't hear the calls for reform from parents and politicians in Cleveland, where the educational monopoly was so ineffectual that the government had to take it over, or in New York, where families put their names on a three-year waiting list for public vouchers to escape the failing public schools, or in Detroit, where school board members were often threatened by parents who thought they were part of a conspiracy to mis- or under-educate their children. And surely the NAACP, while supposedly championing the rights of the downtrodden, didn't hear the cries from residents of Washington, D.C., in 1997 for a voucher program for their district, described as the worst in the nation.

The futile exercise of Black citizens who sought *real* help, not more feel-good "I am Somebody!" speeches, explained why more and more were abandoning traditional leftist policies for Black Power initiatives such as parental educational choice, African-centered curricula, charter schools, and site-based management.

In the course of the Black community's campaign for justice, the NAACP, the ACLU, and PFAW—all self-professed advocates of equality and bastions for the poor—redefined themselves by their opposition to school choice and defense of plantation politics. By choosing to support the failing and corrupt status quo, they had become what they claimed to despise most: racists.

Don't get me wrong. There is no doubt that the NAACP has served an invaluable function for Black civil rights in this country and, despite its philosophical fallacies, remains a viable, important organization for Black and other minority citizens, functioning well as a watchdog for institutional racism, insurance redlining, and political double standards. The NAACP has certainly moved America closer to the vision of the Founding Fathers, in which all possess inalienable rights. As social analyst Ralph Wiley, author of *Dark Witness*, notes,

> Just because you don't need the NAACP this minute doesn't mean you might not one day, if only to look something up; or that your sons and daughters might not need it in order to get in touch with the Legal Defense Fund to help overturn pending disaster posing as legislation proposed by "Angry White Men" who now have their feet up on the congressional furniture. Even in the most obtuse sense, the NAACP might help someone focus who might otherwise wind up massaging your car with a brick.[9]

Wiley's point is well taken. But somewhere along the way, the NAACP got stuck in the groove of victimization and racial politics.

The NAACP scorecard for hotels and other businesses (a report card on affirmative action) is another excellent example of this dichotomy. Few would criticize the project, and most would agree with its purpose, although national studies show that only a small percentage actually follow the NAACP recommendations. But that's not the point. From a Black nationalistic standpoint, the real question is why the NAACP does not criticize the major Black organizations—including the Black Congressional Caucus and Black lawyers, accountants, and engineers—for spending millions of dollars each year on conventions at *White* hotels and convention centers? What would happen if these so-called advocates for Black equality and economic parity actually practiced what they preached and patronized Black travel agencies, Black cab drivers, and Black hotels, filling their bellies with food cooked on a Black stove by Black hands in Black-owned restaurants? That's what Black nationalism and the emerging Black leadership is talking about. That's where the NAACP is out of focus, apparently afraid to alienate its funding sources, who are often more interested in whether the hotel employees are in a union, if the corporation's loss of revenue will chill the possibility of purchasing a lifetime membership or of sponsoring a Freedom Fund reception, or how a loss of revenues will affect Whites.

Civil rights in America is nothing without silver rights: the attainment of economic opportunities and self-sufficiency. Equal opportunity is nothing without an educational foundation from which to spring forward.

Even renowned educator and writer Cornel West, who describes himself as a radical Democrat, and was touted as the most likely successor to Chavis, believes that the NAACP's preoccupation with race has hindered and hurt the organization. While rightly highlighting the national problems of racial discrimination and racial violence, NAACP leadership, like other traditional Black leaders, including Rev. Jesse Jackson and John Jacobs (executive director of the Urban League from 1982–94), have "a preoccupation with race. . . . The mandate from their organizations . . . downplays the crucial class, environmental, patriarchal and homophobic determinants of Black life chances."[10]

West is no advocate of Black nationalism, asserting that it hurts racial harmony (again, that illusory dream that does not address fundamental problems) and "reinforces the fragmentation of U.S. progressive efforts that could reverse this deplorable plight."[11]

West also acknowledges that the NAACP and Black Left leadership have overlooked or ignored the plight of the poor and of Black Americans. In his book *Race Matters*, West writes:

> The vast depoliticization and electoral disengagement of Blacks suggest that they are indeed disenchanted with Black liberals and distrustful of American political processes, and a downtrodden and degraded people with limited options may be ready to try any alternative.[12]

He further agrees with Black conservatives (whom he disdains), that the Black liberal leadership has not addressed the economic realities facing Black America. He continues:

> Obviously, the idea that racial discrimination is the sole cause of the predicament of the Black working poor and very poor is suspicious. And the idea that the courts and government can significantly enhance the plight of Blacks by enforcing laws already on the books is even more spurious. White racism, though pernicious and potent, cannot fully explain the socioeconomic position of the majority of Black Americans.
>
> The crisis of Black liberalism is the result of its failure to put forward a realistic response to the changes in the economy. The new Black conservatives have highlighted this crisis by trying to discredit the Black liberal leadership, arguing that the NAACP, Urban League and Black Congressional Caucus and most Black elected officials are guided by outdated and ineffective viewpoints.[13]

West, like others on both sides of the ideological fence, however, notes that Black America has not embraced conservatism because of its myopic belief in the goodness of those who have perpetrated injustices and its alliance with the GOP. Thus, while conservatives should be applauded for taking the moral high ground and championing self-actualization through entrepreneurship, they have not acquired much more than a small foothold in the Black community because institutional racism is still pervasive, and political agendas continue to overshadow moral right. Black liberal (Left) leadership is indeed inadequate, but Black conservatism is tainted by its association with the Republican Party, or so the theory goes.

Like far too many Black politicians, the NAACP has put the party before the people. Indeed, as it has refused to change its tune, to listen to the masses who are hungering for immediate, pragmatic solutions to neoslavery and despair, the NAACP has been missing in action.

Perhaps the NAACP doesn't want to admit its mistake: the quest for integration, that dastardly solution to all of America's ills, that effort to tap into the moral conscience of America, the grand experiment, *failed*. And we witness the ramifications on the streets of urban America today.

FINANCIAL IMPERATIVES

When Mfume became executive director of the NAACP, his philosophy underwent a startling metamorphosis. It did not escape the attention of many on the Black Right that Mfume, a staunch champion of Black empowerment when a congressman, had put his new party before the people in a conciliatory move. It was widely held that Mfume's transition was rooted in an attempt to bail out the financially strapped organization. He vowed from day one of his administration that resolving the organization's crippling debt was his top priority.

It is a sad reality that many Black organizations and movements are forced to seek funds from outside their membership—usually at a political price—in part because Black Americans do not support our own to a great enough extent. The NAACP's new check-writing friends included interests aligned with those at the farthest left of the Democratic Party, and the teachers unions, which, as I have discussed in other chapters, have a vested interest in maintaining the status quo. The NAACP's multimillion-dollar debt limited its freedom of movement and expression, and the organization's odd opposition to educational reforms and political independence—against the wishes of its constituents—highlighted its financial and philosophical straitjacket. As I have noted, there are two auxiliaries in the Negrocracy: those who compromise but use White support to advance the cause, and those who are pawns of the funding sources. The debate continues to be waged over which side the national NAACP has taken. To paraphrase a comment made by Howard Fuller noted during a forum on school choice in 1997, in order to advance your cause you can get in bed with entities you may be philosophically opposed to, but you don't have to get under the covers.

It is not unusual for corporations to buy acceptance or shield themselves from NAACP attacks through the purchase of lifetime memberships, sponsorship of NAACP conferences, and the purchase of corporate tables (with prominent listings in the programs) at their Freedom Fund dinners and banquets. This hush money paid out to the NAACP has reaped big dividends over the years, especially in the area of educational reform where the organization finds itself in bed with teachers unions, missionaries, and the Democratic Party. Their agenda, although masked by racial rhetoric, is essentially to benefit White America, particularly the poverty pimps or missionaries whose livelihood is directly connected to Black poverty.

The NAACP has always had the scent of sanctimony about it. Like most national Black civil rights organizations, it is generally beholden to interests outside of Black America for its financial wherewithal. And where agendas conflicted, the purse-string holders would yank the organizations back into line. The NAACP was constructed in its early years by wealthy East Coast White and Jewish interests, which ultimately led to cofounder W. E. B. DuBois leaving the organization in frustration, questioning whose agenda the organization was following and who would really benefit. Following a White knight is not unethical, and in some cases it is practical and morally beneficial. But if history is the indeed the best judge, more often than not, when White Americans define the Black agenda and lead our struggle, we are either detoured, co-opted, or sabotaged. Following White leadership of the Black movement is like lending money to a friend—but the consequences of the inevitable fallout are far more serious.

As Amos Wilson notes in *Blueprint for Black Power*:

> The best that White-funded organizations can achieve is a repetitive and tired call for government support, private (White) investment, job training, affirmative action and other solutions which affirm and strengthen the very system that is the major source of suffering in the Black community. Thus creative, courageous, imaginative, novel and innovative ideals, solutions and possibilities escape this dependent intellectual Black elite.[14]

History has also shown that when a Black organization comes under the philosophical control of Whites, the Black voice is muted or misinterpreted. In the case of the NAACP, White corporate sponsors and Jewish interests used their decades-old influence over traditional civil rights organizations to have Nation of Islam leader Minister Louis Farrakhan ejected from the thirty-year anniversary celebration of the March on Washington in 1993. He went on to organize the phenomenally successful Million Man March two years later, using his platform to declare the irrelevance of traditional civil rights organizations, with Chavis, former head of the NAACP, at his side. In a grand show of unity, Minister Farrakhan offered a portion of the funds raised from the March to help retire these organizations' debt, freeing them from the chains of their new Massa's.

The ultimate example of the financial double-bind is the NAACP's recent association with People for the American Way (PFAW), an organization founded by *All in the Family* creator Norman Lear and other Hollywood players that espouses the liberal/missionary agenda similarly advocated by the NAACP. It is rumored, although never publicly affirmed, that PFAW helped retire the NAACP's extraordinary debt in exchange for putting someone in Blackface at the forefront of opposition to school choice and to slow the Black Power movement. PFAW must have learned a lesson from the Milwaukee teachers union, which was accused of racism for its opposition to school choice. Apparently, Mfume was all too happy, or at least fiscally pragmatic enough, to see this self-centered, one-sided venture as being mutually beneficial.

Instead of dealing with the fundamental life-and-death issues of the Black community, the NAACP under Mfume and new NAACP national chair Julian Bond (who replaced Myrlie Evers-Williams in February 1998) began an aggressive—if not successful in any significant way—campaign focusing on the conduct of American corporations, including hotels and other industries, that failed to meet established affirmative action goals. The NAACP also marshaled its forces for a Million Youth March in Atlanta to counter a similar crusade by former Nation of Islam leader Khallid Muhammad to be held in Harlem that same weekend. (The Atlanta march, with the support of traditional civil rights organizations, focused its slant on voting and affirmative action. Khallid's Harlem march stressed self-empowerment, nation building, self-defense against mounting police brutality and White supremacy groups, and a declaration of war against drugs, crime, and illiteracy.) In addition, Mfume spearheaded campaigns to lambaste the U.S. Supreme Court for not having a representative share of Black clerks, and expanded the scope of the effort to deflect attacks against affirmative action programs. Not by coincidence, each of these efforts was nonthreatening to the status quo and to the NAACP's financial support base.

Additionally, the NAACP spearheaded an attack on federal welfare reform efforts, going so far as to challenge President Bill Clinton—at least until his administration's mounting problems with financial and campaign investigations and his personal sexual scandals forced the organization and Black Democrats into silence. Criticizing Clinton under those circumstances was counterproductive, and so the NAACP and the Black Congressional Caucus found themselves in a precarious situation: continuing the attacks would further erode the president's national Black support base and feed right into the Republican strategy. Remaining silent would allow for the further entrenchment of Welfare to Work, lifetime limits for aid, and other programs that Clinton not only signed into law, but, as a New Democrat, philosophically embraced.

Again, the NAACP found itself in an awkward position. The civil rights organization essentially remained mute on teen pregnancy, single-parent households, youth gangs, drugs, and other social ills that feed welfare. By opposing welfare reform, it ignored the culture of entrenched poverty, despair, and antisocial behavior that welfare could breed. Yet the organization refused even to sit at the table to discuss programs calling for a new moral tone or empowering the poor to break out of the cycle of poverty. While on track in questioning the insignificant and often meaningless work and educational components of Welfare to Work programs, many hold the opinion that the NAACP's long avoidance of programs that might lift the poor out of poverty had contributed to the problem. Being able to sit next to a White family in the welfare office or to occupy a place at the front of a bus to the food pantry is not what those who looked to the NAACP for solutions had in mind.

Indeed, the NAACP was curiously silent during the decade leading to President Clinton's introduction of welfare reform, even as Black leaders made note that welfare trapped people in poverty, destroyed Black families and fueled generational dependency. Interestingly, the NAACP, quick to lambaste Nation of Islam leader Minister Louis Farrakhan for his chastisement and questioning of Jewish leaders, was strangely silent when he declared a decade ago that "welfare spelled backwards is 'farewell'—farewell to human dignity and self-respect."

While leaders like Mfume and Bond have planned demonstrations and other campaigns to question the worth of welfare reform nationally, Rev. Flake takes the tack that the debate is nonsensical. Welfare reform is now a national mandate based on a nationwide consensus and is advocated not just by Republican leadership but also by Democrats, led by President Bill Clinton, who campaigned for the presidency espousing an end to welfare and quickly signed into law the measure as drafted by House Republicans. As such, welfare reform is not going away. Instead of questioning the mandate after the fact, Flake argues, Black leaders should seek to humanize it and, where and when possible, to control the training process while creating job opportunities in our own community (as the Opportunities

Industrialization Center and the Private Industry Council have done in Milwaukee). We are the stakeholders in the process and have a vested interest in ensuring that families are empowered by the welfare reform process.

MAKING PROGRESS

Aside from attacks on bigotry and the consistent and justifiable cry for diversity in the public and private sectors, there was and continues to be little to attract the Black grassroots to the NAACP. Indeed, the Black community remains desperate for an agenda and leadership to challenge the assimilationist status quo, within both the political and the civil rights structure. Their opposition to those tenets is helping to fuel a growing acceptance and power of the Black nationalistic and Black Power movements. All share a common belief that the traditional civil rights coalition has diluted Black strength by its blind acceptance of the Democratic Party and liberal Left agenda; that its misleadership has left Black America worse off than it was before the Depression Era's New Deal; that integration has destroyed Black communities, made us educationally impotent, and culturally paralyzed us. Traditional Civil Rights movement groups such as the NAACP find that their aging ranks aren't being replenished by enough young adults and that unless they change their focus their sun may be setting early in the new century.

It would be instructive if Black Americans were provided with the opportunity to judge the opposing philosophies of Mfume and Rev. Flake on their respective merits, unencumbered by rhetoric, misinformation, or personality conflicts—and devoid of White intervention, media interpretation, or political sound-bites.

It would be immensely beneficial if the Black Left stated their case and nationalistic Black leaders espoused their philosophies, and the masses were given a chance to choose between them—or adopt various elements of each—en route to setting their own Black Agenda, untainted by those with a vested interest in slowing or derailing the Freedom Train.

We should never forget or take for granted why those outside our community wish to control or influence our struggle.

Malcolm X brought clarity and strength to the debate in the 1960s, offering an alternative that had the effect of empowering Dr. Martin Luther King Jr.: White America made King the preeminent Black leader so as to lessen the impact of Malcolm X. We see the same mechanism at work even today, where White America gives Rev. Jesse Jackson more entrée because it feels threatened by cultural nationalists such as Conrad Worrill and Asa Hilliard. Those on the Left—the traditional path upon which most mainstream Black organizations have trodden since the

1940s—have apparently deemed that the Black nationalistic movement is a threat that can undermine its friendships and allegiances and must be destroyed at any cost.

That's why the Julian Bonds and Manning Marables of the Black Left feel it necessary to attack Minister Farrakhan and, to a lesser degree, Ben Chavis, Conrad Worrill—and even Dr. Mulana Ron Karenga, the creator of Kwanzaa, a seven-day African-American holiday premised on African-centered morals, principles, and family values. Black conservatives have also felt their wrath because they, too, threaten the civil rights status quo.

School choice thus becomes the battleground on which this philosophical battle is waged, but it is not the war. The war is really over the direction of the Civil Rights movement going into the next century. Should it continue on a pointless meandering train of assimilation, or should Black Milwaukee—or Black America—board another train fueled by self-determination and community building, a train that we alone must engineer?

A MANIFESTO FOR PARENTAL SCHOOL CHOICE:
FIFTEEN LESSONS LEARNED DURING THE STRUGGLE

We will either find a way or make one.
—HANNIBAL

s we discussed the bold initiative called Parental School Choice in 1989, few of us envisioned the movement we would spark, the eyes we would open, and the changes that would spring forth. Our battle for school choice has altered the educational and ideological status quo in America and ignited similar quests for educational freedom around the country—calls and campaigns for reform, for equality of opportunity, for Black and low-income empowerment. Millions of dollars would be spent, blood would be let, and wounds would be opened that would never heal. Perceptions would be changed and friendships lost. The political landscape would be permanently changed because of the decisions of our army of activists and parents led by Williams, Courtney, Harwell, Cleveland, Virginia Stamper, Sisters Callista and Virgene, Pilar Gonzales, State Senator Gary George, State Rep. Spencer Coggs, and Brother Bob Smith. Later, the army would splinter into new branches and others would take leadership positions. And as news of our successes in Milwaukee reached the national spotlight, they would spark similar calls for reform and empowerment across the land. Brothers and sisters in Cleveland, Washington, D.C., Indianapolis, and elsewhere are now replicating our crusade—and others are sure to follow.

Hopefully, these activists will learn the importance of organization, planning, and coalition building, recognizing that political affiliations and labels take a back seat to the grand purpose. In the struggle for equality of opportunity, the ends justify the means, and we have none but ourselves to rely on. If those who follow our lead are lucky, they will link with people of shared vision—or even those with over-lapping agendas they might otherwise take issue with. We learned early in the campaign that the greatest impediment to the Black agenda is our unwillingness to look beyond the propaganda of our so-called friends in order to forge new alliances to advance our cause. Generally, when we looked beyond the superficial political barriers, we found common ground from which to grow. There are many forces on both sides of the political aisle with a vested interest in keeping African Americans at the bottom of the totem pole, and yet there are also many individuals whose political labels obscure a genuine sincerity and desire to help.

If asked, we will tell those who seek to replicate our campaign to look at the prize and not to concern themselves with the wrappings. In that spirit, I offer fifteen lessons of the choice struggle—with the acknowledgment that we are still fighting and still learning.

1. The shadow of slavery still looms large over our community.

This shadow clouds our judgment and shackles the minds of many Black leaders. It instills a sense of inferiority in those who stand under it. It has many African Americans believing that "White ice gets colder, White cars drive smoother." They subconsciously hate their Blackness and so denounce Black nationalism as separatism, African-centered curricula as voodoo, and our efforts to correct (His)story as irrelevant or as Black racism. They will fight even harder than the Massa' to maintain White supremacy and equate Black empowerment with betrayal of the benevolent White father and benefactor.

School choice symbolizes an escape from the "good life" of vassalage and captivity. Those of the clouded mindset will fight tooth and nail to maintain the status quo, for they believe that it will bring security and the opportunity to be accepted. This belief is false.

Though unsubstantiated, this belief illuminates the classic Black paradox that pits the House Negroes (slaves) against the Field Negroes (slaves). There are essentially two types of House Negroes: those who make the most of living in the slave owner's big house (mansion) by either appealing to the Massa' to better the conditions of the slave's brethren or—more radically—spying on, disrupting, and sabotaging the household and system of slavery. Conversely, there were those slaves who were so corrupted and brainwashed by false promises of acceptance, extra scraps from the table, or easy work inside the cool confines of the stately home that they not only forgot they were slaves—human chattel—but also were willing to sell out their captured brothers to maintain their privileged lifestyle.

This scenario provides a viable analogy for the modern-day battle over the so-called public school system by the grassroots Black community. In many cases, today's battle pits the assimilationists (the happy House Negroes) against the nationalists (the Field Negroes seeking freedom at any cost). The analogy also conjures up an assessment often attributed to Black leader Malik Shabazz (a.k.a. Malcolm X) that the institutions many Black leaders fight for are not in truth our institutions but rather plantation big houses. As such, many Black leaders are fighting to maintain or offer placebos within the framework of the status quo institutions that essentially hold America's have- nots hostage.

Subconsciously, Black Americans (and many Whites for that matter) make distinctions between institutions we can truly claim ownership of—that serve our interest or empower us— and those that facilitate a different agenda or are out of our realm of control, and thus are not truly public.

Malcolm X noted that Black people who use the article "the" instead of the pronoun "our" when referring to government are not making a slip of the tongue but instead are espousing a critical reality for Black Americans, just as our ancestors who toiled under the whip as captive Africans referred to "the" plantation and "the" big house.

Easily, a case can be made that MPS is not "our" system (nor White Milwaukeeans' for that matter) but "the" system—a self-serving dominion for which our children are fodder and fuel. As proof, the system's administrators have historically turned a deaf ear to the public's cries and have arrogantly defended substandard products. For the illness of the district they usually blame the victims, the parents, rap music—or even El Niño, if they can't think of anyone else. MPS is a public school system only from the perspective that our public dollars flow through it. In truth, we have little control over how those dollars are spent, and our quest for academic accountability has resulted in little more than superficial change. The electoral process has not afforded the community an avenue for meaningful input; rather it underscores the ineffectiveness and fallacy of the so-called democratic electoral process, and public control over the entrenched bureaucracy.

Private schools like Harambee are in fact more public than the government/ system/Establishment schools that have ill-served an entire generation of Black Milwaukeeans (and New Yorkers, Chicagoans, and Clevelanders, for that matter). In contrast to MPS, Harambee is a parent-owned and -operated school: a perfect example of site-based management and a true neighborhood school, existing solely to serve our children and the community. Its curriculum is geared to maximize our children's potential and is refined and modified to match social and cultural norms.

Its administration eagerly responds to its clients/owners, who serve on its board, volunteer for school events, coach its teams, and contribute as tutors.

No doubt, Harambee Community School epitomizes what a public school should be. Conversely, MPS, although serving an 80 percent minority population, continues to optimize options for the majority of the minority. No wonder some believe that the system is actually a factory to supply clients for social services, inmates for the prison system, and employees for fast-food chains. That assessment may seem a whimsical generalization, but to those who have fought for change while generation upon generation of children have been left by the wayside or detoured to the welfare system—or worse—it is a sobering reality.

Call this conspiracy theory flippant if you will. But then look at the evidence: each year through 1998, an ever-increasing number of Black children have dropped out; the collective grade point average of Black children has remained abysmally low; and the performance gap between Black and White children has remained consistently wide. Judging from the complaints uttered by the mass media and the Milwaukee Metropolitan Association of Commerce and by the number of graduates forced to take remedial education classes at the Milwaukee Area Technical College, a high percentage of alumni are incapable of using their diplomas for anything other than place mats. (No wonder a majority of MPS teachers, according to Polly Williams, send their children to private schools.) All of this occurs as the system seems to bend over backward for the last handful of middle-class White children, providing them with quota seats at specialty schools and allowing them to attend neighborhood schools while Black and poor children are bused in an elaborate system that defies logic. If not a conspiracy—a very dark shadow of slavery—then what? Are the educrats so callous that they do not hear the cries, do they not care that their apathy is destroying a city, undermining the future tax base, continuing a destructive cycle?

The system refuses to budge from entrenched indifference or to respond to cries from the business community, the media, parents of all ethnicities, and even elected officials. If the Milwaukee, Washington, D.C., Los Angeles, Detroit, or Baltimore school systems were businesses, they would be bankrupt—or subjects of a class action lawsuit. By all measurements, they are failures, unwilling or unable to manufacture marketable products that meet corporate or community needs.

Private schools such as Harambee, Urban Day, and Messmer must respond and produce or they will go out of business. And they do so because of—not in spite of—the public they serve. That's what schools should be about, and that's what school choice is about: expanding opportunity to those who are underserved and providing examples of academic excellence. The established private institutions show what can and should be done: they involve the same parents that union officials say are apathetic and unqualified, they educate the same children educrats and poverty pimps say can't be educated because of "genetic predispositions," and they empower families that social scientists theorize are disengaged or uncaring.

Not only has school choice enabled low-income families to make private public, it has also confirmed the importance of self-determination and self-governance within our community, giving credence and merit to the founding principles Jewish and German Americans used to establish strong communities. School choice is true democracy at work. It provides a blueprint for parental empowerment, for a societal revolution to take back those institutions that have become part of a conspiracy to maintain a system of class apartheid. Educational reform in Milwaukee has opened a Pandora's box, and America is now being forced to redefine government, public, and community to reevaluate the concepts of government versus governance and dependency versus self-determination.

School choice is a powder keg that will obliterate the plantation walls, freeing the slaves and moving America back to the vision of the Founding Fathers—sans their belief, of course, that Africans were inferior.

2. School choice is but a way station on the Freedom Train track.

The school choice campaign is grounded in a battle to determine the direction of the Civil Rights movement—whether we will stay the course of assimilation and accommodation, allowing others to control our culture or will seize command of our own destinies, looking inward for our community's definition.

If the choice movement can be used as a gauge, the pendulum has shifted from assimilation toward Black nationalism. Many in the Black community have concluded that the integration crusade has run its course—but not before splintering our social network and undermining our cultural foundation. Black Americans will never stand on equal ground until we approach the table with a dish in our hands instead of with our hands out.

At this civil rights crossroads, Black America must choose the path to social, economic, and spiritual empowerment and parity. This path is nationalism—cultural, Black, or communal, take your pick. Black America must look inward for wisdom and strength and (re)build a mighty community within a community, a neighborhood within a larger community. We can be part of, but distinct. Separate but desegregated. Integrated, but not assimilated. American, but African-American. We should strive for and accept assistance but not direction from the larger society to create a "multicultural" Caesar salad instead of some mystical melting pot in which we would surely lose our flavor.

It is the assimilationists' fallacy that others will solve our problems, take from their pockets to enrich us, allow us to maintain our culture within the confines of the so-called melting pot, give us equal status, and acknowledge our contributions to the world stage. In our hands are Black America's fate, future, and fortune. And entwined with the destiny of Black Americans are the interests of women, minorities, and America's have-nots. America cannot be America until we are all afforded an equal opportunity to rise or fall on our own merits, until race is a source of distinction and not disadvantage, and until the stage can accommodate diversity without dictation or distraction.

Those who formed the foundation of the school choice movement utilized the principles and concepts of nationalism in their quest to tear down the plantation walls and to empower themselves and the Black community in the process. That crusade has sent shock waves throughout the status quo and provided a blueprint for school reform and community building.

The laws are now in place. The battle has now moved into the era of silver rights: economic empowerment, self-determination, and nation building. The era of big East Coast–based organizations agitating for massive governmental programs is over. They do themselves and their worthy legacy and great heritage harm to rage against the mighty and unstoppable tide of Black empowerment.

3. *"Ten thousand ants can eat the mighty elephant."*

This African adage was realized in the various victories achieved by the crusading army of Black parents and activists who took on the mighty Establishment—teachers unions, the Milwaukee Public Schools, the Democratic Party, and the White media—and won. On their own, the governor, MPS Superintendent Robert Peterkin, and Polly Williams failed to get school choice legislation through. But when Williams joined forces with the Black masses, we were able to accomplish what others thought impossible. Truly, there is power in numbers, but an organized Black campaign fueled by conviction and passion can accomplish much.

Indeed, the Milwaukee school choice crusade was successful only because it was engineered by Black people. Previous efforts failed because those who would be most affected by the program were not involved in the decision-making processes. But when the fight for school choice became a bottom-up movement it was inevitable that change would come.

Campaigns such as the school choice referendum in California failed because they were top-heavy. Sponsors imposed their philosophies and solutions on the poor from on high. They refused to pay heed to the lessons of Milwaukee and paid the price. A movement by poor Black families and pragmatic Black leaders can accomplish what traditional coalitions cannot.

Thompson learned that lesson the hard way when he advanced a proposal in early 1998 to take over the Milwaukee public school system if it did not achieve several modest academic goals. He was politically crucified (ironically, by the local teachers union, a union-backed group of Black clerics, and the Black Democratic Legislative Caucus) for his well-intentioned but misguided suggestion. Had he sought out parents, secured their endorsement, and provided them with a say in his process, his effort would not have been met with such a negative response.

Civil rights organizations, Black leaders, and political entities should pay heed to the strategies that made the Parental School Choice initiative a reality. The NAACP, for example, no doubt would benefit from honestly assessing the needs and desires of those it purports to help. If 80 percent of the Black community supports school choice, does it make sense to oppose it?

4. A lie unchallenged is assumed to be truth.

School choice opponents have consistently tried to alter the debate or otherwise undermine the program by introducing lies and distortions. If unchallenged, a lie that is told often enough becomes truth—this, apparently, has been our opponents' chief tactic. However, as a North African proverb affirms, "He who conceals his disease cannot expect to be cured."

To our advantage, most African Americans have lived the American lie so long, we can see it in total darkness. Some still have blinders on, or naïvely accept the propaganda of the teachers union and educracy at face value, but most of us have learned to openly challenge duplicity at every turn. Unfortunately, that's often easier said than done; the enemies of Black empowerment have vastly more resources at their disposal. In the Milwaukee campaign, they were supported by both daily newspapers, the so-called liberal newspaper, and several radio stations. Additionally, the local teachers union controlled not only the school board but also the State Department of Public Instruction.

We prevailed through persistence, good organization, tenacity, and luck. It didn't hurt that we had right and justice on our side, but those valuable assets had to take a back seat to sound research, public debate, and articulate leadership. Central to our campaign was our ability to quickly challenge evasion and half-truths, and to raise questions about the motivations behind the falsehoods.

In their desperation, the opponents of choice generally shot from the hip. For example, opponents first charged school choice would cream off the best students. That was so obviously a lie that they later had to recant, particularly after a well-respected researcher challenged it with irrefutable data. A study by University of Wisconsin–Milwaukee sociologist Sammis White showed that the overwhelming majority of choice participants are students from low-income families—most with highly motivated and concerned parents, but who were nonetheless failing in the public school system. For them, private schools were a last resort. Additional research by John Witte, who was hired by the Department of Public Instruction, showed immense parental satisfaction with students' new schools.

Choice opponents also alleged that there is no private-school accountability, which borders on being absurd. While there are some schools with independent or corporate boards or boards run by religious dioceses, each has mechanisms for redress and all must abide by state and federal nondiscrimination codes, consumer protection clauses, and a truckload of state regulations. Parents also have the last say because they can always protest with their feet. Through collective action, dissatisfied parents can even force schools to close.

Some of the opponents' assertions were so nonsensical they actually helped our cause. Felmer Chaney's statements that the program hurt Milwaukee's public school integration process and that "anything all Black is all bad" certainly backfired. Also, Milwaukee Teacher's Educational Association's President Paulette Copeland's contention that school choice is deficient because it doesn't affect the one hundred thousand students left behind in MPS was interpreted by many to mean that although the program was beneficial, it should not be continued since it was limited to only a small number of children. Using that logic, one could say the system should abandon every specialty program and magnet school because they impact only a small number of students.

The most inflammatory lie was that school choice steals money from the public schools—as if that money is the public school system's to begin with! Per-pupil funding is state (taxpayers') money designated for the express purpose of educating children who are residents of the state, as mandated by the state constitution. This constitution does not differentiate between rich and poor, Black and white, public and private. The money is allocated for education, not specifically public education, and thus can be and is used for a variety of educational purposes as long as they promote the public good. The money is to be used for our children wherever they go. As Howard Fuller said during a recent school choice rally, "The height of hypocrisy in America is for people whose children are taken care of to oppose school choice for poor parents. They argue that to let these people go means that you would destroy the system. The question is—is it about the system or is it about our children? Choice is not the issue in America. The issue is who has choice."

If the schools were truly *public*, we would not be engaged in this great debate— we would control the institution, it would address our needs, and Black and White citizens would not have had to file a lawsuit to desegregate and to end institutional bias against minorities and have-nots. They would not have chained themselves to bulldozers to stop the building of schools in areas they objected to, and the governor would not have had to threaten a hostile takeover in 1998 because the system is failing a majority of its minority and low-income students. Even if the takeover had occurred, it is questionable whether the schools could have converted to "public" institutions. The school choice/educational reform movement taught us that change must be bottom-up, not top-down. Parents and community leaders must be at the front line of this crusade to steal the Establishment system away from the educrats. In the process we must redefine *public*, providing parents with options to suit their aspirations and cultural/theological preferences.

That process will result in true desegregation and freedom of opportunity— and, hopefully, an end to the lies of the education Establishment.

5. One West African adage states "I am because we are." Until we understand the realities of that maxim, the Black community cannot move forward as a political or economic entity.

A significant percentage of the 20 percent of Black Americans who oppose school choice are middle-class professionals. Although research is sketchy at best, it is commonly assumed that most have jobs in the public sector or ties to unions. A significant percentage of opponents believe that choice is a right-wing conspiracy or that it will destroy an already weakened public school system and thus further hinder African-American children, but I contend that research will find that many are caught up in the Black caste system, or are House Negroes who fear the competition for jobs from those who would emerge educated as a result of new opportunities through school choice.

The Black urban professional (Buppie) opposition to school choice brings to light the class struggle that has undermined various campaigns to empower the have-nots. Within the framework of the two Americas are two Black Americas. In some respects the divide that separates them is widening.

The Black disenfranchised and disheartened see the world through different eyes than those more fortunate. Their needs are much more basic, their hurdles much higher. Everyday survival is the challenge, not acquiring home equity loans, trips to the Caribbean, or second cars. For the have-nots, education is the passport out of the culture of poverty and despair, while to the Black middle class it is often a conduit, a procedural stepping stone in a relatively charmed life (by Black standards).

Of course, today's Black middle class faces its own challenges. Milwaukeeans are hindered by the concrete—not glass—ceiling and institutional bias that has defined the city. A 1998 Urban League study showed that while Black Americans make up nearly 50 percent of Milwaukee's population, they represent less than 9 percent of corporate Milwaukee's middle-management workforce.[1] That startling statistic should be even more reason for Milwaukee's Buppies to ride the same Freedom Train as the Black have-nots. For in the final analysis, neither of us can make true progress without the other.

Maybe it's a matter of perceptions—the inability of many Black middle-class citizens to see through the eyes of the have-nots. Maybe they think they've made it and others should follow their example of hard work and a strong moral foundation. Maybe they discount the additional barriers facing the have-nots, such as the dismal quality of public education. Of great concern is that many middle-class citizens have chosen to side with the oppressive status quo over the masses at the bottom of the social, economic, and political ladders. Their actions are generally coated in fiscal or psychological, shadow-of-slavery paint. Too many Black haves have forgotten whence they came and that they have a responsibility to keep the door open so that others may follow. That's a basic tenet of cultural nationalism that would serve all members of the Black community well.

Not all members of the Black middle class oppose school choice or are apathetic to the plight of the Black have-nots (who in Milwaukee and throughout America represent the vast majority). In fact, historically, most conductors on the Freedom Train have been members of the Black middle class, including many individuals at the vanguard of the school choice, charter school, and Black Power movements. A 1996 survey conducted by Ahmed Mbalia, Ph.D., for the Milwaukee-based Black Research Organization reveals that, using traditional definitions, there is a stronger base of nationalistic thought among the Black middle class than among any other group.

But opposition from the others flies in the face of history, culture, and ethnic code.

To them we say, and say again: school choice levels the playing field, opens the door to cultural equality, and corrects a fundamental injustice.

6. *Black parents do care and will make informed choices for their children if given a choice.*

Walter Farrell and the dozens of White missionaries who insultingly asserted that poor Black parents couldn't make informed decisions for their children are wrong—even dangerous. But their comments did reveal the condescending and denigrating mindsets of many of those who impact public policy.

It makes you wonder just how most liberals really perceive the Black community. Do they really think poor Black people are in need of tutelage, that they do not possess the intelligence to make informed decisions for themselves and their children? Do these so-called friends of Black America actually think we cannot rise above social welfare programs, that we are inherently immoral? Do they assume that poverty breeds a less motivated, less disciplined, less cultured individual?

When you think about it, their patronizing attitude toward poor Black Americans—often announced so solemnly and with such conviction and sincerity—sounds a lot like Charles Murray's theories, doesn't it?

What's the difference between a condescending liberal and a right-wing demagogue? One smiles in your face as he leads you to the slave ship, saying it's for your own good, while the other simply makes no pretense of his intentions. It's safe to assume they go home together, too.

Many Black parents are the manifestation of the system that bore them. Many are shell-shocked after decades of beating their heads against the bureaucratic wall or spitting into a strong wind. Many have simply given up, frustrated into inaction by the system's antipathy and psychologically scarred from being told that their voices did not matter.

Such frustration is compounded by the fact that many Black Americans are already weakened by the lingering effects of slavery. African historian Taki Raton declared in a 1997 presentation in Milwaukee at the Black Holocaust Museum that many Black Americans are "brain-dead as a result of the socialization process that has eroded their self-worth, that told them they are subhuman or uncultured savages, convinced them that they were inferior in every respect."

Raton asserts that the impact of slavery has yet to be reconciled, that the conditioning and socialization process has been passed on from generation to generation and is today responsible not only for our self-hatred and low self-esteem but also in many cases Black antisocial behavior. Indeed, we are playing out our slave mindset, uncomfortable before White authority, weakened by a socialization process that has left us culturally impotent.

The assimilationist movement has reinforced that mindset, telling Black children they can only learn if sitting next to a White child, that their self-worth is determined by adherence to Eurocentric norms and standards of beauty, that they can only be accepted in White America if they abandon their African culture.

However, the cultural nationalist movement—the school choice crusade in particular—has awakened a sleeping giant. It has focused Black energy on a specific tactic for self-empowerment and proven that we can make positive strides toward equality of opportunity. The nationalist movement has instilled in the Black urban poor a realization that they can improve the quality of their children's lives immediately and use the same strategies to improve the quality of life in their community. Through school choice, Black parents in Milwaukee—who for generations found themselves shunned and ostracized by the very institutions that supposedly served them—have found the opportunity to positively impact their children's lives. They are now part of the system, with valued input in the process.

White America should embrace and applaud this movement because Black empowerment and community control will lead to healthier communities, stronger institutions, higher quality of life, better educational offerings, and new jobs. Collectively, these developments will have a direct impact on the social ills that plague urban America. Citizens who are educated are less likely to find themselves on welfare or supplementing the prison population. Educated men are less likely to indiscriminately impregnate Sally, Sue, and Mary Jane (or Quintella, Shaneka, or Monessa).

America has a stake in public education, in school choice, and in Black empowerment.

7. Nothing will change unless we change it ourselves.

The school choice movement grew out of decades of frustration over the unwillingness of the MSB to implement policies to enhance the quality of education for Black children. No amount of protest or prayer moved the body to react until a clear alternative—school choice—was enacted.

MPS Board Director John Gardner has stated repeatedly that the modest reforms instituted by the MSB during the last five years have come as a direct result of the board's preoccupation with school choice. The board is aware of the growing disenchantment with the quality of education, Gardner said, but has remained entrenched in its antipathy for two reasons: MPS is a monopoly, and the poor have nowhere else to go. The MTEA is in truth a puppeteer, pulling the strings of a majority of the board, and it is in the union's best interest to maintain the status quo. As Gardner has noted, MTEA and board protestations that complaints about the inadequacy of the public school system have arisen from the business community, the conservative Right, and the Governor are falling more and more on deaf ears.

Indeed, even the *Milwaukee Journal Sentinel* (the liberal and conservative daily newspapers, which merged on April 1, 1995) now calls for a major overhaul of MPS and describes the school board and MTEA as major impediments to quality education for Black children. The White media, which fought school choice, charters, and several major reforms authored by former Superintendent Howard Fuller, is now frightened by the ramifications of an uneducated populace and as a result is embracing school choice and charters.

The *Journal Sentinel* has even allowed Greg Stanford, its top Black editorial writer, space to editorialize in favor of school choice. The newspaper did not go so far as to endorse the program, but its opposition is weakening in the face of overwhelming support for the program and a growing acceptance that the real enemies are not the slaves seeking to escape the plantation, but the slave owners. Indeed, one could conclude that the *Journal Sentinel* was moving close to our position as we entered the last year of the century. On several occasions the paper editorialized for curbing busing for the failed desegregation movement, and against the union-endorsed school board candidates in the spring elections. In fact, the *Journal Sentinel* and *Milwaukee Community Journal* found themselves endorsing the same candidates, and later both publications editorialized in support of a proposal by State Reps. Williams, Riley, and Shirley Krug to shift state aid for desegregation transportation to neighborhood schools.

The Democratic Party's stranglehold on the Black vote has also weakened, not necessarily from a supportive standpoint, but from a moral and philosophical perspective. Democrats had to remove their masks and step from their perches of moral righteousness to wage the battle against Black empowerment. And who could explain or justify his position of denying poor Black families the same right to choose that most of the Limousine Liberal set enjoyed? Their hypocrisy provided us with a new political realism, confirming a long-feared assumption that we were but pawns in a political game whose rules we did not fully understand.

Conversely, it became obvious that our coalition with the Republicans would not develop into a broader confederacy. There were many within the GOP structure who viewed school choice not only as a moral issue but also as an inroad to the Black community throughout the campaign. Wisconsin Governor Tommy Thompson and future House Speaker Scott Jensen were visible through the crusade for school choice, building bridges, and offering assistance from the sidelines. In cooperation with State Rep. Polly Williams, they oversaw the Republican support base and openly portrayed parental school choice as an opportunity to forge a permanent alliance with the Black community that would pay political dividends. Which it did—in 1994, Thompson received an unprecedented 39 percent of the Black vote. But apparently their vision was not shared by enough of their Republican colleagues, whose political and cultural myopia had previously been called into question by Jack Kemp, J. C. Watts, and others who proudly referred to their brand of inclusive Big-Tent politics as "bleeding-heart conservatism."

That dichotomy pushed some African Americans into realizing that maybe we should expand our campaign to a new political horizon that would include our own party—one that solely represents our interests and worldview. There will be issues and campaigns on which we can work with Republicans, and many more on which we can ally with Democrats for mutual benefit. But if nothing else, the school choice struggle revealed that neither major political entity truly has our best interests at heart. They are essentially different wings of the same bird. When push comes to shove, the more the Left moves toward the Left, the closer it gets to the Right—and vice versa.

Black America has failed to recognize how its blind allegiance to the left wing of the "Republicratic" Party has left it politically impotent. Most civil rights leaders will agree with the adage that "Republicans ignore us, while the Democrats take us for granted," yet we do little to assert ourselves or to maximize our political strength. Instead of being prostituted by the Democrats, we should establish our own party, or at least become political pragmatists, working with whomever and whatever supports our immediate interests. Minister Louis Farrakhan planted a valuable seed when he declared at the conclusion of the Million Man March that Black Americans should no longer support Black candidates merely because they are Black. "We've tried that," the Nation of Islam leader said during his keynote address at the October 16, 1995, march. "Instead, Black Americans should support whichever candidate supports our agenda," he advised.[2]

When the smoke clears, Black America is alone.

We must use our numbers, our moral right, our common purpose and destiny as catalysts to change our social and cultural conditions from the bottom up. After all, when you're on the bottom, there's nowhere to go but up. And no oppressor can get his foot on your neck when you're standing up with your shoulders squared.

8. There is a steep price to be paid for independence. No one emerged unscathed from the crusade for justice and equality of opportunity.

You have to be thick of skin to go outside the political and social mainstream to empower your people. Like Howard Fuller, Zakiya Courtney, Polly Williams, and me, you must be able to look beyond the inevitable attempts to assassinate your character. The MCJ also suffered financially for its support, which dissuaded other Black newspapers from endorsing our crusade. Each of us found ourselves under attack by the Establishment media and certain House Negroes (such as Leon Todd and Walter Farrell) with histories of putting their personal and financial interests above that of the Black community. Interestingly, the House Negroes attempted to portray us as sellouts for forging partnerships outside of the Democratic Party boundaries in order to advance our movement. Such censure is a tactic as old as the plantation and underscores the dichotomy of the Black struggle in America. The attackers, under the thumb and financial control of the new plantation bosses, condemned us for seeking to escape. Too many of our people are brainwashed into believing that we must operate within predetermined political parameters, yet will openly admit that Democrats are the lesser of two evils. The reality is that neither Democrats nor Republicans have ever—or will ever—prioritize the needs of African Americans over their core support base and long-term agenda. Neither political entity is blameless in creating and maintaining the American apartheid system.

Black politicians are consistently punished for bucking the partisan political status quo. State Representatives Polly Williams and Antonio Riley found themselves ostracized for their support of school choice. Both were denied choice committee assignments and efforts were even made to gerrymander Williams's district. Some insiders later suggested the punishment leveled against Williams and Riley was intended to sway the four other local Black Democrats (State Senators Gary George and Gwen Moore and State Representatives Leon Young and G. Spencer Coggs) from their support for school choice when the initiative was expanded to include religious schools. That point is open to debate, but what is certain is that the four Democrats did withhold support, despite the fact that the program was overwhelmingly endorsed by Black constituents.

History had warned us of the political price Polly Williams and Antonio Riley had to pay for putting the people before their party. Another defining lesson was provided years earlier when State Senator Gary George's dream of a congressional seat was undermined by his Democratic Party colleagues because he strayed from the party line. George's crime was mentioning during a campaign speech that he hoped to work whenever possible with President Ronald Reagan to advance issues of concern to Black America. He certainly wasn't embracing the GOP platform, and it may in fact have made cultural sense to work when feasible with whomever was in power. But to Democratic Party officials, George was a traitor. "I am a Democrat, but I am first an African American," George asserted before the hammer fell and Democratic Party leadership crucified him for his political blasphemy. His national career aspirations, as well as any hope of a statewide office as a representative of his chosen party, were derailed. But that didn't stop him from asserting himself from within his new political prison cell.

After the affront, the state's lone Black state senator moved toward greater political autonomy, on several occasions bucking the party and operating outside political boundaries to advance programs that benefited his constituency, who collectively represented the poorest and most disenfranchised in the state of Wisconsin. He openly conversed with Republicans and independents and threatened to "sell" his vote to Republicans to advance legislation to benefit the Black community. His national political ambitions were forever soured, however, and over the next few years he found himself in a constant battle with Democratic Party leadership. Eventually he was removed from Joint Finance and replaced by Gwen Moore, who had been elected to the state senate in 1992. Rubbing salt in the open wound, Democratic Party caucus leaders later named Moore president pro tempore, despite George's seniority.

As the deciding vote in a deadlocked senate during 1997–98, George even flirted with the idea of declaring himself an independent, using his swing vote to control the direction of the state senate and key legislation. His actions brought a steady stream of attacks from Democratic Party colleagues, provoking George last summer to call the party leadership "racists . . . uninterested in the welfare, much less the empowerment" of Black America.

In one respect or another, almost all of the officers in the school choice army found themselves targets of the status quo or victims of the political establishment. George, Riley, and Williams lost choice committee assignments and were ostracized in other ways as well; they found their legislation stifled and their support base minimized. Fuller, Zakiya Courtney, Brother Bob and myself found ourselves ridiculed and second-guessed in the Establishment media (left *and* right), or attacked by black gatekeepers and House Negroes for challenging the Negrocracy and civil rights status quo. More often than not, the criticism came from those with ties to the MTEA or the poverty pimp empire, although that fact did not lessen the sting or ease the pain of the wounds.

But it was a price we accepted, acknowledging the words of Frederick Douglass that "power concedes nothing without demand," and that there are no wars without casualties, no bloodless coups.

9. Black independent schools are a serious threat to the educational status quo, public schools, and the Eurocentric culture.

While Polly Williams's long-term goal was to develop a community of Black independent and religious schools, a short-term goal was to draw attention to the success of Black independent schools through parental school choice. She wanted the public school educrats to acknowledge this success, explain it, and then replicate it.

Former MPS Superintendent Robert Peterkin's flirtation with school choice grew out of a series of meetings with Black independent and community schools that offered to work with MPS. The issue of autonomy blocked that marriage, but the first brick was laid. Peterkin was quick to recognize the worth of Black independent schools and saw them not as competitors but as compeers. He was open to collaborations, but the teachers union and some school board members had other ideas.

Site-based management and African-centered curricula are seen as threats to the educational status quo because they empower parents and children. It was no coincidence that MPS Board Director Leon Todd attacked the African-immersion model at Malcolm X Middle School, a specialty school conceived by a male Black task force to address the problem of Black males at risk of failure and dropping out. The school board watered down the original African-immersion proposal, which called for all-male elementary, middle, and high school academies offering African-centered curricula and staffed exclusively by Black educators.

Todd's opposition was not rooted in the quality of education at Malcolm X Middle School—under Black control, the school made the most remarkable turnaround in district history. In cahoots with the MTEA, Todd feared that the African-centered curriculum countered Eurocentric socialization. Todd, the union, and the educracy feared that as the program showed success, new Black parents would push for expansion and the opportunity to control the educational process, weakening the Establishment stranglehold.

Malcolm X Middle School staff and parents approved a referendum in 1996 to become a charter school, an act that would have given them even greater autonomy. But the MTEA interceded, suggesting any teachers who agreed would lose their pensions and seniority within the MPS educracy. The ploy worked. The campaign was killed and never resurfaced, leaving parents frustrated and disenchanted. This time, however, parents had other options, including school choice and charters, which were by then authorized by state legislation for the University of Wisconsin–Milwaukee, Milwaukee Area Technical College and the city of Milwaukee. Despite the opposition, in 1998, the city of Milwaukee granted charters to three schools, including Zakiya and Tony Courtney's Khamit Institute, which provide innovative offerings to Milwaukee's urban poor.

Black independent schools provide Black children with a cultural foundation and self-esteem and thus threaten the grip of the public school plantation system and its apartheid ideology. Because schools are the primary conduit for socialization processes, it should not be surprising that many Black children emerge from public schools with low self-esteem, warped values, and a misunderstanding of their people's contribution to world civilization. A strong case can be made that the public school system intentionally and maliciously instills a sense of inferiority in Black children.

As Carter G. Woodson observed in his historic 1933 education manifesto *The Mis-Education of the Negro*, ". . . the so-called modern education with all its defects . . . does others so much more good than it does the Negro, because it has been worked out in conformity to the needs of those who have enslaved and oppressed weaker people."[3]

Woodson says that the purpose of education is to empower, in part through recognizing and examining a group's contributions to world history. "The mere imparting of information is not education," he said. "Above all things, the effort must result in making a man or woman think and do for himself or herself just at the Jews have done in spite of universal persecution."

Asa Hilliard, Fuller E. Callaway Professor of Urban Education at Georgia State University and African-centered-education proponent, concurs with Woodson, adding that there is obviously a conspiracy afoot to miseducate or undereducate Black children in the public school system. He points to dozens of superior independent and public schools under Black control throughout the country as evidence of what can be accomplished and questions why these successes are not duplicated. As part of a research project, Hilliard traveled the country observing and documenting the success of schools where Black children not only excel but also far outperform White suburbanites. One of these schools, Marcus Garvey Private School in Los Angeles, is located in L.A.'s poorest neighborhood but routinely challenges the best students in the state in academic contests—and wins. Hilliard revealed that Garvey's third-graders challenged sixth-graders from one of L.A.'s most popular magnet schools and beat them. What is even more surprising is that only three of Garvey's thirty-three Black teachers have college degrees.

Imagine that. This is the highest-achieving school I know about, a school that issues a standard challenge where they will let you pick the test, spot you two to three grade levels, and will outperform any students you bring against them. The principal is a by-product of the public school system who go fed up hearing teachers and administrators declaring that Black children couldn't learn; that poor children couldn't learn. Here is proof in an institution where only three of the teachers have degrees. What does that tell you?

I deliberately found schools in the worst neighborhoods . . . gang-infested neighborhoods . . . schools in the housing projects . . . where dope is sold, but ones that still produce the highest achievement inside those islands of hope in those seas of despair. Too many public schools, even those with well-meaning white teachers, contribute to the problem through their

low expectations of Black and poor children. On top of that, the bureaucracies and administrations are corrupt and more focused on
self-perpetuation than educating the urban child. . . . Some people say the
schools are failing. I say they're succeeding tremendously. They are doing
precisely what they're intended to do . . . cripple and disable [black] children.[4]

Black Americans believe that there is a conspiracy to limit their children's educational opportunities, which have far-ranging political and social ramifications.
There are two trains of thought about the motivations behind the conspiracy. The
first theory, advanced by Hilliard and others, suggests that the conspiracy is rooted
in economic and class containment. It posits that technological advances will lead
to an ever-decreasing number of high-paying jobs, and thus it is incumbent to
reduce the employment pool. Ensuring that a large percentage of Americans are
undereducated would reduce the number of competitors for the job market.

The second theory suggests that the conspiracy is the by-product of a racist plot
to slow the inevitable transition of America, and the world, to a colored majority.
This theory is rooted in what Francis Cress Welsing and other Black social analysts
describe as the "last gasp of White supremacy." While proponents of White
supremacy cannot maintain numerical strength, they will maintain control over
the resources and finances, in part by keeping Black, Brown, and Yellow people out
of boardrooms and controlling the lion's share of financial resources, goods, and
services.

A conspiracy to miseducate Black children may sound farfetched, but if there
isn't a conspiracy afoot, how else to explain the abysmal state of public education—
or the unwillingness of public schools to duplicate successful programs—or the
variance between achievement rates of Black independent schools and public
schools that serve the same populations? Is Charles Murray right? Are Black children genetically inferior? Do poverty and out-of-wedlock births stifle learning and
hinder achievement?

Hell, no! Such assertions are absurd. The truth of the matter is that those in
power will do anything to maintain that power. At the root of most civil rights
campaigns is the battle over power allocation—for every civil rights gain, someone
had to give up control or power. When women won the right to vote, they in
essence took power away from men. The battle over school desegregation was
fought over allocation of resources and the power of knowledge. School choice is
but the latest battleground, where the have-nots are waging a war to empower
themselves through quality education. That action threatens to take power away

from the establishment, the status quo, the educracy. It threatens White supremacy and the last vestiges of American duality, American apartheid—the concept of two Americas. The Establishment's hypocritical actions—whether hiding behind the mask of a union member, teacher, or Democratic "friend"—is a stunning testament to the lengths to which it will go to keep Black America out of the Caesar salad. School choice threatens to tear down not only the plantation walls, but the walls of prejudice, lies, and institutional racism.

Obviously, Black children possess the same skills, potential, and intelligence as children of any other ethnic group in America. Most are on the bottom because they have not been allowed to excel, to reach their potential. Along with school choice statistics, Harambee, Urban Day, and Bruce Guadalupe schools have clearly demonstrated that Black students can and will excel in a setting in which high expectations are joined with parental involvement, a good curriculum, and teachers who love children and see their greatest gift as being able to empower them with knowledge.

10. School choice may not be for everyone, but we must find a way of helping those who fall through the educational cracks.

For families subscribing to the Culture of Poverty, whose children are at risk of failure or dropping out or who exhibit antisocial behavior and have all but been abandoned by the public school system, school choice may be the best and only hope. As a result of school choice, charter schools, and public/private partnerships, Milwaukee provides the greatest number of educational options available in America today. Personalized attention and communal networking in private, religious, and Black independent schools can offer immense benefits to low-income families, particularly single-parent households. But that does not mean that all who can benefit will benefit.

There is a genuine fear that a large percentage of those in need will be left by the wayside just as in the War on Poverty and in welfare reform. True, the number of seats available through choice and charters is limited, but there are also self-imposed barriers. Unfortunately, some families won't avail themselves of these unique opportunities because of apathy, misguided values, or lack of knowledge. This scenario underscores one of the greatest challenges of urban education: what to do with those who have fallen though the educational cracks.

How do we address and deal with this major segment of our community—the children of the Culture of Poverty who make up the greatest number of dropouts, and the social misfits who have shifted the primary responsibility of teachers from education to maintenance and discipline? We must recognize that if we don't claim them, the streets will. All social indicators reveal that most poor children who do not follow a spiritual, cultural, or educational path will instead turn to crime and social dependency. If children's parents are apathetic or are themselves the victims of a fragmented culture and value system, if miseducated children are essentially left alone to raise themselves, what role should the community, the reform army, and nationalists play? Should we abandon them, as the public school system clearly has? Should we seek bold solutions such as orphanages or boot camps to take them out of their unhealthy environments and away from the social chaos that underscores the culture of poverty? How can we deal in the long term with this social dilemma without addressing community mores, starting with the deterioration of the Black nuclear family?

This all may seem far removed from the school choice debate. But it isn't. For at the root of the Black Power movement is the goal of building a strong, vibrant and culturally attuned community. Our culture is grounded in an appreciation of family and a communal spirit. We can't more forward as a nation unless we at least try to take our brothers and sisters with us.

11. Missionary politics do not necessarily benefit those whom they are supposed to help.

Indeed, the missionaries have their own interests at heart; in many cases they are also the poverty pimps. Poverty is big business, and guess who profits from it? From prisons to social work programs, millions of dollars flow through the poverty industry, much of it earmarked for programs and jobs that seek to alleviate Black misery.

Welfare reform programs provide a perfect example of financial benefits associated with poverty. In Milwaukee, for example, the YWCA, Goodwill, and Opportunities Industrialization Center, three agencies with overlapping interests, share nearly $60 million in running Welfare to Work programs. As a result, welfare reform has employed more people than any industry in Wisconsin and has created a new middle class of caseworkers, consultants, and managers.

Teen pregnancy is another social ill that has enriched a new middle class. Not coincidentally, although most pregnant teens in Milwaukee are African American, most of the dollars allocated to arresting that social ill go to White agencies, many of which are operated outside the city.

An incident of a few years ago casts an interesting light on the poverty industry. A White suburban organization won a Milwaukee County bid to run a teen-pregnancy prevention/intervention program. Interestingly, the agency's proposal included subcontracts with two of the city's largest Black agencies. Under review, it was learned that the White agency would pay the Black agencies approximately half of the grant, even though the Black agencies would be required to do all of the counseling and follow-up. In fact, the White agency didn't even have a staff of social workers trained or interested in dealing with the urban population. So what did they do for the 50 percent? Administered the program from afar.

Alcohol and drug rehabilitation is another booming business linked to the poverty industry. Here again, most of the dollars flowing into that field end up in the hands of White suburbanites, who are enriched based on Black misery.

Interestingly, most of the aforementioned social ills can be traced to dysfunctional families and an inadequate education system. It is no coincidence that more than 70 percent of prison inmates are functionally illiterate, that a majority of teen mothers are high school dropouts, or that most welfare recipients don't have even an eleventh-grade education.[5] The question is, since abysmal education fuels one of the country's most lucrative industries, is there an incentive on the part of the poverty pimps to maintain the educational status quo? In other words, the more successful the public school system in ensuring that few options are available to the urban poor, the greater the clientele and job security of the poverty pimps.

Polly Williams once theorized that if you follow so-called antipoverty dollars, you'll run into the opponents of school choice. That's sadly true, giving Black America another reason to look cautiously at the plethora of programs in place supposedly to benefit the urban poor. Often those programs are set up merely to allow people to suffer painlessly. Before being ousted some years ago, Barbara Burke-Tatum, the head of the Social Development Commission, said that the goal of antipoverty programs "should not be to make people comfortable in poverty, but to empower them to break the shackles of poverty." School choice has a similar goal.

A final point about White missionaries: What does it say about Black leadership that the most active and politically attuned civil rights groups (meaning organizations fighting for and setting the Black agenda) are White-controlled? In Milwaukee, the most publicized groups are Association of Community Organizations for Reform Now (ACORN), PFAW, Sustainable Milwaukee, and Jobs with Peace. Each of those organizations is incorporated and run by Whites, most of whom are suburbanites. Most of these groups understand the value of fronting Black spokespersons or field workers, but in each case the administration and brain thrusts are White.

These groups have publicly opposed school choice, neighborhood schools, and Black independent politics. Yet in the same breath they have loudly declared their solidarity with Black America, their commitment to civil rights, and their desire to make America live up to its principles of equality and justice for all. They want to lead Black America by the hand, because they know what's best for us. In a nutshell, they must lead the parade, conduct the band, and tame the animals (African Americans). The new White American Left, the catalyst behind the assimilation movement and civil wrongs movement have been covertly pulling the strings for decades and are quick to chastise and slander any Black leader who veers from the party line.

An illuminating case in point: A leader of Sustainable Milwaukee (a leftist civil rights/missionary group) and Progressive Milwaukee (its political arm) for two years, County Supervisor Roger Quindel made a startling statement to me as we were leaving the Charles Sykes radio show. I've known Quindel for more than a decade, having followed his career as a social activist and, more lately, a county supervisor. Quindel is a liberal's liberal, a decent guy who strongly believes in curing America of its social ills and attaining equal rights for Black Americans. Quindel and I had been somewhat at odds over the last few years because of my move toward cultural nationalism in general and advocacy of school choice in particular. On this particular day, following a heated hour-long discussion on a variety of topics, including a debate over whether custody of a Black child whose mother has just died should be given to a well-to-do White suburban couple or to his low-income relatives (citing cultural and psychological reasons, I pushed for the Black relatives, while Quindel stressed the goal of integration and benefits of wealth), Quindel blurted out that he personally liked me, and didn't question my sincerity, "but it's obvious you're confused, and you apparently don't know what you're involved in. You need to come aboard [Sustainable Milwaukee]; *we know what's best for y'all.*"

I was so shocked by his statement and his matter-of-fact manner that I was rendered speechless. "We know what's best for you." Isn't that what the missionaries said as they led my African ancestors to the slave ships and told them they were worshipping a false God?

A point of clarification: Not all White liberals are conspiring to undermine Black empowerment initiatives. Many are sincere and color-blind. There are many who—out of religious orientation, Black friendships, open-mindedness, and a good education—are truly good citizens who can view a person as a person, not a color.

There are also those in the extreme Left—socialists and communists—who would willingly go into battle for Black America. Many Black Americans gravitate toward socialists and communists, because these parties have consistently stood with Black people to protest injustice and racism. But they, too, want to impose a White-dominated political/economic system that would in many respects undermine African-centered thought. It is obvious that those on the extreme Left discovered long ago the necessity of linking their trailer to our Freedom Train to advance their own agenda. Sadly, many Milwaukee White radicals exposed their hold card (a trump card in bid whist, or the first card—which is face down—in poker) and patronizing attitude when they refused to join our movement, suggesting instead that it was a plot by far-right Capitalistic-Imperialistic Pigs who were seeking to break the union and privatize all public schools. That these radicals refused to give us credit or respect for orchestrating a movement rooted in Black Power paradigms was disheartening—and eye-opening.

Many, if not most, of Quindel's contemporaries and colleagues say they believe in equality and justice. Yet it is difficult not to interpret their patronizing attitudes as a form of prejudice that is just as insidious as the overt bigotry that defines America. Moreover, it is obvious that many liberals—from Quindel to State Representative Barbara Notestein—believe they are carrying out a just, moral mission. As such, they do not see themselves as condescending or paternalistic. In effect, the Quindels and Notesteins don't view their victimization politics as racist because they truly believe they are moving America forward (albeit at a pace that benefits them alone). They want to continue giving Black America a handout instead of a hand up, and one has no choice but to wonder whether their calls for social welfare are rooted in true concern.

Indeed, although they would publicly deny it, most liberals and conservatives share a subconscious feeling of ethnic and cultural superiority. White supremacy is part of the socialization process, part of the Eurocentric culture on which this country was founded. To believe otherwise is foolish. In fact, most Black Americans subscribe to the same belief; they have been socialized to believe that they are inferior. That is why assimilation is generally considered the grand design, the ultimate solution.

Many Black Americans are willing to sacrifice culture and identity in an expectation that they will be absorbed, will be honorary White Americans, will be accepted. That's what the integration movement is about. But following that idea to its logical conclusion, America will only be the America envisioned by the Founding Fathers when and if there is total miscegenation, what I euphemistically call the Tiger Woods Solution: All Americans will be light-skinned and slant-eyed, with rhythm, a good command of the Queen's English, and skill in golf.

To the true integrationist, the idea of Black Americans stepping out of the shadow of slavery and building a nation within a nation is nonsensical.

There can be but one culture, one people, one vision. To believers in the assimilation cure-all, school desegregation, affirmative action, and housing integration are but tools to move America to a raceless—not simply equitable—society. And since White America is unwilling to move to Black America, as Milwaukee's school desegregation process clearly showed, Black America simply must move to White America—to accommodate and compromise not only our bodies but also our cultural selves to become Whites in Blackface. We must reject our history, our contributions to civilization, and, indeed, our predestined role in the universe.

This will not happen—not in my lifetime or in that of my grandchildren's children. If current trends continue, the race question will be resolved through attrition, a moral transformation sparked by some international calamity, or through various forms of racial miscegenation—if it is to be solved at all. Projections indicate that America will become a minority-majority country in two decades, with African and Hispanic Americans being the dominant groups. Assuming that minorities' political and economic strength grows at the same rate as our numbers, the power paradigm should shift. Couple that inevitability with interracial marriages, multicultural programming, and a swelling spiritual movement, and one can predict that America will grow much closer to the vision espoused in the Constitution. I would suggest that racism will forever be a reality in America, but it will not be the impediment it is today.

In truth, Milwaukee in many respects is following the lead of South Africa: black people control an ever-increasing number of political positions while the community they represent remains essentially economically depressed and educationally deficient. This condition is not an accident. It is the by-product of institutional racism and can be changed only through total miscegenation or through black self-determination and empowerment. The power paradigm must be shifted. Black Milwaukeeans must use mechanisms such as school choice to break the chains that bind. We must first realize that our socioeconomic shortcomings are a direct result of our total dependency on others to survive, our lack of cultural identification, and our self-hatred, which is a direct manifestation of a socialization process developed to keep us in a state of second-class citizenship. The power, the strength to break the chains, will come from tapping our inner resources and spirituality.

There are those of all political stripes who work as hard as they can to stop or slow Black progress. It may be erroneous to say it that their motives are racist or sexist. But there actions are surely about refusing to concede power.

12. They still don't get it. Apparently, state and local educrats, the MSB, the MTEA, and other defenders of the status quo don't see the writing on the wall.

MPS has been sued and boycotted. Most recently, Governor Thompson has even threatened to take over the district because of the grossly inadequate educational services it provides. The latest statistics compiled by MPS and presented in Milwaukee Catalyst's 1998 publication *Act on the Facts*[6] and the Milwaukee Education Trust's annual report show that fewer than half of the students will graduate, and only slightly more than a third are proficient in reading and math. Yet the board continues to hide its head in the sand, the MTEA blocks every major reform proposal, and the educrats continue to blame the problem on poverty, out-of-wedlock births, the return of bell-bottom pants, and Snoop Doggy Dud's music.

The MTEA orchestrated the 1995 school board elections, sponsoring five candidates who control the balance of power on the board—including the three Black board members. The MTEA has reportedly set aside a significant cash reserve of more than $100,000 to sponsor several candidates again in the 1999 elections and to pit candidates against John Gardner, the only citywide board member and one of the three directors who publicly endorse school choice and other educational options for low-income families. The union has gone so far as to approach several high-profile Black activists with promises of money, resources, and marketing to run against Gardner.

Further evidence includes the selection in 1997 of Alan Brown for superintendent instead of Acting Superintendent Barbara Holmes, a Black woman who has ties to former Superintendent Howard Fuller and who has children in the public school system. Brown, strangely enough, is the former superintendent of the Waukegan, Illinois, School District, which has the distinction of being the fourth worst school district in all of Illinois. Also, criticism of Brown by the Waukegan chapter of the NAACP added fuel to the fire over his appointment. Brown's selection sparked a firestorm of criticism among progressive Black leaders, most of whom theorized that he would be a puppet of the board. Thus far, he has proven them correct.

As frustration among parents, the business community, and lawmakers has grown, so has public support for choice. It is time for the political game-playing to stop. The primary opponents of educational reform in general, and school choice in particular, simply must realize that a poor education system hurts everyone.

13. No permanent friends, no permanent enemies. Not everything is Black and White.

The school choice campaign brought to light the sad reality that counted-on allies and friends could quickly turn against us when we espoused an agenda of self-empowerment and aggressively undertook strategies to shift the power paradigm in our favor.

Liberal Democrats, who propagandize themselves as champions of the poor and crusaders for Black equality and justice, are quick to draw a line in the sand when it comes to programs—such as cooperative economics, independent political campaigns, and school choice—that truly empower the downtrodden. It was liberals, who have for decades lambasted Republicans and the Right for maintaining segregation, who themselves assumed a racist posture as they blocked the private school doors through which low-income parents were trying to pass. Shamelessly, these Democrats then attempted to justify their behavior, hypocritically questioning the motives of Republicans who extended a lifeline to the drowning victims. Would Democrats really rather see Black children drown than watch the Black community accept a life preserver from their political adversaries?

Republicans have proven through word and deed that they are far less attuned to the civil rights struggle or plight of Black America than Democrats, although there is support among the GOP for various Black empowerment programs, which the party characterizes under the political flag of self-help. The GOP has a greater stake in empowerment and thus supports drives for majority Black legislative districts in Wisconsin and, consistent with its platform, supports job training over welfare—although its fiscal allocations rarely match the prognostications. The state of Wisconsin also maintains one of the strongest minority business enterprise programs in the nation. In fact, while the city of Milwaukee and Milwaukee County have abandoned minority business enterprise programs for "disadvantaged" programs, the state has maintained and strengthened its commitment.

Along the same lines, state Republicans have supported Black educational initiatives, from the North Division School District Plan to school choice. Those initiatives aside, there doesn't appear to be much movement toward attracting minorities to the party, nor to addressing such pressing concerns as institutional racism (including insurance and mortgage loan redlining, still major hurdles for Black Americans). Quotas to address decades of discriminatory hiring practices are not even on the table for discussion. Neither are Black concerns about the continuation of such regulatory enforcement programs as the Community Reinvestment Act. That said, there are obviously mutual interests worthy of a date or two, but it's obvious we won't be getting married anytime soon.

It is clear that there are friends, if not allies, on both sides of the political fence, just as there are enemies. The mistake is to blindly label someone an insensitive racist—or a fair-minded friend of Black America—because of his or her party affiliation.

Similarly, we were careful throughout the school choice debate not to make a blanket indictment against public school teachers. Obviously, there are incompe-

tent teachers in the MPS system. There are also many teachers with low expectations for Black children. Prejudice and racism abounds. But many, many teachers
are sincere, competent, highly motivated professionals who are stifled by an
entrenched, self-serving bureaucracy, an educracy that limits their efforts to provide a quality education to the have-nots. The school board and teachers
union—which often operate contrary to the interests of teachers—are the main
culprits, seeking to continue a socialization process that fuels White supremacy.

One of the key lessons learned through our battle to provide opportunities for
poor children is that when push comes to shove, the labels take a back seat to the
interests of those in power. It all comes down to the haves versus the have-nots.
Whatever their affiliation, those in power will do all they can to maintain their
power base.

It is amazing how far the opposition will go—and how readily certain Black
cronies will help them—to carry out an agenda obviously contrary to the community's good. There are many Black opponents of choice who are sincere in their
beliefs, and others who go along with the status quo naïvely or for selfish reasons.
But the Leon Todds, Joan Hollingsworths, and Walter Farrells are a different breed.
These paid pawns are dangerous to the community because they are clever enough
to confuse the issues, smearing good people's names in the process.

"Some of the worst racists are Negroes with Authority," as the Southern saying
goes. Director Leon "Uncle" Todd is a classic example of a House Negro who will
do anything to protect the Massa' and maintain the status quo. He has partnered
with an "Aunt Jemima"—Joan Hollingsworth, a controversial public relations consultant who has made no secret of her love for green over Black—to sabotage and
undermine the school reform movement. Both Todd and Hollingsworth have
financial ties to the MTEA and philosophical ties to People for the American Way.
Part of the Todd/Hollingsworth strategy was to use a small but well-financed group
of Black ministers to declare their opposition to school choice. The effort fell short
of its goal of turning the Black masses against the program. Plan B was the character assassination of school choice leaders.

Todd has also waged a campaign to close two African-immersion specialty schools
even though they have shown the most significant increases in student achievement
in the district. Todd's rationale is rooted in his belief that African history and culture
are decadent. He claims that the program, which has won national acclaim and is
replicated in urban areas around the country, "teaches voodoo."[7] Ironically (and
thankfully), neither of the targeted immersion schools are in his district.

The other two Black MPS board directors are Charlene Hardin, who came
under attack in the White media for business indiscretions, questionable financial

ties to the educracy, and her dismissal from a position within MPS (a fact that wasn't disclosed until after her election) and Joe Fisher, who fellow director John Gardner, a choice supporter, has charged is a union apologist. Fisher, a former MPS teacher whose political campaign, like Hardin's, was paid for by the MTEA, has been ridiculed by Gardner for having "sold out the children of MPS and the tax-payers when he worked out secret deals with the MTEA" that resulted in a recent contract that many analysis say will bankrupt the district.

I don't know if William Rogers, an instructor of African American history at Lakeland College, coined the term "Negrocracy," but his theory is premised on a long-rumored scenario in which outside interests control the direction, scope, and heartbeat of the Civil Rights movement through ordained Black leaders. The Negrocracy, explained Rogers during a lecture at Khamit Community School in summer 1998, consists of a select group of Black leaders whose actions and agenda are controlled by White special interests. The Negrocracy can be traced back to the American abolitionist movement and included such early African leaders as Frederick Douglass. History no doubt judges Douglass as a true Black hero and an instrumental agent in the first civil/human rights movement—one who knowingly allowed himself to be sponsored by White benefactors to advance his agenda of ending slavery and, later, of assimilation of the Negro into American society. Not all members of the Negrocracy before or since have allowed themselves to be used for the greater good. In fact, many were truly pawns of special interests on the Left and Right whose sole agenda was to slow the inevitable progress of the Freedom Train.

Such was the dichotomy of the Negrocracy.

Over the next hundred-plus years, many Black leaders have used or been used by the supporters of Negrocracy to direct the Black movement. Some were poverty and victimology pimps who sold their credibility for a few dollars, leading Black America down dead ends. For most, however, the coalition was a means to an end. One of the most illuminating examples of the Negrocracy at work was the efforts of Booker T. Washington, who accepted the support and guidance of White corporate and political America in exchange for the opportunity to open doors for America's Black have-nots. Some today may call Booker T. an Uncle Tom, yet that would be far from true; if he committed a crime by joining the Negrocracy, he had impressive company, ranging from W. E. B. DuBois to A. Philip Randolph to Dr. Martin Luther King Jr. Some today suggest that Booker T. Washington was a classic nationalist who, unlike the NAACP or SCLC, rejected integration as the cure-all and sought Black empowerment through job skills and community building. His legacy exists today in the form of Tuskegee Institute and thousands of journeymen for whom he paved the way. Those who subscribed to the Negrocracy often faced a difficult decision: to accept the assistance (with obvious strings attached) or to go the longer route—underfinanced campaigns that, in many cases, encountered hostile resistance and violent confrontation.

Obviously, that paradox continues today. The prime examples are leaders of the NAACP, who find their strings being pulled by corporate benefactors, labor unions, and missionary groups such as PFAW. Those groups have effectively stalled the Civil Rights movement, focusing on occasional discrimination suits, cries for justice and integration, and efforts to convince the frustrated and disenchanted Black masses that they must remain shackled to the plantation walls. The last thing these puppeteers want is to empower Black America.

Surely there is evidence of a Negrocracy attempting to circumvent the school choice movement. It involves key Black choice opponents in Milwaukee, including Leon Todd, Walter Farrell, and, to a lesser extent, Joan Hollingsworth and Paulette Copeland. Locally, the Negrocracy is well represented, and it is no coincidence that those who spoke out the loudest against school choice and its proponents also hold membership in this unique club. But these local subscribers' motivations are not exactly as pure as Booker T. Washington's.

Hollingsworth, for example, is a paid organizer with financial ties to the MTEA and political bonds to obscure missionary White political groups such as the Labor and Farm Party and the Reform Party. Hollingsworth's quest to be included in the Negrocracy is rooted in both her desire to assimilate—to be accepted by Left of Left Whites she seemingly idolizes and for whom she is willing to sell out her people—and her desire for the Almighty Dollar (which, given her public pronouncements, is probably the stronger motivation).

Todd's motivations are similar, although his illogical and even sophomoric attacks on school choice and African-centered curricula puts on public display his ignorance, racial self-hatred, and lack of cultural self-esteem. Farrell, easily more intelligent and articulate than Todd or Hollingsworth, sees himself as a gatekeeper. His philosophy (like Todd's) is tainted by a personal hatred and jealousy of Howard Fuller and by envy and chauvinism toward Polly Williams and Zakiya Courtney. Also, Farrell's continual flip-flopping support for choice (often he claimed he supported it; at other times he denounced it as a conspiracy of the Right) and the fact that he hid his consulting relationship with the MTEA throughout the school choice debate say a great deal about his character. But that is often the case with certain power- or ego-driven members of the Negrocracy who are used as paid pawns and who put dollars before ethnic loyalty. Sadly, that's a situation with which Black America must come to grips: often things are not black and white, but rather shades of gray. Not all Black leaders or spokespersons are moved by the grand ideal of Black advancement, equality, and justice. There are many House Negroes in our midst who are not in the big house to spy or disrupt.

The school choice debate makes friends out of enemies and enemies out of friends. It often blurs the distinction between Black and White. We have learned that there are indeed issues of mutual concern that can be advanced if we play the game and extend a hand across the political, ideological, or cultural aisle. We must take criticism with a grain of salt while we seek whatever help is available to tear down our plantation walls. Once again, as Howard Fuller observed, "while politics does make strange bedfellows, you don't have to sleep under the covers."

For Black America, the struggle will have to be waged under new rules, in strange battlefields—and sometimes with new and stranger bedfellows.

14. Black America is in denial about the roots of its social dilemma—and the solutions.

It's time we separate fact from fiction and take a cold hard look at what is the by-product of institutional racism and what is our own doing. Can we blame the KKK for Black-on-Black crime and violence? Can we blame the Republicans for teen pregnancy? Can we put the onus for fatherless children on the conservative Right? Racism remains a major impediment to Black progress; it limits our options and detours our dreams. But it is a stretch to suggest that there are bigots littering our ghetto streets or that the KKK forces us to refer to and treat each other like "niggers" (a term I detest). Indeed, we are in denial about the extent of barriers to Black progress and the real obstacles to empowerment. Too many of us don't support our institutions, protect each other, honor our women and men, and raise our children with a reverence for God, community, and self. The shadow of slavery looms over too many Black heads. And until we turn inward, tap into the greatness that flows through our veins, until we seek our own course and control our own destiny, we will continue to be second-class citizens.

Racism is still pervasive in America. White supremacy is real, and apartheid exists. No doubt, those strong forces have negatively affected the Black mindset. But we can't blame racism for all of the problems that plague our community. Nor can we afford to use it as a crutch. Most of those who contribute to our social anarchy, to our socioeconomic and political status, stand among us. Racism doesn't control us.

It's time to wake up, to step out from under the shadow of slavery.

15. For too long others have spoken for us.

Black press founders John Russwurm and Samuel Cornish were right. As long as we allow others to speak for us, to misinterpret our desires and agenda, we will languish in second-class citizenship. Our Freedom Train will be stuck at the station or will cling to a track that may provide a wonderful view but will take us nowhere significant.

The school choice campaign taught us that the opposition will not go to any lengths to maintain the status quo. However, we have proven that ten thousand ants can eat the mighty elephant. When all is said and done, America must learn that Black Americans—poor, uneducated, or even dysfunctional—have an inherent power stronger than any opposing force.

Chapter 11

WHERE ARE THEY NOW?
A POLITICAL BIOGRAPHY

We are engaged in nation building.
—MARCUS GARVEY

T he lives of the key officers in the school choice army and its opposition were forever changed by the war. Some officers found themselves
propelled into positions of national prominence. Others were punished for their adherence to misguided agendas or their unwillingness
to place the needs of the Black masses over those of political parties. Some faded
happily from the public view; others resented being victimized for their actions and
beliefs.

WALTER FARRELL

Among the leading opponents of the school choice movement, Walter Farrell,
Department of Community Education instructor at the University of Wisconsin–
Milwaukee, remained a thorn in the side of choice proponents until he was unceremoniously knocked from his perch as a columnist for the *Milwaukee Courier* and
was booted out of his job as a radio talk show host at WNOV. Farrell found out the
hard way that there are repercussions to slander, and he was lucky to leave the
radio station in one piece after lambasting Black leader Mike McGee in 1998. In
true Farrell style, he lambasted McGee and his plan to carve out a separate
Black enclave, going so far as to suggest that McGee, a former alderman and
founder of the Milwaukee Black Panther Militia, has misappropriated seed money
for the project. McGee was not amused and publicly declared his intent to "kick

Farrell's ass." Soon thereafter, Farrell received a pink slip from WNOV management, which also owns the *Milwaukee Courier.*

McGee, one of the Black community's most respected and powerful Black leaders, was just one of a dozen or so individuals Farrell targeted for vicious attacks as part of what was clearly a campaign to undermine the emerging Black nationalistic movement. Not coincidentally, most of the victims of Farrell's attacks were supportive of school choice. His motives were soon under community scrutiny, as the *Milwaukee Journal Sentinel* revealed that Farrell had applied for a superintendent's position in Minneapolis (his name had been suggested for Milwaukee's superintendency the year before by Leon Todd) and that he was a paid consultant for the MTEA.

Without his Black media forums, Farrell was left to rely on his weekly appearance as a pundit on the *Mark Belling Television Show*, a weekly news and information television show carried on the local ABC affiliate station. Farrell remains a player to the extent that he can maneuver around his new credibility problem. However, he is a clever and resourceful individual who can't be counted out. He continues his "mentorship" of School Board Director Leon Todd, helped to orchestrate the candidacy of Board Director Charlene Hardin and maintains his camaraderie with Milwaukee's Black elite.

LAURI WYNN

Lauri Wynn all but disappeared from the public limelight after the Wisconsin Supreme Court's 1991 ruling affirming the original school choice program. Not only was she extraordinarily silent throughout the debate to expand school choice to religious schools, but she removed herself from a leadership role in the debate over charters although her input was supposedly sought by the teachers union, which needed a Black point-person to help derail that initiative.

Though her service was primarily behind-the-scenes, Wynn remained active in the NAACP. She was also involved with a small group of Black ministers led by Rev. Roy Nabors, who waged a short but highly publicized campaign to derail choice, charters, and serious school reform. That campaign, however, quickly fell apart when the *Milwaukee Community Journal* questioned the origins of a $20,000 ad campaign orchestrated by the ministers. It was suggested by many that PFAW and the Wisconsin Education Association fronted the group, which reintroduced a previously rejected public school reform package that had been developed by the former head of the WEA as a cure-all solution to the system's dysfunctionality.

Wynn's role as the chief spokesperson for the antichoice forces was apparently taken over by Paulette Copeland, who was elected president of the MTEA in 1997. Some suggest that Wynn was relieved. Though she remains ardently supportive of the teachers union and opposed to school choice, she often seemed uncomfortable as a spokesperson for an agenda and organization with a history of antagonism and opposition to Black leadership.

In November 1998, Wynn was defeated in a bid to become the second vice president of the local branch of NAACP, a defeat that she took in stride, further exemplifying her grand style and poise. Of all the critics of school choice, Lauri Wynn is the one you just couldn't stay angry at, even if you vehemently disagreed with her position. She was and continues to be a grand lady and a role model—if not for her ideology, then for her courage, tenacity, and perseverance.

FELMERS CHANEY AND THE NAACP

Felmers Chaney followed a course similar to Lauri Wynn's. Though he took an occasional potshot at school choice, he was reserved in his comments as the expanded version made its way through the legislature and ultimately the courts. Some say he was preoccupied with other NAACP matters, which included a precedent-setting settlement against the American Family Insurance Company and an attention-grabbing national discrimination case against the U.S. Postal Service, which has yet to be resolved. The NAACP also championed a voting rights lawsuit to increase the number of Black judges in Milwaukee. The suit was dismissed, although the case generated much interest and highlighted a major flaw in the electoral process. Some suggest, however, that the NAACP would have better served the community through voter registration and education programs. They noted that less than 30 percent of eligible African Americans actually vote, another sign of apathy and frustration with the system.

Chaney's leadership came under fire as the religious school choice proposal was making its way through the state assembly and senate and ultimately the courts. NAACP membership dipped, the office was often closed, and committees were dissolved without formal declarations or hearings. The result was a highly publicized election on November 15, 1998, that included a renegade slate offered by Chaney after he was excluded from the slate developed by a special branch nominating committee. The substitution slate included Chaney, Nate Conyers, publisher of the weekly *Milwaukee Times*, and Lauri Wynn as second vice president. The election, which drew the attention but not the direct intervention of the national branch, was further marred by allegations that anti-Chaney members were not allowed to vote. As a result of numerous challenges, the election results were not officially announced until two days after the election. When the smoke cleared, Chaney's slate was ousted. The new president is Jerry Ann Hamilton, a former Chaney ally who headed a reform slate that included several senior NAACP icons such as Vel Phillips, a former alderwoman and Wisconsin Secretary of State, and Martha Toran, a Democratic Party delegate and retired businesswoman.

Hamilton asserted during the campaign that the branch had steadily lost membership and respect in the African-American community and was AWOL on issues like welfare reform, criminal justice, and educational reform. The local branch leadership needed an infusion of younger members, a greater link to the community it serves, and a mélange of new strategies to attack the myriad problems plaguing Black Milwaukee, she said. Whether that will happen under Hamilton and her new officers, however, is open to question, not only because the organization continues to be led by older activists with roots and agendas forged by the traditional civil rights assimilation vanguard but also because the organization is not seen by the grassroots community as presenting viable solutions to our problems. As a vehicle through which to legally seek redress to civil rights violations or acts of discrimination, the NAACP remains vital. But the fact that the organization has turned a deaf ear to its constituents who have for the last two decades been crying out for empowerment and silver rights says something of great significance. The pendulum has shifted from assimilation to Black empowerment, but the NAACP continues to deny the transition. As Kevin Walker noted in a November 11, 1998, essay excerpted in the *Milwaukee Community Journal* following the NAACP elections, the leadership of the branch, even without 80-year-old Chaney at the helm, continues to espouse an agenda that has long since proven ineffectual, and which lacks support in the African-American community.[1]

Walker believes that little will change under the new officers, in part because younger Black Milwaukeeans and a growing percentage of the new emerging leadership have abandoned the assimilation tactics of the 1960s for more pragmatic and nationalistic strategies offered by such Black leaders as Minister Louis Farrakhan nationally and, locally, Polly Williams and Howard Fuller—each of whom has, remarkably, bridged the generation gap, gaining support from the hip-hop crowd. The NAACP will continue to have a role in advocacy for diversity in the workforce and in the schools and, if it can attract pro bono legal assistance, can continue its tradition of legally challenging discrimination in the courts. But in more fundamental issues of concern to Black Milwaukee—jobs, economic development, housing, and education—the NAACP's agenda is myopic at best.

What will the new leadership mean for school choice? Writes Walker:

Even before Chaney, the local chapter's leadership was so outspoken about maintaining the push to desegregate the city's schools that even after that was accomplished as much as it could, they still strove for numerical integration even after African-American parents had long soured on the discredited goal.[2]

Hamilton, says Walker, is a former Milwaukee Public Schools teacher with strong ties to the MTEA machinery. Thus, she is no better a friend to educational reform than Chaney. She has publicly expressed her opposition to school choice, and even went so far as to get involved with a plan to stop the creation of the Malcolm X Middle School four years earlier, stressing that the African-centered curriculum would not appeal to Whites and thus would not promote integration, the foundation of the NAACP's mission. Hamilton, Walker says, worked with a dissident group of teachers who wanted the curriculum weakened and the school named after the late Supreme Court Justice Thurgood Marshall. (Ironically, just prior to his death, Marshall was made aware of the renaming controversy and reportedly announced his opposition to the school's being named after him, citing reasons similar to Hamilton's.) Hamilton also sided with the MTEA when that union challenged then-Superintendent Howard Fuller's effort to put more Black teachers on the Malcolm X staff, in violation of a school desegregation settlement provision that placed a quota on the number and percentage of Black teachers who can teach at any given MPS school. The MTEA ultimately won an arbitration battle on that point.

Hamilton's current chief allies include MPS Board Director Leon Todd, which means she can be counted on to maintain the status quo of the NAACP regarding choice, charters, and African-centered curricula. The NAACP will continue to be out of touch with Black parents starved for educational options for their children and frustrated by the false promises of integration and the fruitless cries for reform. There may be new captains at the helm, but unless the organization can plot a course that most disadvantaged African Americans can relate to and support, the NAACP ship will continue to cruise in circles.

Walker's assessments are generally accurate, as is his theory that choice opponents' tactics will now shift to character assassination of education reform leaders through media vehicles such as the *Milwaukee Journal Sentinel* and the *Shepherd Express*, which is, as mentioned previously, an over-the-edge leftist newspaper with an anti–Black nationalist editorial slant and ownership ties to the MTEA. The MTEA and PFAW will also front Black opponents to school choice in an effort to defuse criticism that its opposition is racially motivated. Walker believes that Paulette Copeland and Jerry Ann Hamilton will be used as replacements for Wynn and

Chaney. Todd will also continue in his role as chief apologist for the racist policies of the MPS, derailing any substitute proposals that would empower Black families.

Without a platform, Chaney will be limited in his public leadership role; however, it isn't expected he will completely fade from view. He is active with the PFAW campaign to derail school choice and may be thrust into the limelight by that organization. Moreover, as a respected elder statesman, he will be given special status and privileges as warranted by his years of sacrifice and struggle. His opposition to school choice notwithstanding, Chaney remains an icon of import and respectability in the African-American community.

HOWARD FULLER

Howard Fuller, among other key choice lieutenants, saw his career and community status blossom as a result of his efforts. Fuller became superintendent of MPS, where he sought to put into place an educational consortium he called the System of Schools Blueprint. The structure was premised on the theory that a variety of educational options were needed to empower parents and fulfill student educational needs and career aspirations.

Fuller sought to transform the public school system from the self-serving monstrosity that it had become. But the founder of Malcolm X College quickly found his task herculean: decades of bureaucracy and antipathy had virtually fossilized the system. Fuller also found himself sandwiched between the teachers union, whose special interests began and ended with teacher benefits, and the school board— myopic and rudderless, yet controlled by special interests, including the MTEA and the entrenched educracy.

Making matters worse were the ongoing battles with decade-old foe Leon Todd—and this time Todd was essentially Fuller's boss. Todd's all-encompassing hatred for Fuller manifested itself in hundreds of skirmishes that left Fuller exhausted and the education community stagnant. Todd attacked nearly every initiative introduced by Fuller. Two years later, the MTEA was able to orchestrate the election of three more board members and thus essentially control the board by a 5-4 majority. In 1996 Fuller resigned in frustration.

After his resignation, he accepted a position at Marquette University and established the Institute for the Transformation of Learning, an educational research and advocacy group created to enhance educational opportunities for poor children and to right the injustice of a failed and corrupted public education system.

The institute has established half a dozen tutorial and educational satellite centers in Central City churches, providing technical assistance for dozens of private schools, and has launched a program with ministers and community activists to organize parents to deal more effectively with the public school system.

The institute, whose research on educational issues has attracted national attention, was a partner in establishing a Web site (www.epic.com) in conjunction with the University of Wisconsin, the mayor's office, and PAVE. The site offers information on every public and private school in Milwaukee: parents now have immediate access to information enabling them to make informed choices about educational options for their children.

Fuller has also championed the charter school movement in Milwaukee. When MPS refused to accept charters under state law, Fuller masterminded a legislative battle enabling the University of Wisconsin, the city of Milwaukee, and Milwaukee Area Technical College to grant charters. The first three charters were granted by the city in summer 1998 under Fuller's direct scrutiny. At last glance, he was responding to the governor's request to blueprint a major school reform package to be considered in 1999.

BROTHER BOB SMITH

Brother Bob Smith became a pivotal player on the national level, emerging from his quiet perch as principal of Messmer High School to become a chief spokesperson for school choice and Black empowerment. His advocacy of school choice sometimes took a back seat to his promotion of Messmer High School as an example of what can be achieved in an urban setting with high expectations, parental involvement, and a sound curriculum. Messmer was pivotal to the school choice debate, not only because of its academic excellence, but because it was viewed by poor Black and White parents as the ultimate prize in the quest to break the cycle of educational mediocrity. Before the expansion of the program to religious schools, efforts to make Messmer a choice school became a rallying cry of parents seeking better education for their children. As the premier Central City private school, Messmer not only boasted of having the highest collective GPA, the highest Black graduation rate, and the largest percentage of Black graduates who went on to college in the state of Wisconsin, but it also held the distinction of being the only school in the state where the Black and White grade point averages were identical. While the gap between Black and White GPAs in the public system had remained wide during the last decade (provoking questions from Black parents about a conspiracy and institutional bias), at Messmer White and Black students emerged from the classrooms on equal academic footing. The fact that most of its students are from low-income families or are otherwise disadvantaged made Messmer's accomplishments all the more impressive.

Those facts did not go unnoticed inside MPS central administration, nor at the meeting rooms at the state Department of Public Instruction facility in Madison, in conversations between Black women at the beauty salon, or among Black men over a game of chess. It was the topic of discussion in Black churches, at community meetings, and in political circles—on both sides of the aisle. Messmer's success (as well as that of other community schools) is a paradox MPS and DPI have refused to address. To do so would obviously open a Pandora's box of related questions that would undermine the public schools' excuse bank, bringing into question the public school system's inability (or unwillingness) to duplicate the private schools' results. But they are facts that can't be ignored. Personally, I put them out for public digestion as often as possible through the *Milwaukee Community Journal*, and through my weekly participation as both a pundit on WTMJ's *Sunday Insight with Charles Sykes* and a weekly commentator on the NBC network affiliate station in Milwaukee, WTMJ, Channel 4.

Often my commentaries have focused on the words and deeds of Brother Bob Smith, who was impassioned about education in general, but was obsessed when the topic focused on Messmer and the opportunities available for the disenfranchised low-income families through the school choice program.

Brother Bob's voice, a smooth, undistinguished tenor, could send shivers up the spine of choice opponents. Beyond reproach as a community leader and educator, Brother Bob's intellect and quick wit made him the perfect messenger for our campaign.

His unique position and keen articulation of the issues moved Brother Bob to the national limelight, the lecture circuit, and several nationally televised debates on school reform, school choice, and the new shift in direction for the Civil Rights movement. In 1997 he became the first African-American board member of the Bradley Foundation, where he prioritized redirecting the organization's wealth to Black grassroots organizations intent on rebuilding the African-American community through self-actualization programs.

ZAKIYA COURTNEY

Zakiya Courtney and her husband Tony Courtney, a longtime community activist and political strategist, led the parent and community takeover of Malcolm X Middle School, an African immersion school. Defying the union and Todd, the

Courtneys put into place the system's first true site-based management program. After ousting a core group of White teachers who ferociously fought the curriculum, the Courtneys helped turn around the fledgling school.

In a one-year period, the school's GPA increased from the lowest in the district—less than 1.9—to nearly 2.4. The suspension rate was reduced by 700 percent and class attendance doubled. Parental involvement also soared, making the school a model for the district. Equally important, the students were able to acquire something offered in few schools in the district: cultural pride and academic excellence.

The Courtneys moved on from Malcolm X to start their own school, the Khamit Institute, which offers an even stronger African-centered curriculum. Tony soon accepted a position as president of the State Charter School Association, and in summer 1998, the Khamit Institute, along with the Marva Collins Preparatory School and Bruce Guadalupe Community School, signed contracts to become Milwaukee's first charter schools. The MTEA immediately filed a lawsuit to halt the program.

Courtney maintained her position as president of Parents for School Choice and works as a consultant and part-time teacher at Khamit Institute when she is not working with Howard Fuller at the Institute for the Transformation of Learning. She also works with several reform organizations and is a central figure in the choice movement nationally.

POLLY WILLIAMS

Polly Williams has earned international acclaim for her work in spearheading a movement that has changed the educational landscape. Williams was rewarded for her work on school choice by the GOP, which named her head of the assembly's Urban Education Committee, allowing her to set the educational agenda and fine-tune the Parental School Choice Program. Even as the expanded school choice bill was weaving its way through the legislative system, Williams was holding hearings to make the private schools more accountable to parents and students.

Williams also got involved in religious-school choice legislation, amending the bill to expand the number of seats from five thousand to fifteen thousand as well as allow low-income students attending private schools the year before to come under the school choice umbrella. Williams continues to work for educational reform. The mother of school choice has introduced proposals that would limit busing for desegregation and shift resources to neighborhood schools. She is also working on a proposal to increase the number of Black teachers in MPS through an accelerated certificate program and has been talking with interested parties about reintroducing her North Division School District Plan.

Like Brother Bob Smith, Williams found herself much in demand as a speaker nationwide, addressing audiences on the Left and Right, espousing an agenda rooted in Black nationalism. In addition, she has championed the campaign for school choice and Black independent schools through the National Association of State Legislators. In December 1997 she hosted a workshop on educational reform and school choice as the association held its annual convention in Milwaukee.

Williams's foray into political gamesmanship has earned her national acclaim and dozens of local awards. But it also brought her the enmity of the Democratic Party leadership, the teachers union, and several prominent Black national leaders whose liberal politics and watered-down agendas made them the darlings of the mass media and missionary coalitions. By putting her people before her party, Williams has paid a price, including exclusion from Democratic caucus sessions and the loss of committee chair positions.

Williams states that her relationship with the Democratic caucus in particular has always been tenuous.

"I'm not going to smile in their faces if they slap me, I'm going to slap them back. Treat me with respect, support me on common sense issues, and we don't have a problem. But I'm not bowing down, and I told them from jump street that I will never put the party's issues before my people's. Never.

"When we criticized desegregation, they got on my case. When I pushed for the Black school district, they said I was a segregationist. They said the missionaries knew what is best for us. The Democratic Party don't want Black people to have our own agenda, to run our own house. Most of them are patronizing in their approach to Black people. I let them know exactly where I'm coming from and tell them we want to run our own community. If they can't deal with it, so be it."

Williams's relationship with the Democratic caucus reached a breaking point over the North Division School District Plan, which was feverishly opposed by the state and local teachers unions. It was said that the situation reached a fever pitch when several high-ranking Democrats ordered Williams to back away from the proposal and she told them to go to hell. She then went on a crusade to expose their hypocrisy: supporting union interests over those of the Black children of Milwaukee, who were failing in record numbers.

Still stifled by political resistance from her party, Williams then topped her act of resistance with a cherry by meeting with Republicans to gain the necessary votes needed for passage of the North Division School District bill. Much to the dismay of Democratic Party leadership, that strategy worked, and the bill passed the assembly in 1988. It was later killed in the senate, and Williams believed Democrats used a Black lawmaker to table the measure in order to send her a message as well as to ward off any charges of racism.

But the die was cast, and Williams's relationship with her party would never be the same.

More often than not, her liberal colleagues couldn't deal with her straightforward Black nationalist approach to politics and community concerns, and whenever possible, they tried to muzzle her—or at the very least, limit her effectiveness as an activist by putting her on time-consuming and irrelevant committees. They also attempted to dilute her constituency base through reapportionment in an attempt to oust her from office. After that strategy failed, party officials—even several Black officials—simply maintained a distance from her, using their control over the local White media to ostracize her.

Candid as always, Williams confessed, "This is basically it for me . . . I'll never get plum committee assignments, and the chance of me running for senate in a district with a sizable Black voting bloc is impossible. I really don't care. This to me has all been a means to an end. Some of the people in Madison just want to be politicians, to have power, to get in the paper, or be held in high esteem. This, for me, has always been a *mission*.

"All I ever wanted to do was improve the quality of life for Black people. That's why I don't care [about criticism from the Democratic Party]. They can put me in corner, and I'm still going to fight. I'm not in this to make friends. My friends live where I live and have the problems I have because we're Black in America. I don't ever forget that, and they won't let me forget why things are that way."

The fiery proponent of Black Power takes her censorship in stride, saying that she is accountable only to the people she serves, and the Party will always be secondary to her membership in the Black community. Democrats and missionaries may not like Williams, but her power base in the Black community continues to be strong, and her influence and popularity are unequaled among Black politicians.

MIKEL HOLT AND THE *MILWAUKEE COMMUNITY* JOURNAL

As for me, I found myself uniquely positioned to expound on the virtues of school choice and cultural nationalism on both the local and national fronts. Articles I wrote about school desegregation and educational reform earned the 1996 and 1998 A. Philip Randolph Award and thus introduced our struggle to thousands through syndication in Black newspapers around the country. In 1997, while attending the founding convention of the Independent Political Party in St. Louis,

I made what was considered a compelling appeal for the inclusion of school choice in the new Black National Agenda. It was voted in and thus stands as a complement to expanding site-based management and African-centered education as key strategies for forcing change.

In summer 1998, Harambee board members—Sister Callista Robinson, Rhodesia Evans, Kathy Barnes, Judge Russell Stamper, and Cleveland Lee—participated in the National Black United Front annual convention in Houston. During the conference, we were allowed to state our case for school choice and were apparently able to dispel enough myths about the program that it was accepted for further review by that organization as a possible platform item. The National Black United Front now hopes to launch a chapter in Milwaukee next year to offer an alternative to traditional civil rights methodologies.

My main emphasis, however, has been to continue filling the informational void in Milwaukee. I have essentially become a power broker of sorts as a result of school choice, weaving between Democrats and Republicans, liberals and conservatives, using the forums at my disposal to advance issues, to inform and educate, and when necessary to provide balance and to follow the tenet of the Black press: "to plead our own cause. . . . "

The *Milwaukee Community Journal* still finds itself under attack by the MTEA, some MPS School Board members, and traditionalists with fading dreams that America will suddenly awaken from its deep sleep and empower the poor, integrate its institutions, and correct centuries of injustice. The *MCJ*'s influence has continued to grow, and our support base and reception are unequaled among Milwaukee newspapers. I continue to espouse Black self-determination and cultural nationalism as the most viable cures for Black impotency and socioeconomic despair. Apparently, our agenda is gaining a significant foothold as more Black Milwaukeeans embrace its philosophy. A growing number of Black youth and elders espouse an interest in a collective and unified response to oppression and indifference. Indeed, one need only look at the growing Black observance of Kwanzaa, whose seven principals are the basic tenets of Black cultural nationalism—Umoja (unity), Kujichagulia (self-determination), Ujima (collective work and responsibility), Ujamma (cooperative economics), Nia (purpose), Kuumba (creativity), and Imani (faith).

Kwanzaa creator Dr. Mulana Ron Karenga defined Black nationalism as the "political beliefs and practice of African Americans as a distinct people with a distinct historical personality who politically should develop structures to define, defend, and develop the interests of Black Americans as a people. This entails a definition of reality in Black images and interests, providing a social corrective by building institutional and organizational structures that house Black aspirations, and it provides a collective vocation of nation building among Black people as a political end."[3]

THE SCHOOL CHOICE ARMY

Those who enlisted in Williams's school choice army shared an unquenchable thirst for educational reform and Black empowerment. We shared a vision of children reaching their full potential in environments where teachers cared, shared, nurtured, and groomed.

We found ourselves targets of the unions, Democratic Party leaders, and Black (mis)leaders, their attacks intensifying as support for school choice grew in the African-American community. And that support did grow—from 60 percent in 1989 to nearly 80 percent by the time the religious school legislation was signed into law in 1997, according to many research groups including the Black Research Organization, the Wisconsin Policy Institute, and the *Milwaukee Journal Sentinel* marketing department. Choice parents were called misguided pawns of the Right and we, the officers in Polly's Parental Choice Platoon, were treated as if we had committed a crime. Well, maybe we had.

Our crime is that we care. Our crime is that we believe all parents should have the right to avail themselves of educational options they feel are right for their children. Our crime is putting our people before political parties and job security. Our crime is our refusal to accept the status quo, our desire for something better for our children and our community. Our crime is being willing to do whatever is necessary to move our nation forward.

The school choice battle was not about public versus private schools. Nor was it about good versus bad teachers. In many respects it wasn't even about education or school choice at all. The real battle is achieving African-American goals: whether we have a right as a people to establish our own agenda or whether we must continue under the thumb of others. Should we continue down a road of good intentions, missionary politics, and programs that end up mostly benefiting others—programs that chain us as much as slavery did—or will we break the chains of dependency and ignorance?

CHAPTER

12

NOT YET "FREE AT LAST"

If you dream it, have faith in it and struggle for it.
—MARIAN WRIGHT EDELMAN

The 1998 Metropolitan Milwaukee Alliance of Black School Educators (MMABSE) Fall Conference is the largest gathering of Black professional educators in the state. The 28th annual conference, "Ujima! Educating Our Children: If We Don't, Who Will?" was held at the Clarion Hotel and Convention Center, across from Milwaukee's Mitchell International Airport. It was expected that the conference, surprisingly held at the same time as the state and Milwaukee teachers' conventions, would draw three to four hundred Black educators and educational activists. Instead it drew nearly seven hundred, many of whom were non-MMABSE members interested in the workshops, which ranged from a debate on school choice to a discussion about African-centered curricula.

The past few years had witnessed unprecedented local educational reforms that not only signaled a shift in educational politics, but posed unique questions for MMABSE membership. Over its twenty-nine-year history, MMABSE had undergone many philosophical metamorphoses, moving from a fiery rhetoric during the turbulent '70s to a more fraternal tone following so-called metropolitan desegregation. Partially reflecting changing norms in the African-American community, from the late '80s on the organization espoused a more culturally attuned philosophy. The membership of a greater number of radical educators from the private sector as well as younger public-school teachers with nationalistic philosophies has again reshaped the organization, drawing it out as a civil rights player.

Most MMABSE members are working professionals; the majority are employed by Milwaukee Public Schools. All members attest to sharing a concern for the welfare of Black students. But conflicting ideologies within the organization have made for interesting, if not fruitful, philosophical clashes, much along the lines of what has splintered the larger community. Strangely, the organization has never taken a public position on school choice, which may reflect differing opinions on the initiative or officers' unwillingness to take sides on such an explosive issue. It did not, however, go unnoticed that the organization recently opened its own private school; MMABSE is light years away from the obstinate platform of the MTEA.

I was invited to participate in a no-holds-barred debate on school choice, one of the most potentially volatile workshops of the conference. With Zakiya Courtney and Jodi Goldberg, an alternative-school teacher, I was to take on Paulette Copeland, president of the MTEA, Edd Doerr, executive director of Americans for Religious Liberty, and June Harris, education coordinator of the House of Representatives.

Before I was diverted by the erroneous and misleading statements of opponents of choice on the panel, I had intended to provide the Black teachers with a report card of sorts on the status of public education: according to my analysis of the statistics presented in Milwaukee Catalyst's report *Act on the Facts*,[1] the public school system would receive a failing grade. The report from Milwaukee Catalyst, a new citywide coalition of parents pressing for parental empowerment and public school reform, showed that the quality of education in MPS had actually declined significantly in recent years. Even I was shocked by the report, which had been complied using MPS statistics, but as the debate wore on, I felt it imperative to counter the rhetoric of the other panelists.

When it was my turn to speak, I was introduced as the editor of the *MCJ*, a weekly pundit on the Sunday Insight television programs, a board member of Harambee Community School, and a member of the University of Wisconsin School of Education's Advisory Committee. At the podium, I glanced at the notes I had prepared but tossed them aside. I scanned the room for a few seconds, locking eyes with several teachers.

"I was going to talk about this latest report that came from a parent's organization and talk about education in the city of Milwaukee," I said, holding up a copy of Milwaukee Catalyst's report. "But I'm going to leave that alone because we all know what the problems are. Let me just clarify one thing by saying I'm a Black nationalist. I'm not politically attuned to the Democrat or Republican Parties, I think they're different wings on the same bird, and all this bird has been doing is dropping its load on Black America. I just came back from a national convention to try and start an independent Black political party, but that's another issue. I'm about Black empowerment, us controlling the institutions and politics of our community. "

I quickly shifted topics and smiled. "I'm almost tempted to mimic Rodney King and ask, 'Can't we all just get along?' Because what this issue is really about is children, Black children getting an education. I don't care if they get an education in a tree house. If someone tells me that a Black child can get a superior education in a tree house, I'll go get some wood. And if you're serious about educating Black children I would hope you would meet me at the lumberyard. Because we are failing a whole generation of Black children today. Children who will either be in a position of power tomorrow, or they won't be, by virtue of decisions adults make today.

"There's a lot of misinformation . . . which makes our efforts to have an intelligent conversation harder because of the myths and fabrications and distortions of historical fact. I'm in the process of concluding my research on a book right now that's on the history of school choice and educational reform in Milwaukee; the ongoing struggle of Black Milwaukeeans to get quality education for their children.

"Let me correct some myths real quick: neither the Republican Party, the Bradley Foundation, the Conservative Right nor the Wizard of Oz started the school choice movement, I hate to tell y'all who need to think otherwise to support your position . . . Actually, the governor wasn't the first to introduce school choice. The first choice movement . . . was started in 1970 here in Milwaukee and was funded by the Social Development Commission for a Black parent group! The school board killed the proposal, which would have earmarked federal funds to Milwaukee for a choice initiative. That campaign was started because Black citizens wanted an alternative for their children; they were unsatisfied with the quality offered by MPS, and frustrated by the refusal of the school board to equalize resources. That's a reality, you know what it was like in 1970, and it's gotten worse in many respects.

"The second choice proposal came from Thompson," I said, explaining it was shot down by the Democratic-controlled assembly in 1988. "The third proposal, introduced the following year —and you'll be shocked by this one, because it wasn't introduced by Black parents, or politicians, but was introduced by Milwaukee Public Schools administration under Robert Peterkin.

"School choice wasn't a bad idea all of a sudden when he introduced it. The only reason it became an issue, and Polly Williams got involved, was because that proposal had criteria for participation that were insulting and stigmatizing. Your mama had to be from a poor family with no education. They described 'at-risk' as 'dysfunctional' and stigmatized anyone who would participate. So Harambee Community and other Black independent schools' board members opposed it. We did not want our kids to be stigmatized, and we didn't want to lose our autonomy.

"Enter Polly with legislation to amend that proposal. Oh yes, there were some other strange things about that legislation: MPS would be the intermediary and would get money off the top. They could also use the grade point averages of all the students who participated as if they were educated in a MPS school. That said something as well.

"Both bills were shot down in the assembly, but they did attract a lot of attention and interest. Immediately afterwards, Black parents went to Polly to reintroduce the legislation. That's when we all got together, Black activists and parents and school board members, and decided to push school choice as an alternative and as a catalyst for change. No Bradley Foundation, no White folks, period. This movement was generated by Black parents who met every week to talk about quality education, but more importantly options for their children. They were not opposed to MPS, never have been, although we've always had serious problems with the system. It was always about options for the poor. We recognized then, as you do every day, that one shoe does not fit all.

"Would you begrudge a Black kid if he went to Howard University instead of the University of Wisconsin–Milwaukee? Would there be questions about the money then? That's what the issue is. It's about options, it's about discrimination. It's about the natural evolution of the Civil Rights movement, it's about Black empowerment. . . . It's about where our children—and they are all our children—can get a good education.

"We're here today, and MPS is making a few moves to reform today, because of this school choice program. And that's good, isn't it? That some poor Black children attend good schools under Black control is good, isn't it? As for the Witte study, it was garbage then, and it's garbage today. June Harris, education coordinator of the House of Representatives, talked about the Peterson study being biased. Well, the Witte study definitely was. Witte publicly declared before being selected by opponents of choice that he was opposed to the program. He wouldn't let other researchers see his data or question his methodology, but I won't get into all that. I can cite six studies that say positive things about school choice, about academic achievement and parental satisfaction, and benefits to MPS. Another study came from a liberal foundation yesterday that previously denounced vouchers that shows our children are excelling in most of these schools.

"And there's another point. All evidence shows that most of these kids, the choice kids, are two years or more behind when their parents sign them up. They come from poor families and public schools and for one reason or another were failing . . . that's why their parents looked for options they wouldn't have if not for school choice. And let's not forget Witte didn't say they were doing *badly*, but that there was no conclusive evidence after one year and limited documentation. But he could also say that it would be a miracle to reverse overnight the problems these kids brought to the table.

"These schools respond to the families because they are founded on families and have a mission. My oldest son went to Harambee. We have an African-centered curriculum. He had a good foundation. Harambee has a 98 percent graduation rate; 79 percent of the children go on to college. One of my daughters went to public school, that was our choice, and she did well and graduated a few years ago from college. My son went on to college. And four years later he's back here teaching at a private school, in part because when he applied for a teaching fellowship with MPS his application was ignored. Some suggested later that MPS wasn't truly interested in Black teachers, or maybe they had filled their desegregation quota, which the MTEA had maintained as part of its contract. Others have suggested that maybe they saw the name on the application and quickly threw the papers in the garbage. But MPS's loss is the community's gain. Malik, like hundreds of other Black children at Black independent schools, was educated not only in the three Rs but also in the important lesson that Black citizens are part of a social order and they must return to serve the community and open doors for the next generation. Black children were groomed not only to excel academically but also to examine ways in which they can share their success with the community and lead us into the new millennium. That's what this battle is about: who should control the educational process. That's what we should be about; that's what the Black nationalism is about: controlling the institutions that impact our community, public or private. That's the bottom line. Thank you."

It didn't dawn on me until I had left the convention center that fate has a way of bringing us back to important points in our lives, allowing us to revisit our past and to look at situations anew. I often reflect on a passage in of my favorite poems: "And in the end, we will arrive at the beginning, and know it for the first time."

It's been a long, long road I've traveled, but in truth, just a few steps.

My son Malik graduated in the middle of his class at Harambee, but under Brother Bob's, Jeff Monday's, and other teachers' tutelage and caring persistence at Messmer High School he moved from being an average student during his freshman year at Messmer to class vice president and an honor student as a junior and senior. Choosing Messmer turned out to be one of the best decisions I and my son could have made. The academic and cultural foundation provided by Harambee was a godsend and allowed him to navigate the sometimes-difficult waters of high school, which were made even more arduous by my being a single parent active in many community endeavors.

One of nearly a dozen Harambee graduates who moved on to Messmer in 1990, Malik found out quickly that the Harambee family would continue to be involved in his life: several of his former teachers conferred and negotiated with his new instructors throughout his freshman year. In fact, they went so far as advise Messmer counselors not to allow Malik to take freshman English, Spanish, or Algebra because his Harambee courses were almost equal to Messmer freshman courses. Malik could breeze through Messmer's freshman offerings; without a challenge, he might end up with a false sense of accomplishment and his academic growth might stagnate.

We took their advice and Malik excelled. After attending Indiana-South Bend on a basketball scholarship, he transferred to Lake Forest College as a sophomore. He returned to Milwaukee each summer to pick up extra credits at the University of Wisconsin–Milwaukee summer school and worked as a youth counselor for the YMCA during his junior year. That experience had such an impact on him that he switched his major to English and African-American studies and committed himself to teaching. He earned his bachelor's degree the next year, graduating in May 1998, and turned down numerous lucrative job offers in the corporate community to accept a position as a teacher at an inner-city private school (after being ignored by the public school system, which did not even answer his application!). He currently teaches at Blessed Trinity, a Catholic elementary school taken over by Messmer in 1988. He plans to begin his master's degree studies in fall 1999 and some day hopes to start a Black independent school.

My son's success had particular meaning to me this fall morning, nearly two decades to the day after I spoke before startled Milwaukee Public School teachers on this very same street, just a half-mile north of the MMABSE convention site. In a variety of ways, the issues were the same. Now it was about options, not just for me, but for my low-income extended family. I had availed myself of a private-school education for my son based on the prevailing conditions and quality of education offered by MPS. That quality, according to all available research, had actually declined since my presentation more than fifteen years ago.

Sadly, the decisions I was able to make were not within the financial reach of most Black parents with children attending public schools. That's where the school choice program came in. But the movement was about much more than enhanced options for 3 percent of the MPS population. The school choice crusade was sparked by our frustration over a system that is unwilling to change for the betterment of those it is entrusted to serve. The battle for educational options was a response to MPS and union callousness and to a wider conspiracy that has caused us to, in effect, lose two generations of children. The dreams and aspirations of at least fifty thousand children have been stifled during my lifetime. Conspiracy or callousness, take your pick.

Whites have long since seen the truth and abandoned ship, long before the MPS Titanic shuck the desegregation iceberg. The enemies are the myopic helmsmen who refuse to navigate out of the treacherous waters. The enemy consists of the captains who have set a course directly for the eye of the storm. The enemy is the ship designer who supplied the MPS *Titanic* with just enough lifeboats for middle- and upper-class passengers and, as the ship sank, told the rest to suffer in silence as the band played on.

Yes, it's been a long journey over a short distance, and I've been blessed to be able to revisit this place, to arrive at the beginning and know it for the first time. In truth, the more things have changed, the more they have remained the same. My journey, my lesson, has taught me that even though we've torn down some of the plantation walls, we are not yet "Free at last!"

SCHOOL CHOICE CHRONOLOGY

April 1970: The Milwaukee Federation of Independent Community Schools is formed to lobby the state to provide vouchers for low-income parents wishing to send their children to parochial schools. Led by community activist Jesse Wary, the group ultimately appeals to the MSB to apply for a federal voucher grant.

August/September 1970: Forums and informational workshops are held to solicit Black community input and support for a voucher program for low-income families. Although many parents express support, the NAACP goes on record opposing the idea. The Social Development Commission and the Urban League declare their support of the concept. The SDC provides funds for the parents' group.

October 1970: The MSB rejects a resolution that would authorize the superintendent to submit an application for a federal voucher program.

February 1988: Governor Tommy Thompson includes a voucher program for Milwaukee in his state budget proposal. The program would provide tuition scholarships for an unspecified number of low-income parents in Milwaukee to send their children to any private or parochial school.

March 1988: A *Milwaukee Community Journal* editorial calls the parental choice idea worthy of consideration. The editorial points out that this program will offer at least a thousand families the opportunity to receive an educational option denied them because of their economic status.

April 1988: Governor Thompson's choice proposal dies in committee.

January 1989: Thompson unveils a second parental choice proposal. He announces in a speech in Washington, D.C., that he plans to introduce a compromise proposal that would allow one thousand low-income children to attend any nonsectarian private school, and a public school choice version that would allow any student to attend any public school district in the state as long as their enrollment did not hurt local school desegregation efforts. Thompson notes that he is hopeful of securing support from State Rep. Polly Williams, who also attended the Washington, D.C., workshop. Thompson stresses that the objective of the choice program is to "widen the educational opportunities for low-income students and to improve the overall quality of their education."

An *MCJ* editorial declares that the parental choice initiative deserves serious consideration. The *MCJ* asserts that the choice program would provide low-income parents with an invaluable educational option.

February 1989: Thompson's choice bill is officially introduced to the state legislature.

March 1989: Parents and activists polled following a forum and debate on school choice at Milwaukee Area Technical College overwhelmingly endorse the concept.

April 1989: Thompson's school choice program is removed from the budget by the Joint Finance Committee following a hearing in which State Superintendent of Public Instruction Herbert Grover and representatives of the Wisconsin Education Association, the state's largest teachers union, expressed opposition.

An alternative Milwaukee choice proposal is introduced by State Rep. Tom Seery on behalf of the Milwaukee Public Schools. MPS Superintendent Robert Peterkin holds a press conference to announce MPS's role in the drafting of the proposal.

June 1989: Responding to requests from several community schools, Williams tries unsuccessfully to convince Seery to amend his choice proposal. After his refusal, Williams drafts an alternative bill. Both measures are to be debated during budget deliberations in early July.

July 1989: The Democratic-controlled assembly kills both Williams's bill, which would have allowed low-income Black parents to send their children to private nonsectarian schools using funds earmarked for MPS, and MPS's proposal, would have allowed one thousand Black at-risk students to attend one of four nonsectarian private schools. Williams was critical of MPS's version, frst, because it required that participating private schools lose their autonomy, and second, because students would be irreparably stigmatized due to being labeled at-risk. The assembly votes 58-41 to remove MPS's proposal and 54-44 to kill Williams's bill.

August 1989: Williams hosts a series of meetings to gauge community support for choice. She forms a coordinating committee consisting of community activists, parents, and Black independent school representatives to advance a new school choice initiative. A second meeting of the committee is held with State Reps. G. Spencer Coggs and Gwen Moore to discuss strategy. Coggs and Moore agree to cosponsor Williams's bill.

Williams announces that she will introduce a new bill in September that will allow up to three thousand low-income families to send a child to a nonsectarian private school in Milwaukee.

October 1989: The Milwaukee Parental Choice Program introduced by Williams has been put on hold by State Rep. Barbara Notestein, chair of the assembly's Urban Education Committee, until an MPS version of the proposal is introduced. Both versions will then be scheduled for public hearings.

Williams addresses a regional strategy meeting on parental choice. Williams, the only African-American political figure to speak about choice, leads the panel discussions "Increasing Educational Options for Children" and "Minorities and Choice."

November 1989: Thompson gives his stamp of approval to the parental choice bill recently submitted by Williams. Thompson tells a group of Milwaukee reporters that he will "sign the bill in a minute if it makes it through the legislature." Thompson also agrees to lobby for the legislation and guarantees GOP support.

February 1990: During an impromptu speech at the Black Women's Network annual conference, Thompson addresses the issue of when parental choice will be adopted in Wisconsin. He asserts that African-American families should have the same educational options as White middle-class suburban families. Williams's bill would provide low-income families with that option.

State Senator Gary George and MSB Director Jared Johnson add their names to a growing list of political leaders endorsing the proposed parental choice bill. A hearing on the Milwaukee parental school choice bill is scheduled at the MPS administration building. The hearing is scheduled after a barrage of criticism is levied against Notestein for holding the measure hostage. George announces in an interview that he has met with Thompson to discuss the possibility of a special legislative session in the event that the bill does not make it to the floor during the current spring session.

Lawmakers are bombarded with support for Williams's choice proposal at the MPS administration building. Speakers bring insight into how the plan would benefit low-income parents and the MPS system. Major provisions of the plan are outlined by Larry Harwell: the program would be funded by a state grant of $600 per student in addition to the general state aid of $2,400 already allocated for Milwaukee students. After three hours of testimony from parents and officials, it should be hard for members of the Urban Education Committee to find reasons not to endorse this proposed bill.

Howard Fuller, director of the County Department of Health and Human Services, receives a standing ovation during his endorsement of the bill. Fuller encourages the committee to "do the right thing and judge the proposal on its merits."

March 1990: In executive session the Assembly Urban Education Committee votes to advance Williams's parental choice program, 7-6.

The Wisconsin Assembly passes the parental choice initiative, which will allow up to one thousand low-income children to attend private schools in Milwaukee. The bill now goes to the state senate where George is expected to lead the battle for approval.

March/April 1990: George redrafts the choice bill as an amendment to the state budget. He then begins a lobbying campaign to solicit support for the measure within the Joint Finance Committee, which he cochairs. George is said to have threatened to derail several Democratic-sponsored bills if committee members succumb to pressure from the state teachers union to kill the choice bill. George wins: the committee endorses the bill without debate.

May 1990: Wisconsin becomes the first state to host a parental choice bill after the senate approves the measure as part of the state budget.

Since the parental choice initiative was passed by the state senate, local private schools have been flooded with calls. The bill now awaits Thompson's signature.

Mayor John Norquist stands up to the Common Council by vetoing a resolution opposing the parental choice initiative.

At a community celebration sponsored by Williams and several Central City community schools, hundreds of low-income parents are praised for their hard work toward the enactment of the state's new parental choice initiative. Political figures at the celebration refer to the signing of the choice bill as not only a "historic event but also a moment that could change the face of education in America."

George makes reference to the possibility of a lawsuit being initiated by Herbert Grover in an attempt to halt implementation of the program. George says, "That won't stop us."

June 1990: A coalition of public school teachers, the Administrators and Supervisors Council, and Milwaukee chapter NAACP President Felmers Chaney files suit before the state supreme court to enjoin the school choice initiative. Clint Bolick, director of the Landmark Legal Foundation Center for Civil Rights, represents a group of African-American parents in the case.

The state supreme court rejects the injunction request. The school choice program continues pending review by the lower courts.

Williams and a coalition of community schools and parents file suit against Grover in an effort to cease his attempts to sabotage the choice program. The suit charges that Grover undermined the participation of five private schools by attempting to force them to sign an extensive array of regulatory requirements as a prerequisite for the program, virtually converting the schools into public school satellites.

Bolick asserts that Grover had no legal grounds to force the schools to sign the form and requests a revised listing of eligible schools.

August 1990: The state court of appeals unanimously rejects the motion by public school teachers and administrators to halt the implementation of the choice program. A hearing will take place in a few days to examine the constitutionality of the program.

October 1990: Vice President Dan Quayle visits Harambee Community School to witness the progress of the choice participants firsthand. Accompanied by Thompson, Quayle visits with students, choice parents, and the press. The vice president comments that he is immensely impressed by what he observed.

November 1990: The state court of appeals rules that state lawmakers passed the choice initiative contrary to a state constitutional provision that disallows local initiatives in the budget. The judges do not call for the program to halt, nor do they rule on the constitutionality or merit of the program. Bolick stresses that an immediate appeal will be filed with the state supreme court. Bolick is confident that the higher court will overturn the ruling.

March 1991: A group of thirteen African educators visit Milwaukee. They spend two days touring area schools and meeting with educators, parents, and community leaders. One purpose for their visit is to study the parental choice program. The African educators express their gratitude to Williams, saying that the visit was eye-opening for them as they prepare to develop an education agenda for the twenty-first century.

April 1991: A nonscientific survey recently conducted by the MCJ reveals that Fuller is the overwhelming choice of Central City residents to take the reins of the MPS system. Also, 88 percent of those surveyed approve of the choice program.

May 1991: The Department of Public Instruction announces the names of six schools that have shown interest in participating in the parental choice program in the second year of the program: Harambee Community School, Urban Day School, Lakeshore Montessori School, SER–Jobs for Progress, Bruce Guadalupe School, and Woodlands School. The 1990–91 school year begins with 341 students attending the participating choice schools.

July 1991: Williams plans an investigation based on allegations made by several dozen parents that the DPI attempted to undermine the registration process for the parental choice program. She also will ask for an extension on the registration deadline. According to Williams, plans for a parent assistance center will soon be finalized.

August 1991: Registration for choice schools increases 47 percent over the previous year.

October 1991: The choice program receives high marks from an MCJ survey on African Americans' views of the quality of education in MPS. The survey conducted by Malik Communications and coordinated by Walter Farrell and Mikel Holt. Choice is endorsed by 76 percent of those surveyed.

February 1992: A Wisconsin Policy Research Institute survey shows that more than 80 percent of Black Milwaukeeans support choice, and the number is steadily growing

March 1992: In a 4-3 vote the state supreme court sustains the constitutionality of the parental choice program. Justice Louis Ceci advocates for giving choice a chance.

April 1992: In another visit to Milwaukee, Quayle praises the parental school choice program. During a visit to Urban Day School, Quayle commends Williams and Thompson for their roles in advancing the nation's most far-reaching choice bill.

June 1992: Choice opponent Grover has placed Messmer High School's choice application on hold pending an investigation on whether it is a religious institution. An MCJ editorial calls the investigation the latest in a series of DPI attempts to derail the parental school choice program.

PAVE announces that with support from the Bradley Foundation and the Milwaukee business community, it will establish a privately funded voucher program providing low-income families with half-tuition scholarships for schools of choice—including religious schools.

February 1994: Williams unveils a bill to expand the state's parental choice program to include sectarian schools. Williams presses the legislature to act immediately in an attempt to save St. Leo's Catholic School, which may close because of financial constraints. The amended version of the choice bill will include provisions to increase the family income guidelines from 1.75 times the federal poverty level to 2.1 times the federal poverty level.

March 1994: A spokesperson from the Chapter 220 program warns that the state of Wisconsin might face a new school desegregation lawsuit if the parental school choice program is advanced.

August 1994: A new study conducted by a research team from Harvard University and the University of Houston finds that after three years in the program choice students' reading scores have increased by three percentage points, and after four years, math scores have increased by five percentage points over those of MPS students.

   With the assistance of the Landmark Legal Foundation Center for Civil Rights, a group of low-income families files a brief with the U.S. District Court challenging the constitutionality of the state's ban on religious school participation in the choice program. The documents ask the court to rule that the sectarian school ban violates the families' First Amendment rights to the free exercise of religion and their Fourteenth Amendment right to equal protection under the law.

September 1994: Dr. Alexander Lockwood Smith, New Zealand's education minister, spends three days in Milwaukee studying Wisconsin's parental choice program. During a visit to Harambee Community School, Dr. Smith remarks that he is amazed at the level of staff professionalism and the enthusiasm and articulation of the children. He is also impressed with the scholarship of a first-grade class that spoke to him in fluent Spanish and a second-grade class that responded correctly to advanced math questions.

   Staff members, however, were somewhat taken aback by the foreign official's acclamations. Said a teacher, "What do they really expect, that our children can't excel?"

October 1994: A rally to honor four schools who were choice pioneers—Harambee Community School, Urban Day, Bruce Guadalupe School, and Woodland Elementary—is held at Milwaukee Area Technical College. Thompson attends, and parents and community activists call upon him to author a proposal to expand school choice to private religious schools. The governor agrees to explore the possibility.

November 1994: Oral arguments begin in the court case to determine the fate of expanding choice to include religious schools (see August 1994).

January 1995: Thompson says he will put an expanded Choice bill into his 1995–96 budget. The assembly's Urban Education Committee is assigned to review the measure. Black state lawmakers withhold their endorsements of the bill pending review by the committee.

Under Thompson's proposal, a voucher system would replace the current choice program. In its first year, the program would be expanded to 3,500 students in Milwaukee and Madison. In its second year, the program would be expanded to 5,500 participants. Thompson indicates that no new state money will be needed for the program.

Seventy percent of Black Milwaukeeans surveyed by the Wisconsin Policy Research Institute approve of expanding the school choice program to parochial schools.

May 1995: Williams seeks to enhance Thompson's choice proposal. She lobbies for pushing the expansion up by one year and increasing the participation maximum to 7 percent of MPS enrollment. Williams also wants to keep funding tied to the state aids formula instead of shifting it to Chapter 220.

The Joint Finance Committee approves choice expansion by an 11-5 vote and approves most of Williams's amendments. Students who participate in the PAVE program are now eligible to participate in the choice program in the fall. The amended choice expansion measure becomes a part of the 1995 budget bill.

June 1995: The Wisconsin legislature passes the bill to expand the Milwaukee Parental School Choice program to religious schools. Beginning this fall, up to fifteen thousand Milwaukee low-income families (based on federal poverty levels) will be able to send their K–12 children to any participating private school in Milwaukee. The state will provide schools with the equivalent of the state aid to MPS, approximately $3,200 per student.

July 1995: More than one hundred private schools have signed up to participate in the expanded choice program, far exceeding the expectations of supporters. Thompson is expected to sign the budget bill containing the provision next week. Tuition grants in the amount of $3,200 per student will be paid by the state to parents who will in turn sign checks over to the schools. Administrators of the participating schools say they are enthusiastic about the opportunity and challenges choice will bring to their schools.

Parents for School Choice, an organization of choice advocates, has been flooded with calls from parents anxious to sign up their children for the program, despite DPI's refusal to advertise registration.

August 1995: On behalf of the MTEA, the American Civil Liberties Union files suit for an injunction against the expansion of the school choice program to include religious schools. The Institute for Justice attempts to intervene on behalf of the parents and children who have already signed up for the program. Clint Bolick, the Institute for Justice's litigation director, says that he will do everything in his power to see that there is no injunction filed against the program. He also says that he wants to remove the constitutional cloud from over the head of the choice program.

The NAACP holds a press conference during which Chaney expresses his opposition to the choice program.

More than four thousand parents have shown interest in participating in the expanded choice program in only a week after its passage through the legislature.

The state supreme court hands down an injunction prohibiting the distribution of state funds for students attending religious schools under the expanded choice program. This decision will affect about 3,300 student applicants who have already signed up for the program, most of whom were going to transfer out of public schools. Williams calls the ruling a temporary hurdle and is confident that the final outcome will be in favor of religious school choice.

Political, religious, and civic leaders join PAVE officials at Holy Redeemer Christian Academy to announce that more than $350,000 has been raised to help two thousand children barred from attending a religious school because of the court ruling. PAVE Director Dan McKinley announces that the organization plans to raise $1.6 million to allow low-income children to attend the religious schools of their choice. McKinley calls the PAVE scholarships a lifeboat for parents seeking private school education for their children.

September 1995: With the school year having started and the injunction still in place, children and schools are suffering. Some children have to leave the schools they planned to attend and find an alternative school. Several of the religious schools have made the decision to let the students stay while they absorb the costs, hoping the injunction will be soon lifted.

Fuller (no longer superintendent) testifies at a congressional hearing on religious school choice. Fuller declares that "the only way to correct the miseducation and undereducation of poor Black children is the use of a two-pronged strategy utilizing educational reforms of the district and alternative strategies such as the continuation and expansion of choice."

June 1996: Twenty-three private nonsectarian schools have been approved for participation for the 1996–97 school year. Registration is set to begin on July 1.

The Black Research Organization (BRO) announces that, working in conjunction with Williams's office and a coalition of Central City private schools, it will conduct a quarterly evaluation of private schools in the state's parental choice program. A spokesperson for Harambee Community School says that the research will furnish parents with additional information about the participating schools and will offer a mechanism for the schools to police themselves.

July 1996: John Benson, state superintendent of public instruction, orders the deadline to be extended to July 15 as a result of erroneous information supplied to the media by the DPI. The DPI contends that the press release that should have announced the July 1 registration deadline for parental choice schools was typed by temporary workers and probably was never checked for correctness prior to being released to the media.

August 1996: A ruling by a Dane County judge maintains the court injunction of expansion of the parental choice program to include religious schools. The same judge does raise the ceiling of eligible participating students from fifteen hundred to fifteen thousand for nonsectarian schools.

January 1997: Judge Higginbotham rejects the religious school expansion plan, which was recalled to the circuit court for consideration after the state supreme court deadlocked. In a fifty-one-page ruling, Higginbotham says that expanding the program to include church-run schools violates the state and federal constitutions and that government must never establish or prefer any religion. He sends the matter to the court of appeals for further review.

February 1997: Two public-interest law firms defending Milwaukee's school-voucher program ask the Wisconsin Supreme Court to bypass the court of appeals and immediately consider the constitutionality of including religious schools in the program.

April 1997: The Wisconsin Supreme Court refuses to hear the Milwaukee school choice case, and allows a lower court to rule first on whether low-income children can attend religious schools at state expense.

May 1997: PAVE announces a plan to raise $4.5 million for the 1997–98 school year for low-income Milwaukee families with children attending private and religious schools. PAVE will continue helping 4,300 scholarship students until the legal issues are settled.

July 1997: Bolick asks the three-judge panel at Wisconsin's District IV Court of Appeals to lift an injunction excluding religious schools from the school-choice experiment in Milwaukee. The appeals court agrees to expedite the case.

August 1997: The Wisconsin District Court of Appeals finds unconstitutional the inclusion of religious schools in the Milwaukee Parental Choice Program.

PAVE receives a $2 million challenge grant from the Bradley Foundation to help support students while the legal battle over school choice continues. A community fund-raising campaign is organized once again.

October 1997: The Wisconsin State Supreme Court agrees to review two lower court rulings against the religious school choice program.

June 10, 1998: The state supreme court affirms the constitutionality of the religious school choice program. The ruling is hailed by parents, educational reformists, and other supporters of civil rights. The *MCJ* calls the decision "the second emancipation proclamation."

July/August 1998: More than one hundred schools that have signed up to participate in the new school choice program are flooded with calls from prospective enrollees. It is projected that the schools will not be able to handle the total number of prospective students.

August 1998: The number of choice participants has swelled to more than six thousand. Hundreds are on waiting lists.

November 1998: The U.S. Supreme Court affirms the constitutionality of Wisconsin's school choice program by refusing to review the case. The high court action leaves intact a ruling by the Wisconsin State Supreme Court that said the program, which expanded three years ago to include religious schools, does not violate the U.S. or Wisconsin constitutions.

"By declining to review the Wisconsin ruling, the Supreme Court leaves intact the most definitive court decision to date, which solidly supports the constitutionality of school choice," says Bolick.

December 1998: While three hundred representatives of the teachers union and the NAACP rally to blast school choice, more than five hundred parents, children, and community activists hold a rally to praise the initiative. The antichoice rally is sponsored by PFAW, a national organization that has partnered with the local branch of the NAACP and MTEA to undermine school choice. PFAW advertises that choice will hurt public education by taking money from the failing system. The organization plans to undermine the program, which is supported by more than 80 percent of Black Milwaukeeans. At the PFAW rally, Rep. Jesse Jackson Jr. denounces choice. Ironically, Jackson attended a private school.

At the pro-choice rally a group of Black ministers announce their intent to launch private schools. Speakers call the NAACP and PFAW hypocrites for their opposition to the progressive initiative and their support for the teachers union, which has worked to derail every major public school reform initiative in the last twenty years. Speaking at the pro-choice rally, Fuller declares, "[Choice] came after we tried everything else, after we tried to start our own district because they [MPS] wouldn't educate our children. We told them, if you won't educate our kids, let us have our own district. When they turned that down, we came up with choice. Now, for the first time, the money goes to parents and not the bureaucracy.

"That's the real reason they are having their meeting tonight. It's because they are mad because we changed the system, we shifted where the money goes, from schools that don't work to parents who care. Now low-income parents who had no power, have power. And that's scaring them."

March 1999: More than two hundred Black educators, politicians, and civil rights leaders representing more than thirty cities convene in Milwaukee for a four-day conference to discuss educational options, including school choice and charters. The conventioneers listen to the success stories of Black independent schools and Milwaukee charter advocates. Black elected officials from Pennsylvania and Florida seek ammunition for advancing school choice proposals in their respective legislatures. At the conclusion of the historic convention, participants vow to put in place a national network and to spread the word on the national reform movement, which has its roots in Milwaukee.

February–April 1999: The MTEA joins with PFAW to orchestrate a half-million-dollar campaign to maintain control of the MSB. At stake are not only five seats—including those of Black board members Leon Todd and Joe Fisher—but also the citywide seat held by John Gardner, the most vocal supporter of school choice on the board.

The union supports the reelection of Todd, Fisher, and Sandra Small, each of whom were previously endorsed by the MTEA and have been outspoken opponents not just of choice and charters but also of major reform proposals. Todd has also denounced African-centered curricula and has supported quotas on the number and percentage of Black teachers at any given school. The MTEA supports another antichoice candidate in an open seat.

Much of the union/PFAW campaign strategy is directed toward Gardner, and eventually these organizations declare their campaign to be a referendum on school choice. As such, national media scrutiny is focused on Milwaukee, where the election will pit reformists and supporters of choice and charters against the status quo.

Estimates are that the MTEA and PFAW will utilize four hundred workers and telemarketers and spend upwards of $500,000 on an advertising campaign—an unprecedented amount for a school board election.

March 1999: A group of prominent African-American ministers form a new organization called Clergy for Educational Options (CEO) and announce their intent to start new schools under the school choice and charter programs. The first president of CEO is Pastor Cheryl Brown, a widely respected cleric and founder and principal of Believers in Christ School, considered a leader in educational excellence.

April 1999: In a resounding statement, all five school board candidates supported by the MTEA and PFAW are defeated at the polls. Proponents of school choice, including two new Black board members, now control the board. After the election they clarify that while they support educational options for low-income children—including school choice—and will promote charters as another reform option, their priority is to make MPS the school of first choice through the infusion of innovative programs, greater teacher accountability, and a greater emphasis on site-based management and decentralization. School choice will force MPS to compete, which is healthy for the district and beneficial to all parents and the community.

School District Fails Blacks, Foils Reforms

By George A. Mitchell

A group of black community leaders in Milwaukee is challenging the public-school monopoly's failure to teach children from poor families. These leaders want greater authority to try what national and local research shows will work: high standards and expectations, more parental responsibility, and greater accountability to parents for results.

This effort challenges the way urban schools are governed and would mean a transfer of power from bureaucrats and union leaders to parents, principals and classroom teachers. If successful it could cause a reappraisal of how American cities address the minority education crisis.

The Milwaukee school establishment has reacted as any strong monopoly would; it has tried to crush any discussion that might legitimize the proposals, which include either a new, independent school district or more autonomy within the current system. These reactions highlight the dual crisis in American public education—the failure of most poor minority children to learn and the stubborn refusal of urban school teachers to discuss reforms that research shows could make a difference.

CONDUCIVE TO LEARNING

The main source of irritation to the education monopoly is the proposed option of creating a new school district composed of several black inner-city schools with a total population of about 7,000 that are now in the Milwaukee Public Schools system, which teaches 95,000 children and is the nation's 21st largest. The system's enrollment is 65% minority. Under the option, Milwaukee's top-heavy central bureaucracy would face certain reductions, because the plan would shift millions in state aid to the new district. The goal is increased academic achievement, resulting from more parental involvement, more accountability to parents, and greater autonomy for educators at the school level.

Research shows these factors are conducive to learning and usually exist in small systems not dominated by an authority-conscious central bureaucracy.

Another essential ingredient for learning is high expectations. Inner-city parents deserve educational leaders with confidence in the ability of their children to learn, yet many of those running the Milwaukee public schools lack optimism. The district's last official plan projects that blacks won't score as well as whites on achievement tests for 10 years. Joyce Mallory, a black member and former president of the school board, scoffs at the suggestion black students could do as well as whites from the suburbs. These educators explain their low expectations by focusing on problems beyond their control—broken homes, teen-age pregnancy—thus attempting to insulate themselves from blame.

One impetus for the proposed district is research by a blue-ribbon state commission that I chaired that studied public schools in Milwaukee and its suburbs. The commission's report identified which schools were working, which were not, and why.

The study disclosed a dramatic disparity in learning between minority children from poor families and white students from middle- and upper-class homes. The gap is widest in the high schools, most of which are integrated. In Milwaukee, the odds are that a black or Hispanic child will drop out of school or be graduated with a D average.

More significant was the finding that educational failure among poor minority children is not universal in the Milwaukee area. The Milwaukee research mirrors studies elsewhere, summarized by U.S. Education Secretary Bill Bennett in publications called "What Works" and "Schools That Work." The evidence is that learning occurs across the economic and racial spectrum when certain conditions are present. Major findings reported by the Milwaukee study:

- Where teachers and parents report effective parent involvement: "test scores are higher, failures and dropouts fewer, and attendance rates higher. Teacher perceptions of [parent involvement] are the most consistent indicator of performance we analyzed."

- "There is a consistent pattern of expectation that develops on the part of students and teachers. . . . The positive schools in terms of performance have the highest reported levels of expectations."

- "An effective school, which in the eyes of teachers has stronger leadership, standards, expectations, and teamwork, performs better with students from low and higher income homes and in the city and suburbs."

A smaller, more accountable school system could help parents take more responsibility for their children and create a school climate responsive to parental input.

The blacks in Milwaukee who are pushing this idea know that "decentralization" efforts such as New York City's have had problems. They believe the key is a true transfer of authority and responsibility. This is demonstrated by four nonsectarian private schools in Milwaukee with an 80% minority enrollment that achieve better results with low-income minority students than the public schools do (at a fraction of the public-school budget). Parochial schools in Milwaukee, with a 25% minority enrollment, also consis-

tently report better achievement for minority students.

The Milwaukee proposal also emphasizes giving poor parents more choice in school selection, the kind already held by many middle- and upper-income parents. Parents in the new school district could enroll their children outside it if they felt a better education would result. Proponents state in their literature that "no child would attend a school in this district if his or her parent did not make that choice."

Race has been a source of controversy in discussion of the proposed new school district. For years, school officials quietly condoned the segregated status of the schools in question. The same officials now shout "Racism!" at the blacks who now propose the separate district and accuse them of wanting to undo civil-rights progress. The school board's attorney has labeled the plan unconstitutional, although it has not even been drafted in bill form yet. And after Republican Gov. Tommy Thompson expressed interest in the proposals, city school officials threatened to sue the state. Proponents of the new district say their bill will encourage and enable white parents outside the district to transfer students to the schools. The proponents believe this will happen when the schools become effective.

Opponents of the new proposal say they have better ways to improve schools. They cite the need for higher taxes to finance lower elementary class sizes, which they claim give suburban schools a big edge.

However, the Milwaukee study commission found "no discernable relationship between student-teacher ratios and any performance measure," a conclusion reinforced by most national research. A recent independent study of metropolitan Milwaukee schools found little city-suburban difference in class size anyway, with 26 students per class in Milwaukee and 24 in the suburbs. The call for smaller class size is largely a way to preserve and create more teacher jobs and justify seeking big increases in state and federal aid.

One area where the district doesn't cut corners is in administrative staff. Despite economies of scale that might be expected in one large district, 17 smaller suburban districts have much lower overhead costs. Milwaukee has two-thirds of the metro public-school students but almost 80% of the administrative staff.

Some important Milwaukee educators reject the effort to stonewall discussion of the black leaders' proposals. Sam Yarger, dean of education at the University of Wisconsin-Milwaukee, says the plan has problems but "puts the right questions on the center stage and deserves serious discussion." He says the controversy it has sparked is predictable, because it "has irritated almost every identifiable interest group in town."

POLITICAL CLIMATE CHANGES

A few years ago, these issues would have had no chance of serious consideration, because they contradict the once-conventional wisdom that more learning requires large infusions of new money and that minority students can't achieve unless mixed with middle-class whites.

Now, the political reaction shows more willingness to discuss the plan. State legislators plan hearings. Gov. Thompson and Democratic Assembly Speaker Tom Loftus say the educational issues merit study. Mr. Loftus asked authors of the plan to discuss it at a national conference on minority education later this month. Three of five major Milwaukee mayoral candidates say the proposal warrants a close look. The school establishment's resistance to change, except on its own terms, remains one of the biggest obstacles in poor children's advancement.

Mr. Mitchell, a Milwaukee real-estate and education consultant, chaired the 1984–5 study of the area's schools.

APPENDIX

C

A NOTE FROM
THE PUBLISHER

This is a book for all Americans, whether or not they are interested in the issue of educational choice. Why? Because Mikel Holt is asking what it means to be a citizen and live in productive communities in today's world, something that many Americans are asking themselves. Holt argues that educational choice is a fundamental civil right. He is correct. As one reads this book one must ask how we have gotten to a place in our political history where citizens must battle entrenched bureaucracies and public sector unions for the right to choose their children's schools. Why has the issue of choice become problematic? How is it that we—a country whose ideal was that citizens could attain good government through reflection and choice rather than by relying on coercion and accident for our constitutions—now have so little real choice?

The historical context of educational choice sets the stage for the issues that Mikel Holt believes we all must address. And it is within this historical context that what the author has to say affects every American. Ultimately, *Not Yet "Free At Last"* is about much more than school choice—it is about how we Americans want to govern ourselves.

We may view the twentieth century as a century of consolidation. Reformers such as Herbert Croly, author of *The Promise of American Life*, argued that we needed to build a nation to replace what seemed like a chaotic patchwork of competing governments and associations. When this drive to build a nation was joined with the emerging role of professionals, we ushered in the century of consolidation. The national government has assumed more and more authority over what was once the province of state and local governments, and the same is true of religious and community associations. The thousands of community chests that have been subsumed by the United Way are a good example.

Education was not immune to this movement. In 1920 the United States had more than 124,000 local school districts, which were governed by citizens. Today we have slightly more than fifteen thousand. School reformers have held that the smallest possible school system capable of producing a high-quality, professionally guided education was five thousand students, and larger schools were desirable. During this period of consolidation we also witnessed the rise of the regulatory state, meaning that, increasingly, states and the federal government made or constrained the decisions of local school districts. We have seen a transformation in what it means to be public. "Government" and "public" have become synonymous.

While there is much that is good in the rise of federal and state interventions, it is becoming clear that we have impoverished or disabled much of our civic space. One of the key attributes of centralization that leads to this impoverishment is the transfer of decision-making authority and power from individuals and communities to "higher" authorities. Over time the concept of citizens as constitution makers and governors has been replaced by the notion of citizens as voters and consumers of professionally provided services.

This is where Mikel Holt's story begins. Holt's book is a political history chronicling an educational crisis that his community has faced for more than thirty years, a period of time in which three generations of African-American children have been lost because of poor education. An activist in the civil rights movement, Holt supported the integrationist-statist model, only to find out that the promise of civil rights became a promise of inclusion in an unresponsive and coercive bureaucratic empire. And this is where the story begins for all Americans. After transferring our rights to self-governing citizenship to the bureaucratic state, how will we get them back?

SPEAKING TRUTH TO POWER

This book has rung true to me since its inception. During my first meeting with Mikel Holt, what struck me was his quiet determination and his commitment to rethink the political principles from which the African-American community should operate. Holt rejects the unsatisfactory either/or choices that have been handed to African-American communities for decades, and is truly committed to striking out on a new path.

For eight years I worked with four groups of African-American women who wanted to take over and own their government housing projects in San Francisco. Their aspirations were fueled by Project Hope, a government program designed by Congressman Jack Kemp and Representative Mike Espy that would allow and enable residents to first manage and then own their developments. Yet in the end there was very little hope in Project Hope. Only a handful of more than five hundred such experiments succeeded.

The obstacles these women faced—bureaucratic hostility, union opposition, community infighting, and unrealistic expectations—are the same obstacles that Mikel Holt chronicles in this book. However, Holt's book does give us hope.

OUT OF THE ASHES

One of the successes of the ill-fated War on Poverty was that it planted the idea of choice in the minds of community activists. It is fascinating that Mikel Holt shows that the Milwaukee scholarship program was not a conservative tactic imported and imposed from afar but rather a community-urged project in response to the consistent failure of government schools. Perhaps the thousands of men and women who gained the idea that they could govern and own their housing developments will in the future rise from the ashes. My experience in housing development was that choice was necessary but not sufficient for success. What was the governing philosophy to be used in building these new self-governing institutions?

THE POVERTY OF MODERN POLITICAL RHETORIC

There are those who will be put off by Mikel Holt's commitment to Black nationalism. However, it is clear to me that Black nationalism is a legacy of racism and reflects a profound poverty in our political rhetoric as a country. What are the alternatives for a community of citizens seeking solutions to problems that aren't being addressed? Holt argues, correctly I believe, that the African-American community must either try to solve problems through the integrationist-statist model—with all its baggage—or move to some variant of Black nationalism. What has happened to self-governing alternatives? Why are we as a country unwilling to grant limited authority to communities or individuals to solve their own problems? Could it be that we lack a coherent set of ideas about how to create self-governing efforts in the "modern" era? Do we feel inadequate as citizens, or are we just too busy to govern the institutions that most affect our lives?

ENABLEMENT IS NOT ENOUGH

There are those on the Right who will argue that Mikel Holt's book is behind the power curve, is old news. They will contend that, after the passage of voucher legislation in Florida in spring 1999, one merely needs to replicate this approach across the country. Their assumption is that once market-like forces are created all our problems in education will be over. There is a mechanistic quality to the argument that one need only exchange one piece of enabling legislation with another and the machine of education will operate effectively. As Mikel Holt demonstrates, when the legislative battles are won, the fight for school choice has only just begun. The entrenched and highly focused special interests surrounding our government schools will continue to fight in courts and communities and through the state bureaucracy to preserve their power. Yet there is even more to this argument.

CONSUMERS OR CITIZENS?

Impoverished notions of citizenship underpin the policy recommendations of both the Left and Right. The Left by and large sees the role of citizens as voting for competing governing elites. The Right expands this a little to see citizens as consumers of government's services, creating competitive forces to make governments operate efficiently.

Here Mikel Holt is most instructive. He provides an answer to why, in April 1999, the citizens of Milwaukee voted in five educational choice advocates over the fierce and well-funded opposition of the NEA, NAACP, and People for the American Way. Over the long years of battling for school choice, the citizens of Milwaukee built a deep and clear commitment to a new set of values to guide their educational enterprises. They have begun to redefine what it means to be a citizen in a self-governing society.

The limits of consumerism are also found in what it means to build and be a part of a productive community called a school. Good schools cannot be built if parents merely drop their children off at the door and allow "professionals" to educate them. We know from experience and research that effective schools are those in which parents, teachers, students, and principals all participate and have a real stake—that is, real authority and responsibility—in outcomes.

EMPOWERMENT CANNOT BE GIVEN

What we learn from Mikel Holt is that at every turn of the road the bureaucratic state (in the form of school administrators, state bureaucrats, or teachers unions) has tried to sabotage efforts to give children a good education. Even as I write this, school choice opponents continue to pour money into Milwaukee. Even after their stunning defeat in the April school board elections, these highly focused interest groups continue to work to destroy choice-based education.

How does one overcome these powerful groups? Clearly not by being mere consumers. The only answer is to view citizens as governors and producers of public goods. Mikel Holt shows us that over a period of time the leaders of the school choice movement not only became hardened by the battles with their opponents but also developed a shared consensus on what it means to be a self-governing citizen and to build self-governing schools. It is precisely this condition that is necessary for school choice communities to withstand the power plays of the opposition. As simple consumers of services they would soon succumb to the exploitation of the opposition. What Holt shows us is a unique and deeply rooted process of constitutional change. Although legal changes were certainly part of the process, here I use "constitutional" to mean that a new community has been constituted through public reflection and action, building a new consensus about the fundamental values upon which public education should be founded. Any legal constitution should rest on such community values.

BUILDING A NEW PUBLIC REALM

In Milwaukee and countless other communities around the country, citizens are beginning to take control of their lives and communities. As of yet we have no coherent public philosophy that guides us and allows us to understand where we are going. My own sense is that we are starting to rebuild the public realm using the animating idea of our experiment in self-governance: that societies of men and women must create good government through reflection and choice. This idea is the moral wellspring of our great country. We can no longer afford either morally or practically to build our public institutions on accident and force.

That is why *Not Yet "Free At Last"* speaks truth to power. Why it addresses our most sacred and profound aspirations. Why it is a spiritual book, lifting our eyes to a Promised Land as Martin Luther King Jr. did during the 1960s. For ultimately it is individual men and women who are the keepers of our great republic. It's time for our policies to enable all of us to play this important role.

IN AMERICA ALL BEGINNINGS ARE LOCAL

This book—especially chapter 10, which sets out lessons learned during the school choice battle—expresses the truth that all beginnings are truly local. If we are willing to reflect and join in common cause with our neighbors, we hold our destiny in our hands. This has always been the promise of America. Mikel Holt believes in this promise, and has worked passionately to realize his dream of being free at last.

—ROBERT B. HAWKINS JR., PRESIDENT
INSTITUTE FOR CONTEMPORARY STUDIES

NOTES

Chapter Two: Local Beginnings

1. U.S. Department of Justice Survey of State Prison Inmates, May 1995, 2.

2. John Hagedorn, *The Business of Drug Dealing in Milwaukee*, Wisconsin Policy Institute, June 1998, 5.

3. Ronald S. Edari, "Black Milwaukee: A Social History and Statistical Profile" (Milwaukee, 1990), 5.

4. Ibid., 13.

5. State of Wisconsin Department of Administration, *Black Population of Wisconsin: A Detail Census Profile*, April 1995, 24.

6. Bob Peterson, "Neighborhood Schools, Busing and the Struggle for Equality," *Rethinking Schools* (Spring 1998): 20.

7. Michael Stolee, "The Milwaukee Segregation Case," in *The Seeds of Crisis: Public Schooling in Milwaukee since 1920* (Madison: University of Wisconsin Press, 1993), 238.

8. Webster Harris and Jeannetta Robinson, MUSIC march participants, interview by author, 1998.

9. Stolee, *Seeds of Crisis*, 239.

10. Ron Johnson, interview by author, spring 1989.

11. Mikel Holt, "Vouchers Pictured As School Stimulant," *Milwaukee Community Journal*, 19 October 1970, sec. 2, p. 13.

12. Barbara A. Koppe, "Critical Test Near on School Vouchers," *Milwaukee Journal*, 26 October 1970, part 2, p. 1.

13. Holt, "Vouchers Pictured As School Stimulant," 13.

14. Ibid., 13.

15. *Milwaukee Sentinel*, 29 October 1970, part 1, p. 8.

16. *Milwaukee Sentinel*, 5 October 1970, part 1, p. 5.

17. Committee for Education Vouchers, *Report on Vouchers*, 1.

18. Ibid.

19. Editorial, *Milwaukee Journal,* 23 November 1970, part 1.
20. Ibid.

Chapter Three: What Went Wrong with the System

1. Larry Harwell, interview by author, at *Milwaukee Community Journal* offices, fall 1997.

2. Bob Peterson, "Neighborhood Schools, Busing, and the Struggle for Equality," *Rethinking Schools* (Spring 1998). "Water bubbler" is a midwestern term for water fountain.

3. Wisconsin Advisory Committee to the United States Commission on Civil Rights, *Impact of School Desegregation in Milwaukee Public Schools on Quality of Education for Minorities . . . 15 Years Later,* August 1992.

4. Ibid., 39.

5. Ibid., 39, 40.

6. Lee McMurrin, "Comprehensive Plan for Increasing Educational Opportunities and Improving Racial Balance in Milwaukee Public Schools" (Office of the Superintendent of Schools, confidential memo, December 8, 1976).

7. Wisconsin Advisory Committee, *Impact of School Desegregation.*

8. Bruce Murphy and John Pawasarat, "Why It Failed: School Desegregation 10 Years Later," *Milwaukee Magazine* (September 1986): 39. Excerpts reprinted with permission of *Milwaukee Magazine.*

9. Ibid., 36.

10. Ibid.

11. Ibid., 44.

12. George Mitchell and William Randall, "Study Commission on the Quality of Education in the Metropolitan Milwaukee Public Schools: Better Public Schools," a report to Governor Tony Earl, October 1985, 11.

13. Ibid.

14. Ibid., 12.

15. Ibid., 19.

16. Ibid., 20.

17. Governor Tommy Thompson, interview with *Milwaukee Community Journal* editorial board, 1987.

18. George Mitchell, "School District Fails Blacks, Foils Reforms," *Wall Street Journal,* 7 October 1987, sec. 1, p. 34. See p. 269 for article in full.

19. Ibid.

20. Ibid.

21. Ibid.

22. Ibid.

23. Ibid.

Chapter Four: Sounding the Trumpet

1. Barbara J. Wood, "The Legislative Development and Enactment of the Milwaukee Parental Choice Program: A Case Study in the Politics of Educational Reform" (Ph.D. diss., University of Wisconsin, 1998). Focusing Event: State Legislature's Joint Committee on Finance SB 31, the Biennial Budget Bill for Fiscal Years 1990 and 1991, which included updated school choice provision for Parents Choice Program/Public Schools and Parents Choice Program/Private Schools in Milwaukee.

2. Felmers Chaney, conversation with author and colleagues, Milwaukee Area Technical College Conference, March 1989.

3. Zakiya Courtney, interview by author, spring 1998.

4. Governor Tommy Thompson, impromptu speech made at Black Women's Network Conference, February 1990.

5. Editorial, *Milwaukee Community Journal*, 7 February 1990, p. 2.

Chapter Five: In Opposition

1. John Witte, et al., "Fourth Year Report: Milwaukee Parental Choice Program" (Department of Political Science, University of Wisconsin and La Follette Institute of Public Affairs, December 1994): 6. Research conducted for the Department of Public Instruction showed that 57 percent of choice families received general welfare assistance of Aid to Families with Dependent Children and 75 percent of choice families were headed by a nonmarried parent. The same research showed that, regarding academic achievement, students applying to the choice program were significantly below the average MPS student on standardized test scores and that students enrolled in Choice "enter very near the bottom in terms of academic achievement." (Witte, "Fourth Year Report.") Moreover, despite MPS claims that the district was financially penalized by choice, a 1999 report showed that real spending, per pupil, had grown 20 percent during the first nine years of school choice. (Howard Fuller and George Mitchell, "The Fiscal Impact of School Choice on the Milwaukee Public Schools," *Current Education Issues*, no. 99–2, Institute for the Transformation of Learning, Marquette University.)

2. Editorial, "Grover Says Choice Plan Raises Legal Questions," *Milwaukee Sentinel*, 3 May 1990, part 1, p. 12.

3. Steve Walters and Gloria Howe, "Grover Raps Bush for Backing Choice," *Milwaukee Sentinel*, 8 August 1990, part 1, p. 1.

4. Aide to Mayor John Norquist (requested not to be identified), interview by author, March 1990.

5. Priscilla Ahlgren, "School Choice Program Transcends Roots," *Milwaukee Journal*, 10 June 1990, p. 1.

6. Editorial, *Wall Street Journal*, 6 June 1990, sec. A, p. 6.

7. Priscilla Ahlgren, "School Choice Program Transcends Roots," *Milwaukee Journal*, 10 June 1990, sec. A, p. 21.

8. Ibid.

9. Author notes from press conference held in Milwaukee involving Felmers Chaney, NAACP attorney, and representatives from MTEA, 1 June 1990.

10. Felmers Chaney, interview by Thomas Mitchell, June 1990.

11. Editorial, *Wall Street Journal*, 28 June 1990, sec. A, p. 12.

12. The Associated Press, *Milwaukee Journal*, 29 June 1990, sec. A, p. 8.

Chapter Six: Pleading Our Own Cause

1. Alan L. Keyes, *Masters of the Dream: The Strength and Betrayal of Black America* (New York: William Morrow and Company, 1995), 95.

2. Wisconsin Advisory Committee to the United States Commission on Civil Rights, *Impact of School Desegregation in Milwaukee Public Schools on Quality Education for Minorities . . . 15 Years Later*, August 1992.

3. "Breier Estimates up to 300 Hard-Core Gang Members," *Milwaukee Sentinel*, 8 February 1984, part 1, p. 1.

4. John Russwurm and Samuel Cornish, *Freedom's Journal*, masthead, 1826.

5. Felmers Chaney, interview by author, 5 June 1990.

CHAPTER SEVEN: SAME TRACK, DIFFERENT TRAINS

1. George Mitchell and William Randall, "Study Commission on the Quality of Education in the Metropolitan Milwaukee Public Schools: Better Public Schools," a report to Governor Tony Earl, October 1985.

2. In 1992, Zakiya Courtney was named executive director of Urban Day School, and the title of principal was eliminated as part of a pilot program in which teachers were given more autonomy.

3. Daryl Michael Scott, *Contempt and Pity: Social Policy and the Image of the Damaged Black Psyche, 1880–1996* (Chapel Hill: University of North Carolina Press, 1997), xiv.

CHAPTER EIGHT: THE SECOND EMANCIPATION PROCLAMATION

1. Howard Fuller, author notes, 9 December, 1998.

CHAPTER NINE: CIVIL RIGHTS AND WRONGS

1. David A. Bostis, "Political Attitudes" (Washington, D.C.: Joint Center for Political and Economic Studies, National Opinion Poll, February 1996).

2. Ibid.

3. Sterling Stuckey, ed., *The Ideological Origins of Black Nationalism* (Boston: Beacon Press, 1972), 1.

4. Floyd H. Flake, "No Excuses for Failing Our Children," *Policy Review* (January/February 1999). Published by the Heritage Foundation. Reprinted with permission.

5. Amos N. Wilson, *Blueprint for Black Power: A Moral, Political and Economic Imperative for the Twenty-First Century* (Afrikan World InfoSystems, 1998), 830. Reprinted with permission of Afrikan World InfoSystems.

6. Ibid., 831.

7. Dorothy Winbush Riley, *My Soul Looks Back, 'Less I Forget* (New York: HarperCollins, 1993), 215.

8. Kweisi Mfume, People for the American Way media kit statement, fall 1998.

9. Ralph Wiley, *Dark Witness: When Black People Should Be Sacrificed (Again)* (New York: Ballantine Books, 1996).

10. Cornel West, *Race Matters* (New York: Vintage Books, 1994), 67.

11. Ibid., 68.

12. Ibid., 82.

13. Ibid., 81–82.

14. Wilson, *Blueprint for Black Power*, 203.

CHAPTER TEN: A MANIFESTO FOR PARENTAL SCHOOL CHOICE: FIFTEEN LESSONS LEARNED DURING THE STRUGGLE

1. Milwaukee Urban League, "African-American Professional Recruitment and Retention: A Dynamic Strategic Planning Process for Greater Milwaukee" (Milwaukee Urban League, Inc., October 1998).

2. Minister Louis Farrakhan, keynote address at Million Man March, Washington, D.C., October 16, 1995. Notes taken by author.

3. Carter G. Woodson, *The Mis-Education of the Negro* (Washington, D.C.: The Associated Publishers, 1933), xii.

4. Asa Hilliard, "Freeing Your Afrikan Mind," audio tape, 1997. Transcribed from tape for Mikel Holt, "Shutting Off the Black 'Brain Drain,'" *Milwaukee Community Journal*, 22 July 1998.

5. George Mitchell and William Randall, "Study Commission on the Quality of Education in the Metropolitan Milwaukee Public Schools: Better Public Schools," a report to Governor Tony Earl, October 1985; U.S. Department of Justice Survey of State Prison Inmates, May 1995.

6. Milwaukee Catalyst, *Act on the Facts*, 1998. A copy of this report may be obtained by contacting Betty Smith at (414) 264-4010 or via e-mail at mkecatlst@aol.com.

7. Mikel Holt, "Resolution by Todd Blasted by Parents, Educators and Historians," *Milwaukee Community Journal*, 20 November 1996, p. 1.

CHAPTER ELEVEN: WHERE ARE THEY NOW? A POLITICAL BIOGRAPHY

1. Kevin Walker, "Chaney Ousted by Hamilton after NAACP Challenge Vote," *Milwaukee Community Journal*, 10 November 1998, p. 1.

2. Ibid.

3. Mulana Karenga, *Kawaida Theory: An Introductory Outline* (Ingelwood, Calif.: Kawaida), 15.

CHAPTER TWELVE: NOT YET "FREE AT LAST"

1. Milwaukee Catalyst, *Act on the Facts*, 1998.

INDEX

ABOUT THE AUTHOR

Mikel Kwaku-Osei Holt is a national award-winning journalist and community activist who has been at the vanguard of the educational reform movement in Milwaukee for the last twenty-five years. He is editor and associate publisher of Wisconsin's largest-circulated and most influential African-American newspaper, the *Milwaukee Community Journal*, and is a member or serves on the board of nearly a dozen local and national organizations. An avowed cultural nationalist, he served as a lieutenant in State Rep. Polly Williams's school choice army.

A Vietnam veteran, Holt is a lifelong resident of Milwaukee. He is listed in *Who's Who in Black America* and *The 100 Most Influential Black Milwaukeeans*. Holt is married and the father of six children, three of whom attended public schools and three of whom have attended or are currently enrolled in private schools.

About ICS

Founded in 1974, the Institute for Contemporary Studies (ICS) is a nonprofit, nonpartisan policy research institute.

To fulfill its mission to promote self-governing and entrepreneurial ways of life, ICS sponsors a variety of programs and publications on key issues, including education, entrepreneurship, the environment, leadership, and social policy.

Through its imprint, ICS Press, the Institute publishes innovative and readable books that will further the understanding of these issues among scholars, policy makers, and the wider community of citizens. ICS Press books include the writings of eight Nobel laureates and have been influential in setting the nation's policy agenda.

ICS programs seek to encourage the entrepreneurial spirit not only in this country but also around the world. They include the Institute for Self-Governance (ISG) and the International Center for Self-Governance (ICSG).

ADDITIONAL RESOURCES
ON EDUCATION FROM ICS PRESS

A CHOICE FOR OUR CHILDREN
Curing the Crisis in America's Schools
Alan Bonsteel and Carlos A. Bonilla

A well-researched solution to America's educational crisis: innovative programs of choice that renew the bonds between school and community.
Paperback. 272 pp., indexed. ISBN: 1-55815-496-5 $19.95

BREAK THESE CHAINS
The Battle for School Choice
Daniel McGroarty

Prima Publishing in Association with ICS Press

The school choice movement has united people of diverse ideologies, religions, races, incomes, and cultures. Together they share a single, heartfelt concern: the future of their children.
Hardcover. 288 pp., indexed. ISBN: 0-7615-0507-5 $23.95

WINNING THE BRAIN RACE
A Bold Plan to Make Our Schools Competitive
David Kearns and Dennis Doyle

The book that woke the nation to the need for education reform.
"Issues a tough-minded call that everyone in education and public policy needs to hear . . . an important book." —Bill Clinton, on the first edition
Paperback. 186 pp. ISBN: 1-55815-166-4 $19.95

RESPONSIVE SCHOOLS, RENEWED COMMUNITIES
Clifford W. Cobb

The first comprehensive study of the conditions that make school choice work, detailing how vouchers can benefit both rich and poor, across racial and ethnic lines.
Hardcover. 314 pp., indexed. ISBN: 1-55815-205-9 $34.95
Paperback. 314 pp., indexed. ISBN: 1-55815-216-4 $19.95

WHAT ARE WE TRYING TO TEACH THEM, ANYWAY?
A Father's Focus on School Reform
Ronald K. Pierce

Fear, frustration, and failure are not things we would choose to teach our kids. So why are these often the strongest lessons children learn in school?
Hardcover. 176 pp. ISBN: 1-55815-239-3 $19.95

800-326-0263   www.icspress.com   mail@icspress.com